Trinity & All Saints

ACCREDITED BY THE UNIVERSITY OF LEEDS

LIS LIBRARY

This book is due for return on or before the last date
stamped below

D1493884

264388 0

STEPHEN BROWN

FREE GIFT INSIDE!!

Forget the Customer. Develop Market*ease*

CAPSTONE

The right of Stephen Brown to be identified as the author of this work has been asserted in accordance with the Copyright, Designs and Patents Act 1988

First published 2003 by
Capstone Publishing Ltd (a Wiley Company)
The Atrium
Southern Gate
Chichester
West Sussex PO19 8SQ
England
www.wileyeurope.com

Reprinted December 2003

CIP catalogue records for this book are available from the British Library and the US Library of Congress

ISBN 1-84112-546-6

Typeset by Forewords, 109 Oxford Road, Cowley, Oxford

Printed and bound by T.J. International Ltd, Padstow, Cornwall

This book is printed on acid-free paper responsibly manufactured from sustainable forestry in which at least two trees are planted for each one used for paper production.

CONTENTS

Free Gifts

GOT THEM OLD, B1–B2, US VISITORS' VISA BLUES

Everyone, they say, has an Immigration Service story to tell and I have more than most. There's something about my face, accent, or demeanor possibly, that sets off their subliminal alarm bells. I get the third degree every time. Without fail. No exceptions. JFK, LAX, O'Hare, Orlando, Newark. You name it, I've been there, got done over, and didn't receive a T-shirt for my trouble.[1]

Naturally, I've tried everything in my power to expedite the immigration process. Friendly smile? Doesn't work. Irish blarney? Don't make me laugh. Silent, glassy-eyed stare into the middle distance? Big mistake.

However, out of all my attempts to effect entry into the United States, none was more disconcerting than my recent kerfuffle in Philly. Not even the time when I failed to wait behind the yellow line, as instructed, and was promptly frog-marched past the roiling multitudes to a welcoming interrogation room, compares to my reception in the City of Brotherly Love.

"What is the purpose of your visit to the United States?" asked the official in that familiar bloodcurdling manner.

"I'm going to a conference, officer."

"Oh yeah. What kind of conference?"

"A marketing conference," I countered (a bit too boldly). "I'm a marketing professor and . . ."

"Tell me something, sir," he interrupted, with sufficient stress on the word *sir* to imply that a detour to Penn Pen's pending, "what is the secret of marketing success?"

"Sorry, what was that?"

"You say you're in marketing, sir. What's the secret of marketing success?"

I was stricken. Staggered. Stumped. Jeez, I thought, I know America is a materialistic country, but I didn't know they'd started testing you on entry! Worse still, what happens if I get the question wrong? We could be talking cavity search territory here. Should I confess that I've spent my academic career attacking the conventional marketing concept? The *American* marketing concept?

Ever true to my beliefs, as only a yellow-bellied marketing professor can be, I hummed, hawed, and eventually ventured, "The customer is always right, officer?"

"Wrong!" he announced authoritatively.

My bowels didn't quite turn to water at this point, but liquefaction was definitely underway. "Wrong?" I whimpered.

"Wrong," he replied. "The customer is king, buddy. The customer is K-I-N-G."

"Whatever you say, officer."

"My wife," he went on amiably, "is in marketing. Multi-level marketing. She sells vitamins and stuff to her friends. She says the customer is king."

Holy moly. I'd found the only friendly immigration officer in the country! Either that, or my arrival coincided with their decennial, half-day customer care training program.[2]

"Thank you, officer," I gasped. "Thank you. I'll try to remember that."

"You do that, buddy. The customer is K-I-N-G. Have a nice one."

Well, what can I say after that? A near run thing, I'm sure you'll agree. My collies, to be honest, have never been so wobbled. Yet, despite this new-found customer focus at the front line of the fight against incoming academicians, I'm afraid I have to disagree with Philly's resident marketing expert. And most other resident marketing experts.[3] The customer isn't sovereign, you see. The customer isn't always right. The customer isn't Number One, because the customer's number is up. The customer is king is dead.

> How can companies best attract customers? One way is to pander to them, to find out what they want and give it to them, as established marketing theory suggests. But there is another way, a way that doesn't involve customer coddling.

Lest there is any misunderstanding, let me make it clear that I am not opposed to customers per se. I am opposed to customer orientation as the primal marketing principle. Companies need customers. They can't survive without them. That goes without saying. The big issue is: How can companies best attract customers? One way is to pander to them, to find out what they want and give it to them, as established marketing theory suggests. But there is another way, a way that doesn't involve customer coddling.

This other way, let me also make it clear, doesn't involve STP (segmentation, targeting, or positioning); it doesn't involve PST (planning, strategy, or tactics); it doesn't involve TLAs (Three Letter Abbreviations); and it doesn't involve AAAs (Alliterations, Aphorisms, and Anagrams). I recognize, however, that many marketing executives are sadly addicted – largely because of the pushers employed by management consultancy cartels – to jargon, buzzwords, and

ACRONYMS (Attempts to Capture Recommendations and Observations in Names You Memorize Successfully). Accordingly, I'm opting for the cold turkey treatment herein. By the time you've finished reading this book, you'll never want to see another 3Cs, 4Ps, or 7Ss inventory again.

Contrary, then, to the contentions of the consultancy conspiracy, marketing is not about customer centricity. What it *is* about is the subject of this book. Read this book and you'll discover the secret of marketing success. But not right away. All will be revealed. Slowly. Gradually. Eventually. Everything, remember, comes to those who wait . . . in line at the register.

Of course, I appreciate that some of you aren't willing to wait. You're keen to know what the deal is. Cut to the chase. Show me the money. Where's the beef, or the take-away at least? You have friends in the Immigration Service, I gather.

Well, I'm afraid you'll just have to hold your horses. As I'll be advocating a philosophy of anti-customer orientation – and suggesting that marketers should tantalize, torment, and torture their way to success – you hardly expect me to pander to a customer like you, much less satisfy your desire for instant intellectual gratification.

Still, I promised you a free gift inside and, as a taster for the forthcoming TEASE framework, I'm going to outline the essence of this book in a single exemplar, an episode of *Will & Grace*. In case you're unfamiliar with this sublime situation comedy, Will and Grace are a twenty-first century Odd Couple, part gay, part straight, all bananas. Grace is an interior decorator, Will is an attorney and, in the episode in question, one of Grace's irascible clients takes a shine and a half to Will. Will pays no attention to his advances and the more he ignores his suitor, the more amorous his suitor becomes. Grace, naturally, is beside herself; she shamelessly dangles Will, as it were, in order to retain the business, and all sorts of connubial complications ensue. It is only when Will turns on the troublesome client, pretends he's seen the light, declares his everlasting love, and expresses his heartfelt desire to spend a lifetime together, that the suitor is frightened off and our demented duo return to a semblance of domestic bliss.

Today's consumer is the irascible client that has been frightened off by marketing's Will-like declarations of undying love and disconcertingly desperate desire to establish a long-term relationship. We've stopped playing hard to get. We're running after them when it should be the other way around. Our once-keen customers can't be seen for a cloud of dust. Our extravagant attempts at ingratiation have only increased their irritation. We've become a pest and pests get ignored, avoided or squashed. Bootlicking kills brands dead.

How, then, do you attract customers when all the Ps in the world don't add up to a hill of beans? The answer is to make your brand alluring, to make your products extra special, to make your organization stand out from the colorless crowd. It's not enough to play hard to get, since that presupposes that people want what's on offer. They have to be persuaded to want what's available and, in a world of identikit products and services, that means attracting attention to your particular offering. It means, among other things, shouting louder than the rest. It means combining hard-to-get with over-the-top to create a hard-to-top attraction.[4]

So there you have it. My argument in a nutshell. Structurally, I should perhaps add, that *Free Gift Inside!!* begins with hard-to-get and gradually segues into over-the-top, though the distinction between HTG and OTT is not clear-cut, as HTT suggests.

However, before you venture forth into hard-to-top territory, I must also make it clear that this book practices what it preaches. It plays hard-to-get by slowly revealing its secrets. It is totally over-the-top in its mode of delivery. I have a thesaurus, you see, and I'm not afraid to use it.

At the same time, I'm aware that this approach is a tad unusual, especially in a field that is characterized by factual, no-nonsense, get-to-the-point publications. Recompense is called for and, in an attempt to ingratiate myself ironically, I've included no less than fifteen, repeat *fifteen*, free gifts inside. Over the top, I know, but we may as well start as we mean to go on.

You don't have to accept my pleonastic offerings,[5] or even take time out to enjoy the hidden musical interludes. But they're there if you want to savor the journey – ten lessons, plus one for the road – rather than rush headlong to our destination. If, of course, you're in a big hurry, simply shimmy from grab quote to grab quote, indicated by signposts in the text, and you'll get the gist of my argument, such as it is.

Some skeptics, admittedly, might suspect that my free gifts are little more than pretentious playfulness, or preposterous padding by another name. Or both. Banish such churlish thoughts, gentle reader. You call it filler. I call it added value. The Immigration Service calls it hard evidence. I'm ready for my close up, officer.

HOW TO WIN BUSINESS AND INFURIATE PEOPLE

O Customer, Where Art Thou?

Pick a marketing textbook, any textbook. Have a look. Take your time. What does it say? No, don't show me. I'll tell you. I'm the marketing mind-reader, remember. It says something about customer orientation, right? Maybe customer care. Perhaps customer driven. Possibly customer led. Surely not customer facing. Hmmm, let me think, could it be customer satisfaction, focus, centricity, sovereignty, or, heaven help us, have something to do with relationships? Hold on. It's coming to me. I've got it. It's a neologism. No, an acronym. No, a noun that's been brutally verbed. *Customerize the company!*

Am I right or am I right?

For forty years or thereabouts, marketers have worshipped at the feet of the customer. The customer can do no wrong. The customer is always right. The customer's will be done. The secret of marketing success, so we're told, involves meeting the customer's needs better than the competition. While such a strategy may have worked when customer orientation was a rarity – when customer care conferred competitive advantage – that is no longer the case. Every organization is customer oriented, or claims to be. Every corporation has bought into the customer-first ideology, if only because there's no credible alternative. Every business boasts a marketing VP, or equivalent, who has read Kotler from cover to cover and spends many a happy weekend at CRM seminars, short courses and customer hugathons.[1]

In this world of customer-coddling congruence, where everyone bar none claims to be customer centric, how can competitive advantage be achieved and, more importantly, how can it be sustained?

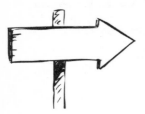

In this world of customer-coddling congruence, how can competitive advantage be achieved and, more importantly, how can it be sustained?

Most marketers seem to think that the answer is to become *more* customer orientated; to not simply satisfy but *delight* the customer; to not simply delight but *enchant* the customer; to not simply enchant but *enthrall* the customer; to not simply enthrall but *enrapture* the customer.[2] Can the customer orgasmatron be far away?

Admirable as this charms race is, it seems to me that marketing is suffering from customer expectations inflation, from adjectival overkill, from a surfeit of superlatives. Long gone are the good old days when satisfaction was sufficient, okay was acceptable and enjoyment an impossible dream. Instead we have a situation where marketers are convinced that *more* customer orientation is the only alternative, that *more* customer orientation is the way to go, that *more* customer orientation is always better.[3]

8

Abundance Unbound

More-ness, indeed, is the modus operandi of modern marketing. The sheer wealth of choice in every conceivable product category is almost mind-boggling in its more-ness. Whether it be detergents, deodorants, dishwashers, or DVDs; chinos, colognes, cornflakes, or cellulite creams; banks, batteries, bottled waters, or barbeque grills; magazines, margarines, motor bikes, or management consultants; SUVs, sneakers, surfboards, or silicon chips; or toothpastes, televisions, theme parks, and tennis rackets, extraordinary abundance is a defining feature of our time.[4] As *Financial Times* columnist Lucy Kellaway trenchantly notes:

> *When I was a child there were two sorts of lavatory paper: hard and soft. Each sort was available in little folded sheets or on a roll. In those days consumers had a real choice, and as far as I was concerned, my parents – who bought the hard sheets – always made the wrong one.*
>
> *Things are not so straightforward now. On the shelves of our local Sainsbury's, loo paper takes up a whole aisle, occupying as much shelf space as the entire contents of the grocer's shop from which my mother used to buy the offending Izal. There is Soft, Super Soft, Quilted, Double Velvet, and Softer & Thicker. There is Economy, Medicated, Recycled, Soft Recycled, Recycled From 100 Per Cent Low Grade Waste, and something called Greencare. Most of these come in a variety of pastel shades: mint green, honeysuckle, snowdrop white, peach, and rose pink. Some have patterns on them and are called things like "bouquet," and "chantilly." In addition, there are wet wipes and a new product offering "advanced personal hygiene."*
>
> *If this is choice, I don't want it.*[5]

There is, Mark Earls[6] observes, "too much of everything." There is, dare I say it, even too much marketing and commentary on marketing. The average marketer is reminded 3,000 times per day that the average consumer receives 3,000 commercial messages per day. Or perhaps it just seems that way. One hundred thousand MBAs are extruded by B-Schools annually, all of them injected with identical marketing ideas from indistinguishable marketing textbooks.[7] The bookstores, moreover, are bunged up with monster marketing manuals, each one bandoleered in bullet points and riddled with boxes-and-arrows diagrams. So competitive is the market for marketing books that they'll come with free gifts before long. Where will it end?

In this world of seemingly limitless choice, the only thing that is scarce is scarcity itself. There is a shortage of shortages. Rarity is rare. One-of-a-kinds now come in multipacks. Increasingly, the marketer's task is to manage in a milieu of more-ness, of oversupply, of superabundance, especially now that the global economy is slowing and gluts are growing.

Contrary to the contentions of copious consultants, commentators, and columnists, however, this management task doesn't require more customer orientation, since there is a surfeit of that as well. More more isn't what we need. There's too much more. A little less more wouldn't go amiss. More isn't always better.[8]

It is possible to become *too* customer oriented and marketing is rapidly heading that way. We have got so close to consumers that we're breathing down their necks.

We are caught up, to put it another way, in what learned marketing philosophers[9] call the Chunky Monkey Progression, where one scoop of Ben and Jerry's signature product is delicious, two scoops are sufficient, three scoops are more than enough, and four means Chunky Monkey chunk-blowing time. Don't ask what happens after five.

Analogously, it is possible to become *too* customer oriented and marketing is rapidly heading that way. We have got so close to consumers that we're breathing down their necks. We have invaded their personal space and they're becoming understandably uncomfortable. As far as customers are concerned, CRM stands for Creepily Repellent Marketers, Peeping Toms one and all, people who make obscene phone calls yet remain immune from prosecution.

Fortunately, there is an alternative to the customer-centric standpoint and this book spells it out. Before we get to that, however, it is necessary to step back and take stock of Lesson # 1, the fairly obvious fact that it is possible to make a bundle in business without being customer oriented. After all, our infuriating day-to-day experiences with rapacious realtors, contemptuous maitre d's, fast-talking insurance brokers, never-turn-up-on-time plumbers, electricians and cable guys, still-waiting-for-the-part body shops, security-deposit-pocketing landlords, bump-em-off-the-flight airlines, and dial 1-800-HOSTILE for our couldn't-care-less customer care hotline, routinely remind us that there are other ways to prosperity beside customer sovereignty.

Free Gift 1: The Disservice Encounter

For Your Inconvenience

Our topic this week is a feature of modern life that really gets up my nasal passages, namely the way corporations do things to make life easy for themselves and then pretend it's for your benefit. You can usually tell this is happening when the phrase "for your convenience" or "in order to provide a better service for our customers" appears somewhere in writing.

For example, I was recently in a big hotel . . . when I noticed that the room service menu said: "For your convenience, a charge of 17 percent will be added to all orders."

Curiosity aroused, I called room service and asked in what way it would be convenient for me to have 17 percent added to my room service charge.

There was a long silence. "Because it guarantees that you will get your food before next Thursday." That may not be the precise form of words the man used, but that we clearly the drift of his sentiment.

There is a simple explanation for why this happens. Most big companies don't like you very much, except for hotels, airlines and Microsoft, which don't like you at all.

I think – though this is a very tough call – hotels may be the worst. (Actually, Microsoft is the worst, but if I started on them I would never finish.) A couple of years ago, I arrived at about 2 p.m. at a large hotel in Kansas City, of all places, having flown in from Fiji, of all other places. Fiji, as you will appreciate, is a long way from Kansas City and I was tired and keenly eager for a shower and a little lie down.

"Check in time is 4 p.m.," the clerk informed me serenely.

I looked at him with that pained, helpless expression I often wear at check-in desks. "Four p.m.? Why?"

"It's company policy."

"Why?"

"Because it is." He realized this was a trifle inadequate. "The cleaners need time to clean the rooms."

"Are you saying that they don't finish cleaning any of the rooms until 4 p.m.?"

"No, I am saying the rooms are not available until 4 p.m."

"Why?"

"Because it's company policy."

Bill Bryson, Notes From a Big Country, pp. 299-301[10]

Herbie Gets a Service

Today I took my year-old car, with less than 4,000 miles on it, into the repair shop at the dealership where I bought it. Why? Seems that every other time I go to start the car, it won't start. I've replaced the starter, the battery, the fuse, the computer chip. But none of that has solved the problem.

When I told the service manager all this, he looked at me with a witheringly vacant stare. "Oh, these new Beetles – they don't start unless you drive them every day."

I thought for sure I must have heard him wrong – after all, he was speaking perfect English. So I asked him again what the problem was.

"You see," he said, shaking his head in pity, "these VWs are run by a computer system, and if the computer hasn't read any activity – namely, you turning it on and driving it every day or so – then the computer assumes the battery is dead or something, and just shuts down the whole car. Is there any way you or someone you know can go down to the garage and start it once a day?"

I didn't know what to say. "If you don't start the car every day, it will die" – what's this, 1901? Am I being arrogant to expect that a car I spent $20,000 on is supposed to start whenever I put the key in the ignition? There aren't many sure things left in the world these days: the sun still sets in the west, the Pope still says Midnight Mass on Christmas Eve, Strom Thurmond still comes back to life whenever there's an ex-First Lady around to grope. I would have thought I could cling to at least one last article of faith: a brand-new car always starts – period!

"Like ninety-five percent of the customers you've sold these new Beetles to," I said, "I live in Manhattan. Do you know *anybody* in Manhattan who drives their car every day?"

"Yes, sir, we understand. Nobody in the city drives a car every day. They use the subways! I don't know why they even sell these cars in the city. It's really a shame. Have you tried writing to Volkswagen? Is there a kid on your block you can get to start it for a few minutes every day or so?"

There's got to be a better way...

Michael Moore, *Stupid White Men*, pp. xix–xx.[11]

As consumers ourselves, we may not like this antediluvian state of affairs. Hell no. As marketers, we may be appalled by such blatant recidivism. Haven't these people read Ted Levitt? As peace-loving, easy-going, mild-mannered inhabitants of this great nation, we may be tempted to take the law into our own hands. Man's best friend is a tire iron, I always say. But as businesspeople, we have to recognize that ignoring the customer can pay dividends.[12] As businesspeople, we know that even though we're supposed to love our customers, some of them are a pain in the rump. As businesspeople, we can't help admiring celebrity chefs like Marco Pierre White, who throws customers out of his restaurant if they dare complain about the cooking or have the gall to ask for condiments.[13] "Condiments? I'll give you condiments! Ketchup, you say? Heinz ketchup, is it? Where's my meat cleaver?"

A Hill of Beanies

There's no need to rush for the cutlery drawer, however. At least, not yet. Let me give you an even better example of anti-customer orientation in action. I am the proud father of three delightful daughters, who are at a very awkward age. They don't believe in Santa Claus but think that we think they do. Thus they continue to write letters to him in the hope that their adoring parents will buy them more Christmas presents than they ordinarily would. These faux-innocent letters usually consist of charming lists of tasteful toys, like six-megabyte Gameboy expansion packs, and come complete with catalogue numbers and recommended retail prices, as well as the infallible catchall "one or two surprise presents, please."

Anyway, our youngest has a bit of a Beanie Baby habit and, if you've ever had any dealings with Ty Inc., the Beelzebubian organization behind Beanie Babies, you'll know that customer orientation is not part of its mission statement.[14] Awkward orientation, contrary orientation, ornery orientation, inconvenience orientation, possibly. But customer orientation? I don't think so.

To the uninitiated, Beanie Babies look like undernourished attendees at the Teddy Bears' Picnic. They are cuddly toys, hewn from the finest velveteen and half-filled with recycled polypropylene. Somewhat reminiscent of old-time bean bags, which loom large in the grade-school memories of many Baby Boomers, Beanie Babies are unfailingly floppy, irresistibly cute, eminently adorable, and blessed with the kind of goo-goo eyes guaranteed to melt all but the hardest hearts. They come in various shapes, sizes, and species, such as Pouch the Kangaroo, Spike the Rhinoceros, Claude the Crab, Ally the Alligator, Puffer the Puffin, Tabasco the Bull, and Smoochy the Frog. They retail at $5–8 on average. They come complete with name tag, birth date, personalized poem, and bags of personality. They want to be your special friend. They really do.

Nothing untoward about that, I hear you say. Behind the seductive smile of the tush-tagged storm troopers, however, lurks a five-star marketing general, a twisted commercial genius, whose sadistic sales strategy puts Sun Tzu to shame. The Beaniemeister is Ty Warner, a 1962 Kalamazoo College grad who spent twenty-odd years as a furry animal wrangler and sometime sales rep for Durkin, the soft toy company. He made his escape in 1980 and, after developing a line of low-price, full-size, plush-wrapped, polystyrene-engorged Himalayan Cats, Ty came up with the Beanie Baby concept in 1993. The first fake-fur covered critters, known to true Beanie Believers as The Original Nine, were released in January 1994, reached critical mass around Christmas 1996, and less than three years later were selling at a rate of 250 million per annum.[15]

Endearing as they are, the success of Beanie Babies is not attributable to their anthropomorphic appeal, nor to the attendant poems, birthdays, name tags, and suchlike. Goo-goo-osity, after all, is a genetic marker of most cuddly invertebrates and personalization has been around since at least the early 1980s, when Cabbage Patch Dolls were being "adopted" by softies the world over.[16] Their success, rather, is predicated on Ty's strategy of customer *dis*orientation. It is a strategy that combines a here-today-gone-tomorrow approach to new product development with a distribution policy

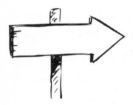

Their success, rather, is predicated on Ty's strategy of customer *dis*orientation.

that is idiosyncratic to the point of incorrigible. Production runs are strictly limited. New ranges of toys are constantly introduced and old models ruthlessly "retired" without warning. All sorts of special editions and promotional tie-ins are produced for sports teams, Broadway musicals, and commemorative occasions. Brigadoon, presumably, boasts the principal manufacturing facility.

When it comes to distribution, furthermore, large chain stores, with their EDI-driven ethic of regular supplies, no surprises and guaranteed delivery times, are deliberately avoided in favor of small-time gift shops, independently-owned toy stores, offbeat boutiques, and airport art emporia. Consistently inconsistent and predictably unpredictable, Warner supplies what he wants to whomsoever he wants and, if the retailers don't like it then they simply do without. Consignments are cancelled, changed, or capriciously completed with whatever Beanies are to hand, irrespective of the original order. There's no point complaining, since Ty is extremely secretive and notoriously incommunicado. The company's telephone number is ex-directory; he doesn't give interviews or throw press junkets; employees are required to sign legally-enforceable gagging orders; above-the-line advertising is expressly eschewed; and, although the

J.D. Salinger of soft toys is alleged to lurk on internet chat rooms, listening in on customers' conversations, this too may be a rumor spread by overenthusiastic Beanieheads.

Don't Infuriate, Infatuate

Be that as it may, the inevitable upshot of Ty's premeditated eccentricity is that his Beanie Baby range is scattered hither and yon. Reason doesn't come into it, let alone rhyme. His tush-tagged treasures can be found in the most quirky, out-of-the-way places, which adds to, rather than detracts from, their appeal. As Stowe and Turkington[17] observe, "When a toy is hard to get, everybody wants it. If it's lying out there in a heap on the shelves like day-old bread, who's gonna care?" Beanie Baby buying is akin to a never-ending Easter Egg hunt, where surprises can pop up in the least expected locations, and secret caches of creatures may be hidden behind the doors of the most unprepossessing retail outlets. For all his Greta Garboisms, it seems that Beanswami Warner has performed the ultimate marketing trick of making brand new, mass produced toys into semi-precious antiquealikes.

More pertinently perhaps, Ty's truffles fetch up to $6,000 apiece. Fist fights among frenzied I-spotted-it-first fans and analogous Babysnatchers are not unknown.[18] Comparative rarities like Squealer the Pig and Pinchers the Lobster can command $2,000 plus on the black market. Billionaire Bear, created to commemorate one billion dollars' worth of Beanies sold, is selling for more than $4,000 at auction. The Princess Bear, issued in memory of Diana, Princess of Wales, is particularly sought after. In a similar vein, McDonald's extra-special, six-week promotion of pint-sized replicas – Teenie Beanie Babies – sold out in less than three days, forcing the company to issue fulsome apologies in all the national news media.

Ty Diet

"Expect the unexpected" is Ty's rallying cry and most would agree that capricious pricing, idiosyncratic distribution, eccentric promotion, haphazard pricing, and standards of customer care that haven't been seen since the lifeboat-lite *Titanic*, are somewhat unusual in the consumer-centric world of modern marketing. Nevertheless, it works. It works brilliantly. It shows that you don't have to espouse customer orientation to succeed. It demonstrates that there's more than one way to skin Zip the Cat. As the Beanie genie himself once sagely observed,[19] "so long as kids keep fighting over the products and the retailers are angry at us because they can't get enough, then I think those are good signs."

All good things come to an end, however.[20] Warner's Waterloo transpired in the fateful year of 1999, when he preemptorally pronounced that Beanie Babies would be exterminated en masse on December 31. This soft toy Final Solution, needless to say, precipitated pandemonium among plush puppy patrons, proselytes, and Typhiles worldwide. True, the apocalyptic occasion would be commemorated by a special black Beanie Bear, The End, but this was insufficient recompense for countless millions of disgruntled Beanie lovers. Never one to look Derby the gift horse in the mouth, moreover, the underworld took note of this looming velveteen massacre, recognized the clandestine commercial opportunity that it represented, and set about robbing retail stores and warehouses. A security guard was slain at a depot in West Virginia, though the subsequent police investigation revealed that he didn't so much lay down his life for Libearty the Bear, as fail to make an illicit delivery to criminal accomplices. Where's Doby the Doberman when you need him?

Beanie rustlers, clearly, are a ruthless lot, but Ty Warner hardly qualifies as a tenderfoot. Not content with announcing the has-beanies Holocaust, he immediately reissued the organization's entire range with a new, "eighth generation" tush tag, which only added to collectors' count-down dementia. Hope, however, springs eternal and it did so in spades when the Mephistopheles of soft toy marketing ostensibly relented. On December 24, a week before Beaniegeddon, he announced an online plebiscite to determine the fate of his hellfire-and-damnation bound menagerie. Should they stay or should they go?

Fast-buck-maker to the end, Warner shamelessly insisted that would-be voters pay 50 cents apiece to participate in the Beanie Baby ballot. The outcome, naturally, was a foregone conclusion, since only the most perverted plushopath would vote for Beanicide or pay to see the innocents immolated. A stay of execution was announced, albeit the rejoicing was short lived. Many enthusiasts had had just about enough and, although Ty's cuddly creatures still smile winsomely at toy store patrons, Warner's end game marked the beginning of the end of the Beanie obsession. Except in my house, unfortunately.

Hermèsmerized

The Beanie bubble may have burst, or deflated at least, but even when it was full of hot air, Ty's draylon-covered dirigible never attained the marketing altitude of the Hermès Birkin. Paragon of purses and acme of chic, the Hermès Birkin is yet another example of anti-customer orientation in action. Up to $80,000 – enough for twenty Billionaire Bears – is necessary before possession of this apotheosis of accessories is possible and, even then, ownership is by no means guaranteed.[21]

To be sure, Hermès purses can be purchased for as little as $3,000, and $10,000 or so will get one that doesn't make you look like a refugee from Wal-Mart. However for die-hard fashionistas the

Birkin is the purse of purses, the handbag of handbags, the holdall of holdalls, the fashion appendage if not quite to die for, certainly worth undergoing life-threatening surgery. Supermodel Kate Moss has one in denim, Naomi Campbell swears by hers, apparently, and rock star Bryan Adams buys them for friends and fellow travelers. Cheaper than a trail of trashed hotel rooms, I guess.

Paragon of purses and acme of chic, the Hermès Birkin is yet another example of anti-customer orientation in action.

Although the House of Hermès, as everyone knows, was established in 1837 as a specialist in saddles and equestrian equipage, it has been making purses for a mere eighty years.[22] Arriviste! In 1922, the wife of the proprietor couldn't find a purse to meet her needs and Emile-Maurice Hermès responded with the Bolide, a sleek valise fastened by the then latest technology, a zipper. Handbag Heaven. A superbrand was born and to this very day Hermès bespoke bags (customers choose their preferred combination of leathers and linings from sample books) are hand-crafted from the finest materials (kidskin, crocodile hide, ostrich epidermis . . . whatever) and sold from the organization's beautifully appointed selection of retail stores (most notably its famous flagship on the rue du Faubourg St-Honoré).

For years, Hermès' best-selling handbag was the Kelly, which got its name in 1956 when the aristocratic actress used one to shield her pregnancy from the paparazzi's prying Pentaxes. However, an accidental in-flight encounter with sexy sixties chanteuse, Jane Birkin, who complained bitterly about the lack of overhead locker-proof luggage, persuaded company president Jean-Louis Dumas to create the bigger, bulkier, but still beautiful Birkin bag in 1984. "Career, cosmetic, and carnal needs contained in a single blissful bag," claims one proud owner.[23] What more could anyone ask for?

Well, nothing. Except that . . . except that . . . except that . . . Hermès, we have a problem. Hermès, there is a big problem with the Birkin.

Birkin Purdah

Despite what you might think, the big problem with the Birkin bag is not the price tag, prodigious though that is. Nor is it the agony of anticipating this season's chic specifications. Crocodile hide is so 2002, don't you know! When are they going to make one in Squealer the Pig's skin? Nor, for that matter, is it the waiting list, which averages nine months or so. A pregnant pause, perhaps, prior to product procreation, pocketbook parturition, and post-purchase penitence? The real problem, rather, is getting on to the waiting list in the first place. Birkins aren't just for anyone, the likes of you and me. The Birkin is a beautiful bag for beautiful people. B-list and above. Haut monde only. Hoi polloi need not apply.

The Birkin, in short, is a blue-blood brand, somewhat scarce and very special. Its scarcity and specialness, however, makes the purse particularly desirable and ensures that its price remains steep to the point of precipitous. The rumor mill, moreover, maintains that Hermès' waiting list can be circumvented, provided one's in the know or prepared to pull the appropriate strings. In this regard, a recent episode of *Sex and the City* revolved around Samantha's attempts to get her hands on a Hermès Birkin. PR-person to the superstar Lucy Liu, Samantha exploits her employer's celebrity to leapfrog the waiting list. But when the magical bag materializes, it is delivered direct to the petulant personality. Wild with Birkin-induced desire, Samantha demands her rightful property, only to receive a pink-slipped reminder of her position in the socialite scheme of things.[24]

True or not, the possibility of jumping the Hermès queue only adds to the mystique of the marque.[25] It's the commercial equivalent of an urban legend, repeated so often that it becomes part of shopping folklore and the fount, furthermore, of fervid consumer imaginings. At the very least, this line-circumventing rumor increases involvement, infatuation and the intention to acquire the "Hallelujah handbag" (Hallelujah, because that's what devotees say when they finally get their hands on one. Jesus Christ is often invoked as well, usually when the credit card statement comes through).

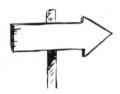

Hermès, remember, is pretty well versed in crocodilian habits. It has the pelts to prove it.

The company, naturally, is deeply sympathetic toward its disappointed customers. It periodically wrings its hands, sheds a tear or two, and apologizes profusely for the "intolerable" waiting times. It has even lobbied the French government over its restrictive employment legislation, which limits leather workers to a 35-hour week. But, as unattainability is one of Hermès' principal marketing ploys – *the* principal marketing ploy, in point of fact – these ostentatious acts of atonement can only be considered publicity stunts at best or crocodile tears at worst. Hermès, remember, is pretty well versed in crocodilian habits. It has the pelts to prove it.

Thunderbirds are Go!

Preposterously priced purses are one thing, I hear you say, and

Beanie Babies are something else again. The former are the preserve of irrational fashion victims, while the latter is a passing pre-teen passion. Both can thus be safely ignored. There's nothing to be learned from either of these objects, you may well be thinking. What you're really thinking, of course, is that you need a more *manly* example of Beanie-Birkin marketing principles in action.

But hold. What have we here? Is it a bird? Is it a plane? Is it a cliché? Yes and no. It's a Ford Thunderbird actually, in the signature turquoise blue, just like the one lovingly caressed by the camera in *Thelma and Louise*. Except this isn't a 1955 original or even one of the later, clunkier models of the 60s, 70s, and 80s. But it looks a bit like the original. More than a bit. It's got the V-8 engine, the egg-crate grill, the decorative hood scoop, the oval, 'luminum-trimmed head- and tail-lamps, the thru-fender, dual-exhaust pipes, the distinctive dashboard arc, and, glory be, the 1955 nameplate on the rear quarter panel. Most importantly of all, it's got the immortal, spread-wing Thunderbird logo on the hood, deck lid, and forward surface headrests of the fluted bucket seats. Man-oh-man-oh-man.

It's a real T-Bird all right.[26] A total head-turner. It even sounds like the original. However, in addition to the heritage 'n' stuff, this one's got traction control, anti-lock brakes, air bags front and side, rear window defroster, dual-zone air conditioning, speed sensitive wipers, cruise control, power steering, windows and door locks, a six CD stereo radio, and five speed transmission, all sitting atop a 3.9 liter, overhead camshaft, 252 horsepower engine, and a shortened Lincoln LS chassis. As two-seater, rear-wheel drive convertibles go, this one's outta sight, round the bend, and burnin' up the freeway. It's almost worth having a mid-life crisis for.

Not everyone, of course, is enamored by Ford's road-hugging, smooth-running, open-topped, perfect tailpipe-pitched, automotive Phoenix. The press corps is carping about its imprecise handling, indifferent performance, uncomfortable seating, tiny trunk, limited headroom, low fuel economy, and lack of optional extras, to say nothing of the manufacturer's make do and mend mentality, which involves pulling together parts, pieces and panels from the other cars in the range, including the unspeakable Taurus.[27] But what do they know? There's more to automobiles than chassis numbers and accessories. This is a living legend reborn. The king of the road is back and a supercharged model, the Blackbird, is in the pipeline. Awesome.

You want one? Of course you do! In turquoise? Doesn't everybody! Try getting one. Only 11,000 were produced for 2002 and its 25,000 per annum thereafter. Tops. This is no P.T. Cruiser, where production was increased to meet demand, thereby detracting from its supercool cachet. No sir. There was a 17,000-strong waiting list before the first T-Bird hit the forecourts and it'll stay that way. Unless, of course, you know someone who knows how to get to the head of the line.

As for colors: Well, if you can track down a turquoise one, consider yourself lucky. Thunderbird Blue and Inspiration Yellow are this year's colors – and this year's only – along with Torch Red, Evening Black, and Whisper White. Next year will see a different range of limited edition color schemes and interior design accents. It keeps the concept fresh, they say. It keeps the dealerships in nicely padded profits. It keeps consumers on their toes. But, what the hell, guys. Look on the bright side. No matter what they gouge us for, the T-Bird is still cheaper than the Hermès Birkin or a backpack full of Billionaire Bears. Where do I sign up?

How to Win Business and Infuriate People?
Sell Them a How-to Book Without Telling Them How To.

Lesson 2

HOW TO COPE WITH CANNY CUSTOMERS

Enlisting Resistance

Many marketing managers, in my experience, have a love–hate relationship with their customers. On the one hand, they know that customers are the life-blood of business. On the other hand, they have to deal with the difficult, demanding, deeply frustrating dilettantes on a daily basis. What's worse, they can't come out and say what they really feel, because criticizing customers is the marketing equivalent of condemning motherhood, apple pie, and the American way. It's just not done. In public, that is.

Consumers, by contrast, are perfectly happy to denounce marketing malefactors, or so the recent anti-capitalist protests in Seattle and suchlike suggest.[1] Yeah, Seattle. That was a turning point, I suppose. Three days of peace, music, and love. Except that it wasn't very peaceful; the music comprised a cacophonous concerto of chanting crowds and cop car sirens; and there was little love lost between the police and the protesters.[2] It also lasted for five days, but that is by the by. Seattle was the defining moment for a generation, a generation built on marketing, brought up on branding, and trademarked from birth. Generation ®.

To be sure, anti-marketing sentiment had been simmering long before the Seattle spillover. The outrage over Kathie Lee Gifford's central American sweatshops; the seemingly obscene profit margins on Nike Air Jordan sneakers; the environmental despoliation attributed to McDonald's, Exxon, BP, Monsanto, and more; the indoctrina-

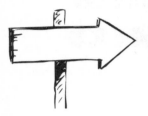

Seattle was the defining moment for a generation, a generation built on marketing, brought up on branding, and trademarked from birth.

tion of school kids through in-class marketing programs like Channel One; and the egregious expropriation of identity politics by allegedly "right on" corporations such as Benetton, all contributed to Generation®'s growing sense that they had been taken for a ride.[3] They had been betrayed by the very brands they had befriended, boasted about, and, not least, blown a great deal of money on. They had succumbed to the spin about customer orientation, corporate responsibility, and the sanctity of the marketplace. They had been revealed as patsies for plutocracy.

Seattle was just the start of it, moreover. Street protesters in London, Prague, Geneva, Davos, New York, Porte Alegre, and Barcelona among many others, carried on where the Seattle vets left off. In Italy, an anti-capitalist was killed by the Genoese carabineri.[4] In France, McDonald's was run out of Millau by the Peasants' Confederation of disenfranchised farmers.[5] In Britain, a burst of consumer boycotts – against Esso petrol, Barclays bank, Triumph lingerie et al. – has been successfully mounted.[6] And, in the developed world as a whole, "Buy Nothing Day" is rapidly emerging as a counter-Christmas celebration,[7] a much-needed respite from the frenzy of consumption that characterizes the rest of the year, Yuletide especially.

Above and beyond everyday acts of consumer resistance, the anti-marketing movement has found an able and articulate spokesperson. Naomi Klein, a born-again mall rat with impeccable radical credentials (her mother was a prominent first-wave feminist and her grandfather organized an animators strike against Walt Disney), has emerged as the voice of Generation ®. Her exposé of the capitalist conspiracy, *No Logo*, was greeted with rapturous reviews, quickly became a world-wide bestseller, and is routinely described as the *Das Kapital* of our time.[8] Not since *The Hidden Persuaders*, observes *The Economist*,[9] "has one book stirred up so much antipathy to marketing."

It is, I grant you, easy to be contemptuous toward No Logo lovers – the Nologoistas. The movement has been condescendingly portrayed as a small group of media-savvy malcontents, full-time students filling time between tutorials, part-time poseurs for whom radical chic is the *dernier cri*, and biters of the marketing hand that feeds them. These are people, after all, who wear Gap jeans and Nike sneakers whilst throwing stones at Gap stores and Niketown.[10]

In a similar vein, Naomi Klein's contention that brands represent "a fascist state where we all salute the logo and have little opportunity for criticism" is not only grossly exaggerated,[11] but it is a bit rich coming from someone whose bestseller was very heavily promoted, is published by a Rupert Murdoch-owned imprint, and who has had the temerity to trademark the No Logo logo.[12] Hell, they'll be

The anti-capitalist collectives have forced their way onto capitalists' agendas. They have used their strength as brand buyers to shape the policy of brand suppliers.

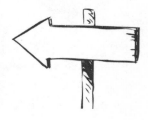

selling *Adbusters* in Barnes & Noble next. Whoops, they already are . . .

So Logo

Although there is something deeply ironic about anti-branding riots led by brand-bedecked protesters, let alone the apparent logophobia of the No Logo logo owner, the effectiveness of Klein's camp followers cannot be denied. The anti-capitalist collectives have forced their way onto capitalists' agendas. They have called multinational organizations to account. They have used their strength as brand buyers to shape the policy of brand suppliers.

Nike, for example, has responded to accusations of third world exploitation by completely revamping its supply chain. Still reeling from the Brent Spar debacle, Shell is just about as eco-friendly as oil companies come. The mighty Microsoft, not exactly renowned for its love-thy-competitor credo, has latterly seen the light and announced its conversion to the modish doctrine of Corporate Social Responsibility. In the wake of the Enron, Worldcom, Tyco, and ImClone scandals, moreover, the 4Ps of probity, purity, propriety, and penitence are the management principles of the moment.[13] Honesty, decency, and "authenticity" are the order of the day.

Free Gift 2: Authenticating Authenticity

One of the most striking things about contemporary culture, according to copious commentators, is the apparent desire for authenticity.[14] Real food, pure water, fresh air, natural cosmetics, organic farming, traditional remedies, genuine antiques, additive-free snacks, unspoilt holiday resorts, hand- built furniture, hand-made suits, hand-thrown ceramics, hand-crafted collectibles, and hand-picked hand-me-downs are the order of the day.[15] Reality TV is all the rage, as *Jerry Springer, The Osbournes*, and *Temptation Island* attest.[16] Real movies, using handheld cameras, improvised performances, and Dogme dogma, are relieving the tiresome diet of special effects-led blockbusters. Real rock 'n' roll, based on bass, drums, and lead, or played on scratchy vinyl albums, is making a comeback.[17] Real art is being championed by the Stuckists, an international movement opposed to conceptual artists' reliance on shallow gimmickry, while advocating a return to painting, sketching, engraving, palletes, brushes, berets, smocks, and all the rest.[18] Reality has even intruded into the otherworldly world of self-help philosophies, as evinced by the dramatic success of "tough love"-disbursing, "authentic self"-espousing Dr Phil McGraw.[19]

A similar reality-led revolt is discernible in marketing. Real brands, those made from natural ingredients or blessed with an illustrious heritage (Kellogg's, Budweiser, Volkswagen), are especially highly regarded.[20] Real customer service – service that doesn't involve cold calls or please hold, press star now platitudes – is particularly appreciated. Real testimonials, from real people (or at least real actors playing real people) are increasingly evident, as Apple's $50 million "Switch" campaign illustrates. Real executives, unobtrusive individuals who work hard and keep a low media profile, are preferred to the headline-hogging, bottom line-massaging management superstars of the pre-Enron epoch. Real television commercials – ads that sell stuff rather than bamboozle viewers with incomprehensible images, subtle allusions, and creatives-at-work self-indulgence – are welcomed like a long lost, if somewhat shady, friend. "There is a feeling of slight relief," Bracewell astutely notes,[21] "when one comes across one of those brightly colored adverts that announce, without further ado, 'It does exactly what it says on the tin!' After the succession of dizzyingly jump-cut, defiantly conceptual, and ultra-fashionable blip-verts, there is something faintly endearing about the hard sell."

At the same time, it is important to appreciate that, for all today's fixation on the authentic, *there is no such thing as authenticity*, only varying degrees of inauthenticity. The unspoilt holiday resort is designed to look unspoilt. The traditional Irish bar is assembled from mass produced, cod-Celtic kitsch. The free-range chickens are free to range around a fetid factory farm. The classic blue jeans are pre-shrunk, pre-faded, pre-ripped, pre-grimed, and, doubtless, pre-impreg-nated with pre-washday adolescent aromas. Authentic authenticity, so to speak, is unattainable. But it can be staged, it can be created, it can be evoked.[22] Our situation, in certain respects, is very similar to the dilemma described by post-modern theorist Umberto Eco: How can a man make a genuine declaration of love when the words "I love you madly" have been used repeatedly and thereby rendered meaningless by generations of romantic fiction writers? His solution: "As Barbara Cartland would put it, 'I love you madly'," which both acknowledges the cliché and makes a declaration of love all the same.[23]

Analogously, how can marketers sell stuff when every sales pitch has been used already, when every advertising treatment has been tried and tried again, when there's nothing left to market but market-ing itself? The most common response, as a glance at today's advertising attests, is to be reflexive. To say, in effect, "As marketers used to say, this product is good. Buy it." "Here we are, trying to make an ad that'll sell stuff, do you think this'll work?" "Marketing research tells us that you like ketchup on your burger. *Voila.*" "Are you sick and tired of car dealers that use scantily clad models to sell their vehicles? We thought not!"

Another approach is to play it absolutely straight. This product is good, buy it. Nine out of ten cats prefer it. Use our shampoo for silky, shiny hair. A painkiller that kills headaches. Fast. The finest food in town. Here. Delivery in 15 minutes. Guaranteed. Cures hemor-rhoids, or your money back (as if you'd ask for a refund . . . as if they'd check if you did).

The fiendish genius of this apparent straight talking is that it works in two ways.[24] On the one hand, good old-fashioned sales pitches work as good old-fashioned sales pitches. This detergent washes whiter. That hire car is best value for money. The other computer has more bells and whistles, but our after-sales service is superior. On the other hand, ostensible authenticity has an air of imputed irony. That is to say, sophisticated, marketing-savvy consumers will surmise that traditional this-product-is-good sales pitches are tongue-in-cheek, private jokes between them and the advertising agency. Straightforward sales pitches flatter their intelligence by intimating that – unlike unsophisticated consumers – they can see through the unsophisticated sales pitch and detect the sophistication behind the unsophistication. The key is to play it dead straight. Don't even hint that there's a double-bluff going on. Deny any complicity. Let ambiguity, inscrutability, and mystery prevail. Insist that it means exactly what it says, on the tin or otherwise. They'll immediately assume the opposite and start imagining all manner of ulterior motives. They'll convince themselves that you're a marketing genius. Others will simply applaud your honesty, forthrightness, and refreshing avoidance of contrivance. You read it here first.

Be that as it may, and notwithstanding the grotesque sight of ever-ethical politicians lining up to condemn the corporations whose campaign contributions they were once happy to accept, there is a very important lesson here for marketers. Generation ® has made marketing an issue, a scapegoat, a fall guy for multinational capital, and marketing executives have been forced into action. As custodians of customer-led, customer-focused, customer-oriented organizations, marketers are duty bound to respond to the concerns of those they are led by, focused on, or oriented towards. There is no alternative, no excuse, no escape.

Indeed, the paradox of today's anti-marketing protests is that the protesters have taken marketers at their word. Marketing has sold the creed of customer orientation so well – *too* well – that consumers now expect to be listened to.[25] For decades, marketing managers have maintained that customer satisfaction comes first, that consumers are the be all and end all of business. However, by portraying themselves as customer-centric organizations (rather than, say, profit-focused) and having reneged on the deal (by rapacious acts of environmental despoliation and employee exploitation), marketers have created a customer-oriented cross for their own backs.[26] So much so, that even the most customer-oriented organizations are feeling the post-Seattle heat. They are feeling it *because* they are more customer oriented than most. The anti-marketing riots are a consequence of, not a call for, customer orientation.

Good to the Last Double Decaff

Take Starbucks. From its earliest incarnation as *Il Giornale*, through the first coffee bars in Seattle, to the 5,200 outlets it operates in 23 countries today, Starbucks has remained completely, totally, absolutely, unapologetically customer centric.[27] Its mission statement – remember them? – aims to "develop enthusiastically satisfied customers all of the time." Note, not just satisfied, but *enthusiastically satisfied*. Not just now and then, but *all of the time*. In fact, it is fair to say that Starbucks not only cares about its customers, it cares about what its customers care about. In three important respects.

First, Starbucks' customers care about their coffee. They must do at those prices. And Starbucks' hard-won reputation is predicated on Howard Schultz's love of and enthusiasm for the beautiful brew. Starbucks, as the founder frequently points out, was built one cup at a time into the – mission statement alert! – premier purveyor of the finest coffee in the world.[28] Granted, the company's success cannot be divorced from Schultz's determination to educate his customers and raise their expectations about what constitutes a good *grande latte* or short *macchiato*. An astute product development program, ranging from the famous Frappuchino and not-so-famous Mazagran to Starbucks' CDs and premium ice cream, has also helped things along. Schultz's pragmatic attitude to consumers' desire for low fat milk and flavored coffees, despite his purist coffee brewing principles, clearly indicate that an astute marketing sensibility is at work. Customers call the shots.

Second, Starbucks' customers care about the physical space in which their espressos, cappuccinos, and, to quote comedian Steve Martin,[29] "half double decaf half cafs, with a twist of lemon," are consumed. In today's get-up-and-go world, where we are expected to keep up, keep on, keep on up, keep on keeping on up, and what have you, Starbucks provides a haven of peace, tranquility, and communal solitude, a place where the cares of the day can be cast off and washed away with the aid of a caffeine infusion or two. The

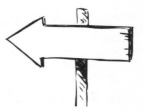

Starbucks operates a hospital for the healthy.

easy chairs, the terrazzo flooring, the tinkling, jazz-tinged soundtrack, the seductive smell of freshly brewed beans, and the retail stage show mounted by Starbucks' strutting, shouting, steam-swathed baristas, combine to create a special space, a third place, a decompression zone interposed between work and home. Starbucks' Band Aid binds the wounds of the modern world. Starbucks operates a hospital for the healthy. Starbucks is a customer-oriented cure for the stresses and strains of consumer society. Starbucks, as Schultz eloquently expresses it, is a place to exhale.[30]

Or should that be exhort? The third sphere in which Starbucks cares about its customers' cares is good corporate citizenship. At a time of rising consumer concern about the west's exploitation of "the rest," Starbucks has gone to great lengths to establish its philanthropic credentials. It resolutely refuses to exploit third world plantation workers and pays substantially over the odds for its beans. It offers health insurance and stock options to its lowliest part-time employees and pays more than the minimum wage. Its environmental consciousness extends to a discount for customers who supply their own beverage containers. It has appointed a Senior Vice-president for Corporate Social Responsibility, publishes an annual CSR report, and, from the company's earliest days in the Pacific northwest – long before consumerism was cool – it has supported CASE, an international relief organization. Unlike most of its rivals in the coffee business, moreover, Starbucks sponsors clinics, schools, and credit schemes in coffee growing communities. Like its left-leaning, right-on customers, in other words, Starbucks wears its corporate heart on its homespun, hand-woven, have-a-nice-one sleeve.[31]

You For Coffee?

Yet, for all its do-gooding, Starbucks is in the eye of the anti-marketing storm. In the Seattle riots of November 1999, its outlets were singled out for special attention by the demolition men and women, as they have been ever since.[32] Such is the attention lavished on Starbucks by the Nologoistas that it is now part of the particularly pernicious triumvirate, alongside McDonald's and Nike, that today's anti-capitalists love to hate. Similarly, Starbucks' arrival in many communities is greeted with placards, picket lines, and vociferous protests by concerned citizens, who foresee the rapid demise of local, independently-owned coffee emporia. Even its record of good corporate citizenship has been contemptuously dismissed as greenwash, mere window dressing, socially responsible play-acting, a caring-sharing front for capitalism red in tooth and claw.[33]

Such accusations, to be sure, are not entirely unwarranted. Starbucks is competitive to the point of ruthlessness, as the infamous Peet's Bar episode proves (when Schultz's former boss refused

34

to sell up, a Third Place opened four doors down). Starbucks is the Wal-Mart of coffee bars, the death knell of small town establishments (its tightly clustered location strategy squeezes the life out of competitors). Starbucks pays above the odds for its supplies, albeit the subsequent mark-up is still astronomical (less than 1% of its beans are Fairtrade certified). Starbucks may be a model employer but many part-time counter-hands don't stay long enough to reap the benefits (such as stock options and health care provision). Starbucks, many believe, is a particularly insidious form of capitalism, one that pretends it isn't capitalist. Starbucks' ostensible

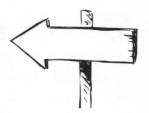

> Starbucks, many believe, is a particularly insidious form of capitalism, one that pretends it isn't capitalist.

opposition to exploitation masks its own deeply exploitative activities. Starbucks, as Austin Powers revealed in *The Spy Who Shagged Me*, is the lair of Dr Evil, a Third Reich place where heinous plans are hatched for world domination. Ooh, behave.

In fairness to Howard Schultz, his organization is a paragon compared to some of its competitors. For all its seeming ubiquity, furthermore, Starbucks is very small beer. It absorbs just over one per cent of the world's coffee supply. Similarly, it is totally unreasonable to hold a single company responsible for the imbalances, injustices, and iniquities that inhere in the arabica business, especially one that is as conscientious, comparatively speaking, as Starbucks. Nevertheless, it is Howard Schultz and his henchpersons – rather than Nestlé, Kraft, or Procter & Gamble – who get it in the globalized neck. Part of this is due to the organization's high profile,

35

which makes it an obvious target. Part of it is ease of access, since it's easier to trash a nearby Starbucks than trek to the nearest Nestlé factory. Part of it is down to Starbuck's positioning as a hip 'n' happenin', third-world lovin' corporation, a stance that practically invites people to critically examine the reality behind the rhetoric.

The hostility, however, is also due to the company's completely, totally, absolutely, unapologetically customer-oriented marketing philosophy. Protesters target Starbucks because they *know* it claims to be especially attentive to customers, because it aims to "develop enthusiastically satisfied customers all of the time," because it listens to the voice of the consumer and will respond to customer demands, no matter how inelegantly expressed. As Ronnie Cummins, director of the US Organic Consumers Association,[34] openly confesses about his contra-Starbucks campaign, "we target them because they're the only big coffee company in the world that pretends to be socially responsible . . . It's better to start with them. Kraft is never going to do anything. When you're the grassroots with limited resources, you have to pick your targets carefully."

The Marketing Reflex

So, what can be done? Many traditionalists might conclude that this state of affairs calls for *even more* customer orientation. That is, to really love the customer, not just love them like before. And if that doesn't work, to really, *really* love the customer, not just really love them like before. And if that doesn't work . . .

I'm sorry, but this more-of-the-same solution won't wash. It won't wash because Starbucks and similar super-customer-centric corporations are at the epicenter of a new customer dispensation, a dispensation that first found expression in the Seattle riots. It is a dispensation where marketers' vastly increased knowledge of consumers – thanks to sophisticated research techniques, humungous databases, and the software to mine the raw material – is counter-balanced by consumers' vastly increased knowledge of marketers and the marketing system.[35]

When Vance Packard published *The Hidden Persuaders* forty-five years ago, US consumers were deeply shocked, and not a little intrigued, by the mendacious machinations of marketing types.[36] Today, however, they are fully au fait with marketers' latest maneuvers. Our television channels and radio stations are chock-a-block with programs and stories about marketing, consumption, shopper psychology, and all the rest. Stand up comics perform lengthy routines on supermarkets, shopping carts, and stereotyped TV ads for shampoo, shaving foam, or sanitary napkins. Glossy magazines routinely appraise their readers of the rationale behind retail store design and the rebranding exercise *du jour*. Sunday newspaper supplements are replete with reflections on, and deconstructions of, breaking advertising campaigns, as well as industry gossip, impending pitches, and account executive shenanigans. Hollywood movies regularly make use of advertising/marketing/retail store settings – *What Women Want*, *Crazy People*, *Clerks*, *High Fidelity*, *Scenes From a Mall*, *You've Got Mail*, *Working Girl*, *Soul Man*, *Pretty Woman*, *Jerry Maguire*, *How to Get Ahead in Advertising* – and, in so doing, reveal the inner workings of the marketing institutions concerned. These inner workings may well be overdramatized caricatures, but they nonetheless raise the general public's overall marketing consciousness.

What this all means is that today's consumers are wise to the wiles of marketers. They possess a "marketing reflex," an inbuilt early warning system that detects incoming commercial messages – no matter how subtle – and automatically neutralizes them. Or, as Bond and Kirshenbaum[37] colorfully describe it, "Consumers are like roaches. We spray them with marketing and for a time it works. Then inevitably they develop an immunity, a resistance." This is particularly true of Generations X, Y, and ®, those who suckled at the marketing teat from birth and speak Brandsperanto like a native. Innumerable empirical studies reveal that they are perfectly capable

They no longer read ads innocently, but look behind them, as it were, to see what the advertiser's up to.

of examining, evaluating, expropriating, and eviscerating marketing campaigns.[38] My own analyses of consumers consistently show that they unfailingly second-guess the marketers' intent. They no longer read ads innocently, but look behind them, as it were, to see what the advertiser's up to. They are conscious of the pitch behind the pitch.[39]

Image is Nothing

Today's marketers, to be sure, are aware that consumers are aware of them. This accounts for the recent rapid rise of reflexive advertising campaigns. That is, advertisements about advertising, or marketing research, or sales promotion, or new product development, or all manner of marketing-related scenarios.

Consider Joe Isuzu. When the phony car dealer, who wowed American TV audiences in the 1980s, was revived for today's marketing-literate consumers, the ads didn't feature Joe's straight-to-camera sales pitches of the past. The commercials, rather, focused on Joe's attempts to sell his big budget advertising ideas to Isuzu's marketing VP and Chief Executive Officer. An extra layer of marketing, so to speak, has been added in the interim.

The Budweiser frogs, furthermore, are not straightforward trade characters of anthropomorphic marketing tradition, akin to Tony the Tiger, Morris the Cat, or Tommy the Tuna. To the contrary, they are amphibian thespians, who have captured the Budweiser voice-over account, despite the protestations of ill-mannered iguanas like Louie. The marketing is the message.

In a similar vein, the iconoclastic Italian outfitter Diesel consistently sells itself by means of an anti-selling message. It takes marketing-savvy consumers as a given and seeks to subvert the norms, clichés, and customer-centric sanctimoniousness of the marketing industry. As Maurizio Marchiori, Diesel's Advertising and Communications Director states about do-gooding, caring-sharing, hug-a-customer-today corporations,[40] "Big brands try so hard to portray themselves as sincere and well-intentioned but it doesn't come across as real, and you can almost always feel the monstrous corporate structure behind it."

Consumers, in a nutshell, are aware of marketing matters. Marketers are aware that consumers are aware of marketing matters. Consumers are aware that marketers are aware that consumers are aware of marketing matters. And so the contrapuntal dance of consumer-savvy marketers and marketing-savvy consumers continues, in an infinite regression of reflexive fractals.

But what are the implications of all this? What are marketers actually doing about it? Are they re-engineering their thinking to cope with today's changed circumstances?

Well, to some extent they are. There is a swelling, if still *sotto voce*, chorus of marketing commentators who refuse to sing the hush-a-bye-customer tune. The literature on innovations, in particular, shows that: (1) customers often don't know what they want; and (2) the customer isn't always right. With regard to the first of these, there is a long line of successful products and services that were initially rejected by consumers, only to go on to great things.[41] This speaks volumes about people's ability to articulate their wants

39

or anticipate their own reactions. Indeed, if consumers had had their way, there'd be no CNN, Sony Walkman, Chrysler Minivan, Motorola cell-phone, Palm PDA, Fox TV Network, Boeing 747, Dyson vacuum cleaner, and Disneyland, to say nothing of microwave ovens, frozen food, electric toothbrushes, and the internet. True, the world might be a better place without the Sony Walkman, Motorola cell-phones, and Fox – no earphone overspill, no annoying ring tones, no *When Good CEOs Go Bad* – but the fact of the matter is that they triumphed because the innovators behind them ignored early customer resistance, rejected focus group or test market findings, and proceeded to launch in the face of universal indifference, ridicule, antipathy. Whatever.

Customer, Schmustomer

The customer, likewise, isn't always right. This is nowhere better illustrated than in Clayton Christensen's seminal analysis of the market for hard disk drives.[42] Puzzled by the fact that world-class organizations repeatedly stumbled when "disruptive technologies" hoved into view – 14-inch disks, 8-inch disks, 5.25-inch disks, 3.5-inch disks, 1.8-inch disks, etc. – he found that, far from ignoring the new idea, the organizations often pioneered the technologies concerned. But they didn't bring them to market. And why? Because their customers were opposed, or indifferent to, the innovation. "There's no call for it." "Can't see the point." "It's not what we're looking for." "Don't waste your R&D dollars on that nonsensical notion."

Unfortunately for the disk makers concerned – Shugart, Micropolis, Priam, Quantum, Western Digital, and all the rest – they paid a very heavy price for paying heed to their customers and their undying devotion to best marketing practice. Some paid the ultimate price, as did others in completely different sectors. Christensen found the exact same pattern in markets as diverse as mechanical excavators, inkjet printers, tabletop photocopiers, personal digital assistants, integrated steel making, and department store retailing. It thus seems that far from being always right, the customer can be the kiss of death. In this regard, never forget that it was customer

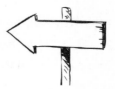

> **Far from being always right, the customer can be the kiss of death.**

orientation that brought you McDonald's McLean, KFC's skinless fried chicken, and Pizza Hut's lo-calorie deep-pan pizza, all of which flatlined at the fast food counter.

My point, then, is that regardless of what the standard marketing textbooks suggest, sometimes the very worst thing you can do is listen to customers. And the same goes for their surrogates. That is, those who purport to speak on behalf of the customer, the ordinary Joe, the regular gal, the man in the street, the stereotypical soccer mom, or, as in Heartmate's remarkable case, the patient.[43]

Heartmate, in case you haven't heard of it, is a hi-tech pump, an artificial device that performs the necessary cardiovascular functions while heart patients are waiting for a transplant. When the mechanism was first mooted by Vic Poirier, it was spurned by the medical establishment. Surgeons simply didn't want to know, consultant cardiologists were contemptuous. The apparatus, they said, could cause organs to atrophy. It would precipitate patient deaths rather than prolong their lives. As a bare minimum, Poirier's heart-assist pump might trigger seizures, strokes, or cardiac arrests. Worse still, the pioneer's prototype had a roughly-textured inner surface, which was sure to create blood clots, the bane of heart surgery. Nothing but an ultra smooth surface would suffice, since the tiniest scratch or imperfection could cause clotting to occur.

However, in keeping with the archetypal against-the-odds trad-ition, Vic Poirier persisted. His heart-assist pump worked. Blood clotted evenly, thanks to the textured surface, and created a collagen lining like a natural heart. The product took off, thousands are implanted every year and the market for cardiosystems devices is now worth approximately $400 million per annum.[44]

Heartwarming as Heartmate's story is, what does it actually mean in practical marketing terms? It means that we are in a strangely paradoxical situation where, on the one hand, sophisticated market-ing-savvy consumers are dissing customer-oriented organizations like Starbucks. Customer-savvy marketers, on the other hand, now believe that listening to marketing-savvy consumers is more of a hindrance than a help.

So, how should marketers respond? Should we become *more* customer oriented, thereby winning back the skeptics? Or should we become *less* customer oriented, thereby avoiding customer-led faux pas?

The answer, of course, is neither. Marketing needs a non-cus-tomer-centric means of attracting customers. It must neither obsequi-ously pander to, nor completely ignore, consumers. Twenty-first century marketing will take place in a world where customers are wise to marketers' wiles and marketers are cognizant of cus-tomer-focused shortcomings. The hills and valleys, so to speak, of ignorance and mutual incomprehension – marketers who are besot-ted by customers and consumers who are apprehensive about marketing's hidden persuasions – have been flattened out. The play-ing field is comparatively level. We are living in a different marketing dispensation and marketing principles must be rearranged accord-ingly.

How to Cope With Canny Customers?
Flattery Never Fails. Tell Them They're Much Too Smart For You.

HOW TO HANDLE HOW-TO MARKETING BOOKS

Levi's Has Left the Building

In October 1999, Levi Strauss & Co opened the flagship store to end all flagship stores in its hometown of San Francisco. A four-story tribute to the peerless apparel company, Levi's Union Square megastore is the embodiment of the brand.[1] It is hip. It is hop. It is hot. It is happenin'. It is sharp. It is edgy. It is something else. It is full of flashing lights, flickering images, startling special effects, and extra-extraordinary features like real time store directories and video periscopes in the vestibule. It has banks of giant TV screens showing the organization's award-winning commercials. It holds the entire Levi's range in stock at all times, including Dockers, Slates, and items only available in Europe and Japan. It contains all manner of Levi's memorabilia, as well as shrines to the individual lines: 501s, 505s, 550s, red tab, silver tab, orange tab, and, naturally, a complete vintage collection of Levi's Classics. Its nu-metal esthetic – all cast iron, concrete floors, and steel tubing – pays homage to the brand's pre-industrial past, post-industrial present, and its then-as-now rugged, riveted, rip-em-if-you're-strong-enough build quality. Levi's, the original and best. Levi's, the blue jeans that built America. Levi's, official outfitters to the young and the young at heart.[2]

If, however, there is one word that best describes Levi's Union Square emporium, that word would be "customized." When it first opened, the flagship store was full to overflowing with personalized touches, from fingerprint recognition and body scanners to offbeat photo booths and shrink-to-fit jean pools.[3] The centerpiece of the third floor was a customization center, where consumers could put their individual stamp on a favorite Levi's garment, newly bought or ancient fossil. These customization services included embroidery, hand painting, laser etching, abrasion work, and beaded, sequined, or rhinestoned heat transfers. Nearby computer kiosks enabled Levi's lovers to log on to the brand's website, Original Spin, where a pair of custom-built pants could be designed, ordered, paid for, and delivered by FedEx twenty-one days later. "Create your own jeans from scratch," it suggested.[4]

On opening day, then, Levi's flagship comprised the epitome of customer orientation. It symbolized the shift from mass manufacturing and marketing, where a limited range of sizes fits all (with a great deal of pushing, pulling, and squeezing), to the markets of one, have it your way, mass customization model that characterizes contemporary commercial life. In this regard, Levi's Union Square megastore was as much a monument to Peppers and Rogers as it was to Levi Strauss & Co.[5]

A Rivet Runs Through It

Be that as it may, they say that the zenith of a civilization, culture, corporation, or, for that matter, brand occurs at the very moment when it is starting to disintegrate, deteriorate, decline, die.[6] Levi's is no exception. Union Square's grand opening came at the very moment when the brand hit the buffers. The megastore wasn't so much a monument to, as a mausoleum for, the once iconic brand. At the start of the decade in which the flagship was constructed, Levi's captured 48% of the jeans market, compared to Lee and Wranglers' 22%, private labels' 3% and others' 27%. Ten years later, Levi's had slipped to 25%, Lee and Wrangler were up to 32%, private labels enjoyed a seven fold increase to 21%, and others were down slightly but still lookin' good at 22%. The American icon, furthermore, saw its revenues plunge from $7.1 to $4.6 billion between 1996 and 2000.[7] A 14% fall occurred in 1999 alone and, according to its then CEO Robert D. Haas, the company barely broke even in that fateful year. When Union Square opened in October, Levi's had already left the building. In marketing terms, at least.[8]

Like all good Hollywood biopics, however, our seemingly down and out corporation is making something of comeback, thanks to new CEO Philip A. Marineau's commitment to the brand, its heritage, and creative thinking.[9] Interestingly, the comeback is based on limiting choice, reducing options, and reinjecting an inimitable air of uniqueness and unattainability into what had become a boringly ubiquitous brand, available in every conceivable customerized option. The cutting-edge Red Collection is made in just three styles and finishes. Small numbers of exclusive concept stores, each named after an obscure allusion to jeans manufacturing, are opening in style capitals like Paris (Nim), Milan (B-Fly), London (Cinch) and New York (Selvedge). The ill-fated customization service, Original Spin, has been cut back to the point of closure. Meantime, the "original" Nevada jeans, found in a coalmine, dating from the 1880s, and bought back by the company for $50,000, have been reproduced in a strictly limited edition, at $400 a pop. While Levi Strauss still has a long road to travel, the cachet that attracted customers in the first place is steadily being recaptured.[10]

Phil and Ted's Bogus Journey

This encouraging development notwithstanding, Levi's *folie de gran-*

deur in Union Square is more than a monument to hubris, an ironic symbol of an iconic organization in trouble. The megastore also symbolizes the chronic state of contemporary marketing, a conceptual megastore if ever there was one. Just as Levi Strauss & Co. thrashed around, desperately trying to capture the charisma of old, so too marketing is engaged in an attempt to reimagine itself. Forty years on from the birth of the "modern" marketing concept, the customer-first approach that Ted Levitt formulated and Phil Kotler codified, marketers are wakening up to the fact that it isn't modern

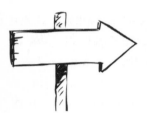

Just as Levi Strauss & Co. thrashed around, desperately trying to capture the charisma of old, so too marketing is engaged in an attempt to reimagine itself.

any more, that it's out of touch, that it needs a rethink, that it no longer works in today's post-Seattle circumstances. A browse in the business section of most mega-bookstores reveals that there's a small but vocal group of doubters, heretics, agnostics, and backsliders.

Clearly, it is impossible to do justice to this clique of marketing critics. They range from former Coke supremo Sergio Zyman,[11] who has apocalyptically announced that the end of marketing is nigh, through Regis "marketing-is-everything" McKenna,[12] who has apocalyptically announced that the end of marketing is nigh, to E-marketing guru Elliott Ettenberg,[13] who has apocalyptically announced that the end of marketing is nigh.

As a rule, however, marketing's millenarians adopt a two-pronged rhetorical strategy: (1) they mount an attack on "old-style" marketing, usually by apocalyptically announcing that – all together now – the end of marketing is nigh; and (2) they offer a "radical" marketing alternative, invariably one with a suitably snappy title. For the purposes of the present discussion, these alternatives can be summarized (snappily, if I say so myself) under the following Eight Es:

- *Experiential* – an emergent school of marketing thought that emphasizes ecstasy, emotion, and the delivery of extraordinary consumer experiences. It exploits the "Wow" factor, in effect.[14]
- *Environment* – an approach that relies on retail store atmospherics, on impressive architecture, on the power of space, place, and *genius loci*. The Niketown phenomenon, in other words.[15]
- *Esthetic* – a stance that espouses art, beauty, and design, everything from quirky Alessi kettles and psychedelic Apple iMacs to the Chrysler P.T. Cruiser and the "feel" of a Mont Blanc pen. Art for mart's sake.[16]
- *Ephemeral* – a net-driven notion based on buzz-building, fad-forwarding, chat-room churning, brand community boosting, and unleashing the ideavirus. In the beginning was the word of mouth, so to speak.[17]
- *Evangelical* – an alternative that taps into the alleged spirituality of consumption. This ranges from the shopping-mall-as-cathedral cliché to the suggestion that CEOs seek solace in the seven deadly sins.[18]
- *Ethical* – a perspective predicated on Anita Roddick's precept of trade-not-aid and eco-conscious consumer behavior. Just say no to rapaciousness, exploitation, and waste. Buy a lipstick, save the world.[19]
- *Eccentric* – an off-the-wall standpoint that wraps itself in hipness, irreverence, and fun-filled frolics. Instantly recognizable by wacky book titles like *Eat the Big Bananas* or *Hey Wendy's, Squeeze This*.[20]
- $E=MC^2$ – an antidote to eccentricity, which contends that marketing is a science, or would be if it weren't for the bananas

brigade.[21] Rigor, Rectitude, and Reliability are what marketing needs right now. Got that?

Easy Money

It is, I admit, easy to be cynical about these exercises in E-type marketing. To many, they are little more than blatant attempts to flog half-baked fads and make a few quick bucks on the management consultancy circuit. However, as someone who has previously poured scorn on fad-fuelled flatulence, as someone who is currently engaged in a brazen attempt to board the fad-wagon, as someone who is nothing if not a hyper-hypocrite, I can only say that skepticism doesn't become you, gentle reader. "Live and let live," is my personal credo. Second only to "Available for Weddings, Bar Mitzvas and Brand Image Audits."

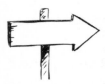

Hey, at least I'm giving you free gifts!

Regardless of what you think about the various forms of E-ffrontery – hey, at least I'm giving you free gifts! – the Espousers, Enthusiasts, and Enunciators are as one in their belief that a change is necessary.[22] New times require new marketing. The old rules no longer apply. The world has moved on and marketing must move on as well. E-volve or else. Even Philip Kotler, the pioneer of "modern" marketing, has joined the E-volutionaries. In his latest book, *Marketing Moves*, the venerable Phil contends that the modern marketing concept has been consigned to the trash can of history, alongside the reviled Selling Concept. A new marketing paradigm – the Holistic Marketing Concept, no less – now holds sway:

Under the holistic marketing concept, the starting point is individual customer requirements. Marketing's task is to develop contextual offerings of products, services, and experiences to match individual customers' requirements. To explore, create, and deliver individual customer value in a very dynamic and competitive environment, marketers need to invest in the company's relational capital covering all stakeholders – consumers, collaborators, employees, and communities. Companies therefore go beyond the business concept of customer relationship management *toward the concept of* whole relationship management . . . *Holistic marketers achieve profitable growth by expanding customer share, building customer loyalty, and capturing customer lifetime value.*[23]

Hmmmm. While many commentators agree that it's time for a change in marketing tack, if only on account of latter-day innovations in information and communications technology, there is a bit of a problem with the options currently on offer. When you actually

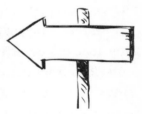

The basic problem with our Eight Emergent forms of marketing is that they still rest on the discredited idea of customer orientation.

examine the above Eight Es, or any other conceptual Electives, Entreaties, Emendations, and Enemas out there, they are misreading the situation and, well, missing the point.

Postmodern Marketing Myopia

Reluctant as I am to take issue with the consultancy industrial com-

49

plex – until such times as a place on the witness protection program is available – the basic problem with our Eight Emergent forms of marketing is that they still rest on the discredited idea of customer orientation. They still espouse a customer-first philosophy. They still place the customer at the center of the marketing universe. The underlying logic seems to be that no matter how sophisticated, or choosy, or antagonistic, or downright difficult consumers become, marketers will continue to bow down to them, only lower than before. And lower. And lower. The spread-eagle has landed.[24]

A related difficulty is that the Eight Es and their ilk are sorely afflicted with what might be termed postmodern marketing myopia. That is to say, the case studies, companies, and campaigns they hold up as exemplars of Esthetics, Ethics, Experiences, or whatever are almost always drawn from the world of business, from commercial life, from the line up of usual marketing suspects. Granted, they occasionally feature not-for-profit organizations, or a token customer-oriented politician, but in the main they focus on the same-old-same-old companies that everyone else has focused on. Levi Strauss and Starbucks, for example.

Be that as it may, if there is one thing the literature on innovation teaches us, it is that radically new ideas often originate from outsiders, from mavericks, from the margins, from the least expected sources. By continuing to concentrate on the business community – the *contemporary* business community – E-type marketers are ignoring alternative role models.

One such model is the arts. Just as the CIA turned to Holly-

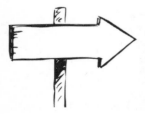

Art is a big, pumped-up, operatic version of real life; it's the lie that tells the truth better than the truth does.

wood's imagineers and scriptwriters in the aftermath of 9/11, so too marketers should sometimes look to the artistic and cultural spheres for inspiration.[25] Music, painting, poetry, plays, movies, stage shows, situation comedies such as *Will & Grace*, acerbic essays by Michael "downsize this" Moore, or novels like Alex Shakar's *Savage Girl* – a wonderful encapsulation of today's reflexive consumer (see Free Gift 3) – can provide insights into marketing matters that are otherwise unattainable. Rather than regard the arts as a particularly recalcitrant industrial sector that badly needs to be taken in hand by modern marketing science – the conventional view[26] – perhaps it is time to recognize that marketing can learn from the arts. "Art," as cult novelist Chuck Palahnuik (paraphrasing Picasso) rightly observes,[27] "is a big, pumped-up, operatic version of real life; it's the lie that tells the truth better than the truth does."

Free Gift 3: I am Not a Target Marketer

"Right now people are nostalgic for simpler times, times when people felt pure and complete in their bodies, when their bodies were all the power they required to satisfy their needs. People today are sick of being consumers. And you have a product that can help. Your product will keep them pure. Your product will restore their innocence. Because your product is, in its very essence, the opposite of consumption. Consuming your product is like consuming nothing at all. Keep this is mind always when designing your campaign. Keep in mind how light this product is going to make buyers feel, how free it's going to make them feel – free of people like you."

Thus speaks Ursula Van Urden, the protagonist of Alex Shakar's first novel, *The Savage Girl*.[28] Trainee cool hunter for Tomorrow Ltd., a cutting-edge market research consultancy, Ursula spots a feral street person living rough in Middle City's Banister Park. Inspired by this savage girl's apparent ability to thrive in the urban jungle, Ursula develops a major marketing campaign based on getting back to nature and the abandonment of consumerism. Middle City consumers, you see, are sated, jaded, cynical, and wise to the wiles of cunning marketing types. Thanks to Ursula's trend-spotting acumen, however, a noble savagery fad takes off. Fake-fur loincloths, exfoliating war paint, bonelike bracelets, high-heeled moccasins, rough-hewn haircuts, and bow and arrow accessories become the order of the day among Middle City's putative postmodern primitives.

As the savage ensemble suggests, Alex Shakar's novel is a wonderful parody of the marketing industry, with its cool hunters, street scouts, and preposterous self-importance. Like all good lampoons, nevertheless, *The Savage Girl* contains more than a grain of truth. Many of the products, services, and concepts described in the book teeter on the edge of plausibility. A discussion of credit cards' metallurgic class system – gold, platinum, titanium, tungsten, etc. – leads to the not unappealing notion of a Plutonium Card. The fashionable journal *Trend* maintains a "Dichter Scale" that registers companies' score on the retroquake of consumer desire. Tomorrow Ltd. captures the account for diet water, a breakthrough product that has all the benefits of ordinary water without making imbibers feel bloated. Middle City's latest theme restaurant is an upscale, five-star diner, which not only looks like an unhygienic greasy spoon, but its Ferrara marble tabletops are indistinguishable from the faux-marble Formica tops of the original. The savage trend, moreover, starts getting out of hand when consumers wear pants made from the hide of sweatshop workers, sprout paste-on bullet entry wounds, embrace see-through tribal masks, and carry designer colostomy bags.

Above and beyond Shakar's squibs at the expense of consumer culture – popular hairstyles include The Whirl, The Deep-fry, The Porcupine, and The Pan-o'-Jell-O – he offers some remarkable reflections on the mainsprings of contemporary consumption. Every successful product, claims Tomorrow Ltd.'s chief executive, is predicated on an irresolvable paradox. It somehow combines two mutually exclusive states and promises to satisfy both simultaneously. Ice cream melds eroticism and innocence. Coffee amalgamates stimulation and relaxation. Air travel offers sanitized adventure. Amusement parks provide terror and reassurance. Automobiles render drivers reckless and safe. Sneakers grasp the earth and help consumers soar free. Muzak is a hybrid of transience and eternity.

The marketer's task, therefore, is to manage this tension, this broken soul, this bifurcated core, this *paradessence* of a product or service. For all their schismatic contradictions, remember, products are the building blocks of the impossibly perfect world that consumers construct on top of degraded, degenerate reality:

> *Our world exists only to hold up this other world, this ideal world. It's the world of our dreams, our desires. It's elaborate, it's heavy, and we carry it around with us everywhere. But we don't mind. The more that's up there, the better. Because up here is where we keep all that's best in us. The more that's up there, the richer our imagination becomes.*[29]

Whatever else they are, however, Middle City consumers are neither utopian nor naïve. On the contrary, they are irredeemably "post-ironic." That is to say, they not only doubt the claims, campaigns, and sales pitches of marketing types, but they doubt their doubts about marketers' claims, campaigns, and sales pitches. As everyone knows, ironic advertising began with Bill Bernbach's classic 60s campaign for the VW Beetle, which included a critique of the product as part of the sales pitch, and thereby successfully circumvented consumer skepticism. But, in a world where irony is the base condition, ironic advertising can no longer work, since it comes across as a straightforward sales pitch. In such circumstances, the task of post-ironic advertisers is not to demystify, or explain, or importune, but to befuddle, to antagonize, to unsettle. Customer orientation is giving way to customer disorientation. The paradessence of post-ironic marketing is dissatisfaction guaranteed.

Sell Me the Old, Old Story

An additional pedagogic possibility is history. Despite what the standard textbooks suggest, marketing was around long before the mid-50s, when Drucker descended from the mount bearing tablets of customer-oriented stone. Many pre-modern marketing campaigns were as good, if not better, than those conducted today. The golden age of marketing was the 1920s, not the 1950s.[30] All of the above Eight Es, ironically enough, were anticipated, articulated, and applied by past generations of marketing specialists.[31] Even Philip Kotler's "new" marketing paradigm is not so new, after all. He was arguing for "new" marketing in his very first book and has identified literally dozens of "new" marketing paradigms in the ensuing decades, all with suitably snappy titles.[32]

Accordingly, the marketing perspective I'll be presenting in the present book – let's call it marke*tease* for the time being – turns the clock back to the approaches, perspectives, understandings, and ideas that prevailed prior to today's customer-coddling, CRM-driven, permission marketing-polluted epoch. It looks to the unorthodoxies of the past rather than the orthodoxies of the present. It taps into the history of marketing, the people, products, and places of yester-year, albeit interlarded with contemporary examples of the same. It also seeks inspiration in the artistic and cultural arenas of bygone eras. Granted, it draws upon some of the ideas – *the old ideas* – articulated by latter-day E-type evangelists. But it does so without the accompanying constraints of customer centricity. We need to break out of the box of customer orientation and, more to the point, we need to break out of the box of the break-out-of-the-box motivational metaphor.

Now, marketease doesn't ignore the customer completely. It ignores the notion of customer orientation. It is predicated on an eternal truth, perfected by sultry maidens of yore and rediscovered by Levi's of late, that more is achieved by playing hard to get than by pandering to a suitor's every whim. It contends that marketers should stop chasing customers and get customers to chase them instead. It posits that, rather than kow-towing to consumers, organizations ought to make life deliciously difficult for them. It maintains that when customer orientation is ubiquitous, customer deprivation is a source of potential competitive advantage. History shows that people want what they can't have and don't appreciate what they've got. It follows that pampering the customer is pointless, especially when everyone else is a pamperer. Customers should be titillated, teased, and tormented. They should be made to beg for some attention. Customers should be forgotten, because it is only by forgetting them that you fascinate them sufficiently to facilitate the transaction.

Such a stance, it must be stressed, is not a substitute for excellent products, efficient logistics, effective communications, expeditious after-sales service, or any other element of the established marketing paradigm. If, however, after two decades of benchmarking, continuous improvement, six sigma, JIT, TQM, QFD, P2P, quality circles, value chains, learning organizations, dancing elephants, world class competencies, and megalomaniacal mission statements, your product or service is not on a par with the best in the business, or Baldridged to the back teeth, then no amount of titillation, teasing, or torment will help.

To the contrary, teasing might be disadvantageous, since it'll only succeed in attracting prospects to your disappointing offering. As first impressions, so they say, are made but once, marketease is not for the defective or deficient, let alone the faint-hearted. It only applies in a context of abundance, such as the one outlined in the first Lesson, where all products are pretty much functionally equivalent and there is very little to choose between them in terms of performance. It pertains, in other words, when some products are better than others, but most are pretty much of a much-ness. As the automobile monitoring organization J.D. Power[33] recently 'fessed up, "There is no such thing as a bad car nowadays, they are all good." The same is true of colas, computers, cameras, chisels, cornflakes, corkscrews, chrysanthemums, copper cables, compact disk players, coffee makers, cat chow, credit cards, cell phones, CRM consultants, and the celebrated Clone Radio,[34] which plays "the songs that sound more like everyone else . . . than anyone else."

There are, of course, *perceived* differences between today's identikit offerings. These differences, as Ries and Trout have been telling us for decades,[35] are primarily due to marketing interventions. Marketing is the difference that makes a difference. The only problem is that marketing itself is increasingly stereotyped and, as a result, brands are becoming less and less distinctive in the eyes of contemporary, marketing-literate consumers.[36] Our identibrands are not only functionally indistinguishable, but marketed by marketers with a 3Cs, 4Ps, Five Forces, customers first-last-and-always worldview.

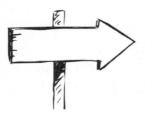

The *end* of marketing – its overall aim or purpose – is to sell stuff to consumers. No more, no less.

Marketease, by contrast is just about as far from the customer-centric norm as it is possible to get. So much so, that many brought up in the "delight the customer" tradition might be outraged at the very idea. It is important to emphasize, however, that the outraged are mistaking the means for the end. The *end* of marketing – its overall aim or purpose – is to sell stuff to consumers. No more, no less. The *means* to that end are something else again.

Delighting the customer is one possible means. Disregarding the customer is another. Disregarding, let me make this absolutely clear, does not mean defrauding, or deceiving, or diddling, or double crossing the customer in any way. Disregarding, rather, is the starting point for – fanfare, drum roll, pause for effect – the Dozen Ds model of customer disorientation (Exhibit 1).

Exhibit 1: The Dozen Ds Model of Customer Disorientation*

Disregarding the customer increases their **Desire**
Denying the customer increases their **Determination**
Depriving the customer increases their **Desperation**
Deferring customer consummation drives them to **Distraction**
Delivering the goods or services inspires **Devotion**
Desisting immediately induces **Disorientation**

*Note, no matrices were harmed in the making of this model. It contains no boxes, arrows, or analogous artificial ingredients. It has not been tested on animals, let alone humans.

Now, I appreciate that the Dozen Ds is a bit of a mouthful and I'm cognizant that you might be unwilling to swallow such an obvious whopper. If you think about it, nevertheless, you'll agree that the model makes eminent sense. In essence, the Dozen Ds rests on the notion that: (1) disregarding the customer draws rather than discourages them; (2) denying the consumer dramatically increases their desire, almost to the point of desperation; and (3) when the much-deferred object is finally delivered, such is the customer's delight that devotion is guaranteed thereafter. The concept, in effect, is predicated on the don't-call-us, we'll-call-you approach employed by generations of show business impresarios over-supplied with innumerable, equally talented, functionally indistinguishable artists.

More specifically, it is based on five key principles, summarized by the acronym TEASE, which will be fully explained in due course. Officially, TEASE stands for *Trickery*, *Exclusivity*, *Amplification*, *Secrecy*, and *Entertainment*. However, there are so many Ts, Es, As, Ss, and Es coming right up that you'll never look ACRONYMS in the eye again. No need to thank me. It's all part of the customer-centric service . . .

The Mother of All Hubbards

For the meantime, let me give you an example of marketease in action; an example that dates from the late nineteenth century, when marketing first emerged from the primordial soup of barkers, boomers, boosters, and bunco artistes; an example that occupies the disputed territory between commerce and creativity; an example that starts with soap bubble blowing, slides into the storm-tossed seas of printer's ink, and ends in hazardous waters off the west coast of Ireland.

According to an eminent Victorian marketer, Thomas J. Barret, "Any fool can make soap, but it takes a clever man to sell it." One such clever clogs was Elbert Hubbard.[37] He made his name in a product category characterized by countless competitors, all selling identical, functionally indistinguishable merchandise, through interchangeable channels of distribution. Almost single-handedly, he transformed the Larkin Soap Company from a low-end, me-too operation into one of the leading mail order companies in the US, alongside Sears Roebuck and Montgomery Ward. This was achieved by cutting out the middleman (much to traditional retailers' annoyance), by convincing consumers that they were getting an excellent "from factory to family" deal (as the anger of circumvented storekeepers "proved"), and by using the cost savings to underwrite an inspired promotional campaign of expensive free gifts. Furniture, pottery, desk lamps, bookcases, upright pianos, and all sorts of "surprise" items were freely available to coupon collectors and bulk purchasers. So popular did the premiums prove that people went out of their way to stock up on soap, much as today's business class travelers happily alter their itineraries to increase their air miles yield. Larkin Clubs, comprising ten or more households who pooled their soap purchases and drew lots for the mysterious premiums, sprang up all over the country, to the additional ire of adroitly-avoided middlemen. Thus was a cult brand born in a copy-cat product category.

Hubbard, however, had only just started. At the tender age of 36, he gave Larkin Soap the shove and set sail for the gilded groves of academe. Determined to become a man of letters, he enrolled in Harvard and unenrolled equally quickly after being haughtily informed that he was a talentless know-nothing. He got even by getting into publishing. Elbert established an anti-establishment periodical, *The Philistine*, which not only settled the score with Harvard highbrows, but also proved surprisingly popular with the general public. Its squibs, satires, and salty self-help proclamations, written in deep purple, adjectives a-go-go prose, were just what his autodidactic audience wanted. At a time when higher education was confined to the well-heeled few and many wannabe middle classes lacked formal book learning, the Mother of All Hubbards purveyed easily digestible cultural nuggets to the pedagogically deprived.

He did it in a humorous manner, moreover, by poking fun at the great and good and playing tricks on the East Coast establishment.[38] On one occasion, he published unattributed extracts from Ecclesiastes and, when the literary elite denounced his pathetic biblical pastiche, took great pleasure in revealing the good book as his source. On another occasion, he got hold of a racy love letter that was doing the rounds of the sporting set and published it as "A Letter by Lord Byron." The literati exploded on cue. On yet another occasion, he published an *Essay on Silence*, a book comprising nothing but blank pages and duly advertised it as "Hubbard's best book," "translated into 57 languages," "nothing ever written, by any author living or dead, has had so wide a circulation."

Elbert's textual tomfoolery was accompanied by an apposite physical transformation. The dapper young man, who charmed the stays off suburban soap-buyers, evolved into a larger than life "character," a sartorially-challenged cross between Oscar Wilde and Walt Whitman. Long hair, longer neckerchief, gargantuan Stetson set at a

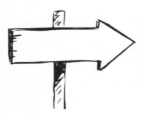

In an era not exactly renowned for its shrinking violets, Elbert Hubbard was a tall poppy.

rakish angle, coupled with a Clinton-sized libido and an unerring eye for self-publicity, served to ensure that his name was never far from the headlines. He was photographed in every conceivable position, in all the right places, with every celebrity worth their salt. He maintained that "life is an advertisement," that people should advertise themselves incessantly, and that those who didn't push themselves (or their products and services) forward at all times, were failing to reach their true potential. In an era not exactly renowned for its shrinking violets, Elbert Hubbard was a tall poppy.

Hubba Hubba Hubbard

Like all tall poppies, Hubbard attracted more than his fair share of scythe-swingers, nay-sayers, and no-can-doers. A self-made man and self-appointed "General Inspector of the Universe," Elbert was ostracized by the elite. Yet he was more than an ivy-league defoliator,

Harvard-baiting hoaxer, or entertaining exemplar of the mannerisms maketh man constituency. He was an artist, a marketer, a firebrand. His masterpiece was the Roycroft Shop, a manufacturing, publishing, and furniture making community in East Aurora, New York, modeled on William Morris's Arts and Crafts movement.[39] Behind faux-medieval walls, the latest printing and furniture making equipment produced a judicious selection of leather-bound books, semi-bespoke house furnishings, and limited edition collectibles. These were sold via mail order and direct to the public, who turned up in ever increasing numbers as Hubbard's fame spread and the communal, back-to-nature, neo-arcadian lifestyle he espoused became the self-help fad *du jour*. Naturally, his Roycroft products were lambasted by everyone who was anyone, not least on account of their prominently displayed brand name and the fact that his prices were beyond the reach of the common man he so loudly lauded. Nevertheless, the Roycroft brand was a raging success. Hubbard did much to kickstart an American Arts and Crafts movement; he nurtured a community of artists, designers, and imagineers in East Aurora; and, indeed, his exclusive collectibles are even more collectible today than when they were first carted out of Colophon Valley.[40]

Above and beyond the Roycroft brand collective, Elbert Hubbard was a prominent management guru, the Steven Covey of his time. His nationwide fame was established in 1899 with *A Message to Garcia* – an eloquent paean to personal empowerment – that was picked up by the robber baronage and reproduced on a massive scale. Never one to look free publicity in the mouth, Hubbard squeezed his celebrity until the mixed metaphors squeaked. He earned a fortune writing "publicity preachments" for national advertisers; he coined countless can-do, successories-style aphorisms for self-help publications; he served as a proto spin doctor for plutocrats, by means of a series of *Little Journey* booklets; he went on huge speaking tours of the country, charging fees of more than

$1000 a night; and he was, in certain respects, a forerunner of the "new age" approach to management, which has come back into fashion of late.[41]

At the time, of course, Hubbard was excoriated for selling out to big business and dismissed as a defender of the indefensible, a court jester for capitalism. The muckrakers – the Nologoistas of the Progressive Era – went to town with Hubbard's attempted exculpation of Standard Oil. Roycroft, likewise, was regarded as a massive vanity operation, managed by someone with a surfeit of self-absorption. He was repeatedly accused of plagiarism, ungentlemanly conduct, and taking sole authorial credit for the work of his 30-strong copywriting team.[42] Hubbard, however, reveled in the attacks, since he believed that all publicity is good publicity ("Every Knock is a Boost"), and often went out of his way to court controversy. Little wonder, then, that even after his untimely death in the *Lusitania* sinking of 1915, the titanic trailblazer's reputation remained sullied in the eyes of East Coast tastemakers. As Carl Rollins observed in the *Saturday Review of Literature*,[43] "this American barker . . . was strange and ridiculous and awful . . . so absurd and so grotesque that it is almost incredible . . . he was beneath contempt, both artistically and ethically."

Hubba hubba Hubbard may have failed the literary litmus test of his time, but his marketing scores are off the scale. Compared to Fra Elbert, Richard Branson is a pip squeak, Tom Peters an amateur, and Anita Roddick a new age nag. When it comes to drumming, Elbert Hubbard is hard to beat. When it comes to pitching, Elbert Hubbard is in a league of his own. When it comes to marketease, Elbert Hubbard is second only to . . . ah, that would be telling.

How to Handle How-to Marketing Books?
With Caution, and not a Little Circumspection.

NOW THAT'S WHAT I CALL MARKETING #1

Free Gift Unplugged

There's a point in most rock concerts, immediately after the up-tempo openers, when the lead singer announces that, "It's time to slow things down a little." This is rock 'n' roll speak for "the boring bit," though it sometimes means "all the boring bits from the latest album, which represents a radical change of direction for the band, which is tanking in the record stores right now, and which everyone either hates or hasn't heard yet."

Hearts sink throughout the stadium. Dancing feet get itchy. The mosh pit stagnates. Unfamiliarity breeds contempt.

Well, we've reached that point in this book and it's time to slow things down a little. Oh yeah! All right!! Rock 'n' rooooooollllllllll.

In accordance with the arts- and history-based ethos of *Free Gift Inside!!*, I'm gonna play you a little medley from that fabulous chart-topper, *Now That's What I Call Marketing*. It consists of mini case studies of famous musicians, all of whom personify the TEASE mentality. I won't explain how they epitomize marketease. The stories speak for themselves. Suffice it to say, that unlike (say) Elvis Presley or The Beatles, whose careers were masterminded by Colonel Parker and Brian Epstein respectively, these musicians were marketing maestros in their own right.

Ladies and gentlemen, boys and girls, give it up for the legendary, the unforgettable, the recently exhumed but lookin' good considering, the one-and-only "Irish Orpheus," Patrick Sarsfield Gilmore . . .

Irish Orpheus

Patrick Sarsfield Gilmore was the U2 of the mid-nineteenth century.[1] Now almost forgotten, he was the most popular musical attraction of his day. Renowned for his spectacular live shows – the high Victorian equivalent of stadium rock – he played to huge sell-out crowds throughout the United States and Western Europe. He toured incessantly; he composed numerous still-familiar numbers, most notably *When Johnny Comes Marching Home Again*; he assembled a professional, full-time band, whose standards of musicianship were second to none; and he paved the way for subsequent celebrity bandleaders such as John Philip Sousa. In fact, Sousa's big break was caused by Gilmore's untimely death in 1881 and for years afterwards the so-called March King was widely regarded as a poor substitute for the flamboyant Irish bandmaster.[2]

Pat Gilmore was born on Christmas Day 1829 in the village of Ballygar, Co. Galway. Originally destined for the priesthood, he ran away to a wholesale merchants, of all places, where he picked up the penny whistle, graduated to the B-flat cornet, joined a British military band, volunteered for service in Canada, and, after extricating himself from the army's baleful embrace, arrived in the United States in 1848. He found a job with Boston's foremost musical instrument makers, Ordway Brothers, where his natural facility for public relations first manifested itself. He formed a minstrel company, Ordway Eolians, which was used to promote the wares of his employers. The euphonious Eolians proved very popular and no doubt would have secured Gilmore's future as an Ordway partner, were it not for the accidental intervention of Louis Jullien. An eccentric French conductor, completely unencumbered with natural reticence, Jullien toured the United States in 1854 and caused a sensation.[3] His enormous 100-piece orchestra, limitless advertising outlay, and even less limitless showmanship, attracted hitherto unparalleled attention. More pertinently perhaps, his impeccable attire, hirsute histrionics, extravagant baton wielding, and totally over the top performances had a profound impact on an ambitious twenty-five-year-old from the west of Ireland.

Pat promptly became a full-time bandleader, took over the nearby Salem Band, forged it into a formidable musical machine, established the famous Fourth of July concerts on Boston Common, and inveigled a gig at the March 1857 inauguration parade of President James Buchanan. The accompanying publicity convinced the novice showman that popular music was the way to go, and he went there with gusto. In 1859, he became sole proprietor of a 32-piece band. He immediately equipped it with shiny new instruments, smartly tailored uniforms and splendidly appointed rehearsal rooms. Unfortunately, Gilmore's outlay vastly exceeded his income and he would undoubtedly have succumbed if the Civil War hadn't arrived like a grotesque fairy godmother.

A Minstrel Boy

Bands are big business in wartime and big bands are bigger business still. Gilmore's bandstand battalion leapt into the breach between the States, where it served with distinction as a Union recruiting agent, home front fundraiser, and campfire camaraderie consolidator. The Irish impresario's moment of glory arrived in 1864, however, when he was asked to organize a concert commemorating Louisiana's reluctant return to the North's refulgent fold. Mindful of Jullien, he assembled a chorus of 5,000 voices, a band of 500 musicians, an enormous drum and trumpet corps and, on March 4 in Lafayette Square, delivered a show-stopping performance of the *Star*

Spangled Banner, America, The Union Forever, and *Hail Columbia.* The last of these was accented with the peals of nearby church bells and accompanied by a battery of cannon, which boomed on each beat of the drum.

Like Lord Byron, Patrick Sarsfield Gilmore awoke to find himself famous. On his triumphant return to New England, our Hibernian headbanger reformed the band, hit the road, took up a residency at the Boston Theatre, began selling Gilmore brand musical instruments, and started thinking about his next spectacular. Never one for half measures, he decided to double everything associated with the New Orleans extravaganza and came up with the perfect vehicle, a national jubilee concert to mark the long-awaited outbreak of peace. Naturally, Boston's musical blue bloods were appalled by the very idea and dismissed him as a mere "salesman of thunder." Undaunted, Gilmore prepared a gaudy prospectus, secured the backing of the business community and city council, both of which recognized a money-spinner when they saw one, and won over local choral societies with the promise of free sheet music, cut price lodgings, and discounted railroad tickets. More than 100 musical societies agreed to participate, the proposed program was distributed, rehearsals began, and an enormous wooden auditorium was assembled in double-quick time. A midway for retail stores and restaurants was constructed nearby; tented hotels were erected on the Common; street car companies put on extra services; musical instrument dealers vied to be appointed official supplier; and one enterprising cough drop manufacturer announced that he would give all of the choristers a free box of Brown's Bronchial Touches.

In the event, every single seat sold out, even at the premium price of $5 per ticket. People came from as far away as California and Texas. President Grant and his cabinet deigned to attend, as did a host of local dignitaries, including several of those who had opposed Gilmore's plan in the first place. Be that as it may, between

June 15 and 17, 1869, Boston rocked to the sound of a 10,000 voice choir, 1,000 piece orchestra, and a 50,000 strong audience, ever ready to sing along. This cacophony was counterpointed with cannon fire and church bells, complemented by the largest drum and pipe organ in captivity, and kept under control thanks to copious assistant conductors sprinkled throughout the performing throng. The program ranged from the trusty *Star Spangled Banner* and reliable rabble-rousers like Rossini's *William Tell Overture* to the solemnity of *A Hymn of Peace*, written for the occasion by Oliver Wendell Holmes. The highlight, however, was the *Anvil Chorus* from Verdi's *Il Trovatore*, which featured 100 fully uniformed and helmeted local firefighters, who marched onstage shouldering long-handled sledgehammers and beat out time on specially constructed anvils.

Heavy metal, or what?

Pandemonium, needless to say, ensued, swiftly followed by pandemonium-plus, with just a hint of hyperhullabaloo. An encore was instantly demanded and instantly delivered. Sadly, one over-stimulated attendee, a certain Ms Dunlap from Chicago, succumbed to the emotion of the occasion by expiring on the spot. Her death could have been a PR disaster. But, ever the quick thinker, Pat Gilmore turned it to promotional advantage.[4] "No one," he intoned funereally, "more pure and gentle, more tender or affectionate, could have been chosen to bear to the angelic choir above tidings of the glorious scene on earth, of the thousands listening in rapt reverence to the sacred songs that inspired the souls of the greatest masters."

When Paddy Comes Marching Home Again

Where to go after that? Where else but double or quits! Enthused by the festival's reception, Gilmore went for broke three years later with his inaugural World Peace Jubilee. Not only was this twice as large as the summer of '69, but it was truly international in scope. It embraced bands from Germany, Great Britain, France, Russia, and Ireland, as well as the matchless waltzmeister himself, Johann Strauss. The great Viennese composer was tempted into performing by Gilmore's promise of a 20,000-strong chorus and 2,000-piece orchestra, the largest ever assembled. True, its rendition of *The Blue Danube* was described by Strauss as "an unholy row such as I shall never forget," but it was clearly a case of never mind the choral quality, feel the orchestral width.[5] Regrettably, the Irish impresario had overreached himself on this occasion. The festival was a flop. Not even a revival of the redoubtable *Anvil Chorus* could pull in the necessary crowds over the three-week event. On one unfortunate occasion, there were an estimated 22,000 people on stage and only 7,000 in the audience. It was all too much, too soon after the Peace Jubilee, and inevitably it ended in financial disaster.[6]

Down but not out, Gilmore gave up on his proto-Ozzfests. With the exception of mini-mammoth concerts in Chicago, to commemorate the rebuilding of the fire-razed city, and at the Philadelphia Centennial Exposition of 1876, the irrepressible Irishman devoted his not inconsiderable energies to polishing a 65-piece band. Immaculately attired, beautifully coiffed, and drilled to perfection, Gilmore's burnished ensemble marched on New York, where it commenced a long-running series of promenade concerts at the venerable Hippodrome auditorium. Although he was forced to compete directly with P.T. Barnum, whose circus shared the venue, Pat more than held his own in the head-to-head hyperbolisms. He kept his name in the newspapers with all sorts of promotional stunts, such as the "duel" he fought with a musical rival and the "war" between two of his soloists, which gave rise to riots among the protagonists' partisan supporters. He also churned out the hits, including *O Let Me Dream of Former Years*, *Freedom on the Old Plantation*, and *Whispers from Erin*; he wrote a new national anthem, *Columbia*, which enjoyed a brief vogue but never seriously threatened the incumbent; he toured the Americas and western Europe with metronomic regularity; he established a successful summer season at fashionable Manhattan Beach; and he kept his musicians in fine fettle by instituting individual encore bonuses of $5 per solo.

Gilmore, furthermore, formulated a forerunner of today's "Opera Babes" by fronting his band with a succession of drop dead gorgeous sopranos. Out of respect for their delicate femininity and spiritual equipoise, Gilmore's babes were excused "lottery concerts" and Sunday performances, though they occasionally played so-called "sacred events." Even these, however, inflamed the God-fearing, Bible-belted hinterland. Good Christian condemnation descended on the blasphemous band and gate receipts blossomed accordingly. Praise the Lord and pass the penny whistle.

American Beauty

Gilmore was still in his pomp when another Opera Babe hit the boards with a resounding thump. So firmly did she hit them on November 15, 1878, that the footlights were still shaking forty years later, when Lillian Russell finally retired.[7] Initially billed as an "English Ballad Singer," albeit Iowan born, bred, and very well fed, Russell made her first unforgettable appearance in a pirated production of *HMS Pinafore*, just as the Gilbert and Sullivan craze was sweeping the United States. More than eighty ripped-off versions of the operetta were touring the country in those heady days before the long arm of international copyright law reached the proto-Napsters of North America. But none had the impact of Lillian's. Although the alluring eighteen year old was only part of the *Pinafore* chorus, her prodigious proportions had a disproportionate impact. Blue-eyed, golden-tressed, amply-enbonpointed, and blessed with an incredible peaches-and-cream complexion, the statuesque chorister was sexual magnetism made flesh. Stage door johnnies, first-night notables, love-struck swains, and a long line of completely bedazzled beaus were as one in their communal abasement before the American Beauty. According to an entranced biographer,[8] "there was something provocative in her blue eyes, the swing of her hips; there was a hint of the coming opulence of her figure and just that touch of vulnerability essential to every love goddess, which was also visible in such successors as Jean Harlow and Marilyn Monroe . . . As the noted impresario Florenz Zeigfeld exclaimed after first seeing her, 'Destiny and the corn fields of Iowa shaped her for the stage'."

Corny perhaps, cheesy undoubtedly, but Lillian Russell was more than just a pretty face. Much more. She could sing like a conservatoire-coached angel. La belle Lillian had an unerring ability to hit high C, repeatedly and without effort. While her voice had a slightly metallic edge – one unkind critic compared her to a whistling kettle – she was prodigal with her pipes. On discovering that she registered eight high Cs per performance, in each of twenty-seven performances per week, the imperious Australian diva, Dame Nellie Melba,[9] was astounded and outraged by turn. "The public," she famously reminded Russell, "never values anything that comes to them so cheaply. Take my advice and give your audience just two high Cs a night. You'll be far more appreciated."

More appreciation, however, was the least of Lillian's concerns. At the height of the Gilded Age, the good ship Russell sailed serenely from triumph to triumph. Immediately after disembarking from *HMS Pinafore*, she berthed in a burlesque of *The Pirates of Penzance*, which was so successful that Gilbert and Sullivan tried to pirate the pirate performer for their own *Pirates* performance, then running at the nearby Fifth Avenue Theatre. Russell demurred and signed up instead for another Tony Pastor-produced pastiche of another popular operetta, *Olivette*. Dressed in loose-fitting boy's clothes, she trilled "In the North Sea Lived a Whale" and concluded each verse with a little jig. The audience reaction to her Baywatchesque jiggling was, well, predictably pheromonic.

Now I know why they call it the hornpipe.

The hormonal hoopla, what's more, further increased with her next role, a double bill of *Babes in the Woods* and *Fun in a Photograph Gallery*, which toured the West Coast in the summer of 1881. By all accounts, *Babes* sent seismic waves of sensuality throughout the Sunshine State, largely on account of Lillian's leggings. Skintight tights were then regarded as the last word in wantonness and the American Beauty give the audience what it wantoned. But only on occasion. Her fashionably sturdy shanks were paraded periodically and never failed to get an appropriate reaction from local light-opera lovers – libretto chewing, in the main. It wasn't so much a case of teasing, tormenting, and tantalizing the customer as a crime against Californian humanity. Indeed, such was the lovely Lillian's allure that one of her many rootin' tootin' admirers shot dead an ungentlemanly cowpoke who cast aspersions on the rosebud's resplendence. Justified homicide was his defense and he was duly acquitted.

Russell may have played the hapless ingénue part to perfection, but professionally she was quite the opposite. An extremely canny businesswoman, who was very well aware of her box office worth, she regularly withheld her musical favors from a succession of theatrical managers. On several occasions she refused to honor written contracts, or even go on stage, until such times as the impresarios met her hefty financial demands. Russell's salary steadily rose from $35 per week to one hundred times that in 1905. She also took a percentage of net profits; ensured that the cost of her costumes – always the latest and most expensive that Paris could provide – was covered by the producer concerned; and, for good measure, top-sliced the sale of tie-in photographs, concert programs, and associated promotional materials. From time to time,

Russell demanded so much that the impresario's acquiescence surprised even her and she was forced to undertake (highly lucrative) tours that she might otherwise have refused. The offers, however, kept on coming and, trouper that she was, the great soprano rarely failed to deliver. Throughout the 1880s and 1890s, she not only bestrode Broadway, but the American musical landscape. She slithered seductively in *The Snake Charmer*, pulsated provocatively in *Patience*, cast a spell over all concerned in *The Sorcerer*, transfixed enamored onlookers in *Reptila, the Girl With the Glass Eye* and, when she commanded the company at Rudolph Aronson's prestigious Casino Theatre, Russell was at one with the musical immortals. Tickets for the songbird's first nights were not only to die for, they were worth several lifetimes in Purgatory.

It couldn't last. But it did. Russell was sufficiently accomplished to adapt herself to changing musical tastes, such as the rise of musical comedy, the decline of comic opera and the vogue for vaudeville. She appreciated, moreover, that as her vocal abilities diminished and a healthy Midwestern appetite slowly took its toll, an adjustment in her roles was called for. Thanks to the coaching of Weber and Fields, the clown princes of American music hall, Russell became a brilliant light comedienne and, eventually, a top-notch character actress.

Professionally, the early years of the twentieth century were just as triumphant as the Gilded Age. Although she epitomized the "naughty nineties," that notorious epoch of red plush velvet, ten course dinners, rampaging robber barons, serious self-indulgence, and shameless conspicuous consumption – the era that Thorstein Veblen famously raged against – Lillian Russell rode the tides of fashion and defeated all those who tried to wrest her theatrical crown. *Lady Teazle, La Belle Helene, The Wedding Day, Hokey-Pokey, American Beauty,* and innumerable others successfully fanned the flames of fandom. What's more, when she occasionally suffered from overexposure and found herself unable to captivate the metropolitan in-crowd, she simply took to touring smaller towns and cities, which paid handsomely to see the legendary Lillian in the flesh. Hence a 1907 tour of 104 one-night stands in *The Butterfly* ranked amongst her most profitable ever.

The Millinery-Industrial Complex

The American Beauty, in sum, had an unerring eye for the public eye. She was a sublime self-promoter and marketer supreme. Her much-reported marital difficulties – one bigamous, another unconsummated – kept the moral majority in a state of perpetual high dudgeon, as did her rumored love affairs (with a circus strongman and Haitian prince, among others) and periodic fits of theatrical petulance. She brilliantly played the box office boosting game of "retirements," "comebacks," "first nights," and "last chances," as latterly perfected by Frank Sinatra and the Rolling Stones. Likewise, law suits against grasping partners (one of which revolved around Lillian's reluctance to reveal her legs), gee-whiz publicity stunts (recording for Thomas Edison, making the first official telephone call to President Grover Cleveland etc.), and the sheer ostentation of her lifestyle (latest outfits, celebrity companions, fabulous boudoir, personalized Pullman car, fleet of automobiles, stables of thoroughbreds, and huge hats that commandeered the entire resources of the millinery-industrial complex) all served to keep the scandal sheets and printing presses working to capacity.

Marketing-wise, her image appeared on everything from cigars and corsets to cosmetics and cigarette cards. She was courted by couturiers, made a mint from milliners and, with her gold-plated, jewel-encrusted bicycles, did wonders for the Edwardian pedal-pushing industry. She marketed her own line of make up, appeared as a catwalk model at the 1910 Chicago Dressmakers' Convention,

73

made several short movies about fitness more than fifty years before Jane Fonda, and wrote a widely syndicated newspaper column disbursing tips on health, happiness, and husband-hunting. The last of these comprised a curious self-help philosophy that mixed elements of Marcus Aurelius, Mary Baker Eddy, and the sure-fire matrimonial clincher of not trying too hard whilst maintaining a modicum of male-attracting mysteriousness. Later in life, Lillian turned her hand to social marketing. She was a leading spokesperson for women's suffrage, sold war bonds like home-cooked hot cakes, and served as a doughboy-drafter first class. So effective a recruiting sergeant did she prove that, when she expired on June 6, 1922, the American Beauty was buried with full military honors. The curtain, in accordance with her celebrated signature tune, had finally "Come Down, My Evenin' Star."

HOW TO TRUMP THE TRICK-OR-TREAT

"Our marketing strategy was to play hard to get. It was a reverse sales technique. If you sit in an office with a contract in your hand, eager to make the first deal that comes along, it's quite obvious to people that the apartments aren't in demand. We were never in a rush to sign a contract. When people came in, we'd show them the model apartments, sit down and talk, and, if they were interested, explain that there's a waiting list for the most desirable apartments. The more unattainable the apartments seemed, the more people wanted them."

So speaks the irrepressible Donald Trump in his best-selling 1987 book, *The Art of the Deal*.[1] Perhaps more than anyone else, Trump understands that selling stuff doesn't involve kow-towing to the customer, be it a merchant bank, a construction firm, a local government board, a casino licensing commission, or, as in this case, would-be purchasers of luxury apartments in Trump Tower. Quite the opposite, in fact. The Donald, as he is affectionately known, is a master of teasing, tantalizing, and tormenting the customer. His brinkmanship is legendary. His negotiating skills are unsurpassed. He has an uncanny ability to size up clients and opponents alike. He is a master of strategic tantrum throwing. He has no time for "fancy marketing surveys" or sycophantic MBAs from Harvard or Wharton.[2]

The Art of the Donald

More than almost anything else, however, The Donald is heir to P.T. Barnum.[3] Everything he does is bigger, better, higher, longer, greater, further, classier, or richer than has ever gone before. He has his name on more buildings than Burger King.[4] His ego is so huge that it takes crampons, oxygen, and sherpas to scale the lower foothills. He knows more celebrities, and their secrets, than J. Edgar Hoover in his pinafored prime. The rise in global warming, they say, is due to the deforestation caused by The Donald's daily press coverage. His hair alone is a work of art, an installation piece loosely based on Monet's *Haystacks* or, possibly, Magritte's little-known surrealist master-piece, *This is Not a Combover.*

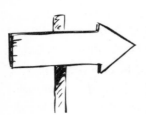

The Donald, as he is affectionately known, is a master of teasing, tantalizing, and tormenting the customer.

At the same time, this Flaxen Saxon openly acknowledges that "Donald Trump" is a necessary fiction, a form of "truthful hyper-bole." It is an act, a role, a persona, a trick, no less, that must be maintained, sustained, and polished at all times. His organization is fuelled by the The Donald's inveterate bamboozling. According to his autobiography, for example, he persuaded the owners of the Commodore Hotel to announce its closure, which bounced the city into making financial concessions to the then penurious developer. His architectural models of Trump Tower were so grotesque that the owner of Tiffany, renowned esthete Walter Hoving, sold him the air rights over his Fifth Avenue flagship, thereby enabling Trump to build a better looking edifice. He fooled Holiday Inns into thinking that his Atlantic City casino was under construction by the simple expedient of hiring every bulldozer and dump truck in town and making them look busy while the suits looked on. He out-maneuvered the honest burghers of Palm Beach, played zoning poker with the town council, and succeeded in turning his 128-room mansion Mar-a-Lago into an exclusive retreat for A-list celebrities.[5]

On several occasions, similarly, The Donald has announced plans to construct the world's tallest building, a sure-fire, hold-the-front-page showstopper, which unfailingly oils the wheels, smoothes the path, and helps guarantee the acceptability of his real, much smaller scale building ambitions.[6] He consistently employs creative counting to convey the impression that his skyscrapers contain several more stories than they actually do. By thus gilding the gilding on the lily, he implies that they are bigger, better, bolder, brasher, the best. The very best. Not second best, the very best. Better than very best. The bestest.

In the early 1990s, moreover, when things were looking grim for him, The Donald repeatedly threatened to declare himself bankrupt, which would have precipitated a blizzard of inter-bank litigation. From this paradoxical position of strength, the great pretender extracted incredible concession after incredible concession from his irate creditors. As he observed in his pomp,[7] "The worst thing you can possibly do in a deal is seem desperate to make it. That makes the other guy smell blood, and then you're dead. The best thing you can do is deal from strength, and leverage is the biggest strength you can have. Leverage is having something the other guy wants. Or better yet, needs. Or, best of all, simply can't do without. Unfortunately, that isn't always the case, which is why leverage often requires imagination and salesmanship. In other words, you have to convince the other guy it's in his interest to make the deal."

Love him or loathe him, The Donald has leverage. The Donald

has chutzpah. The Donald has flair. The Donald has flair on his chutzpah and leverages it unceasingly.

Tease Please Louise

Donald Trump, then, is a master of *trickery*, the first component of the TEASE framework. Marketing, indeed, is a trickster, akin to Loki of Norse myth (and *Spiderman* comics), wily Coyote of Native American legend (and Warner Brothers cartoons), Mark Twain's timeless Tom Sawyer, or Lorelei Lee of *Gentlemen Prefer Blondes*. Trickster figures disorientate, dissimulate, disturb, and deceive.[8] They dissem-

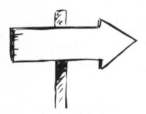

Trickster figures disorientate, dissimulate, disturb, and deceive. Just like marketing.

inate disruption, promote playfulness, and, as often as not, generate good-humored glee (sometimes we laugh at them, sometimes with them). Tricksters interpose themselves between truth and falsity, between what is and what ought to be, between initial desire and ultimate delivery. Just like marketing. It is no accident that trickster figures are frequently associated with marketing (Hermes is the god of the marketplace, after all). It is no accident that marketing practitioners have often employed trickster figures in their merchandise moving maneuvers (Joe Isuzu, Tony the Tiger, the Honey Monster, Joe Camel, Frito Bandito, the Budweiser bestiary, et al.). It is no accident that tricksters occupy a liminal, interstitial, betwixt-and-between position, much the way marketing is situated with production on one side and consumption on the other, with obscurantist academicians to the left and practicing managers to the right, with sizzle above and servility below.[9]

More pertinently perhaps, marketing is regarded as a trickster by consumers. Despite growing awareness of the minutiae of marketer activity, noted in Lesson Two, most people associate marketing with the likes of Richard Branson, Doug Kelleher, Luciano Benetton, Steve Jobs, Jeff Bezos, Phil Knight, Tom Peters, and Donald Trump, tricksters one and all.[10] In the popular imagination, marketers are jumped up salesmen and everyone knows what salesmen are like. They'd do anything to make the sale, even to the point of denying they're after the sale. Especially to the point of denying they're after the sale!

We're Off to See the Wizard

Denial, indeed, is central to the trickster's conniving. There are, in essence, two main modes of tricksterism. The first and most effective of these is pretending you're not a trickster. Intimations of honesty, integrity, fealty, altruism, selflessness, naïvety, and, not least, innocence are especially important components of the trickster mix. They are the cap and bells of the commercial jester. They represent the marketers' natural motley. They are the mask behind which marketers hide, hype, hawk, and hoodwink.

Consider Dean Kamen. Widely regarded as the heir to Thomas Edison, the Wizard of Menlo Park, Dean Kamen is nothing less than the Wizard of Manchester, NH.[11] Like Edison, he presents himself as a preternaturally gifted inventor, a twenty-first century version of the garage-based, gizmo-surrounded, patent-pending technojock, who is obsessive, otherworldly, socially maladroit, and, if not quite the mad scientist of Hollywood legend, certainly several test tubes short of a laboratory. He was an underachiever at school, dropped out of college, was deemed a failure waiting to happen, and, it almost goes without saying, was a multi-millionaire by the age of 25. He made his name with a portable insulin pump which delivers precise doses to diabetics at the appropriate times. This was followed by a suit-case-sized dialysis machine, an array of heart stents, and a gyroscopic stair-climbing wheelchair, the IBOT.

True to the eccentric, uber-nerd archetype, moreover, Kamen lives alone in a huge, gadget-gorged hexagonal house, designed by his good self; he commutes to work by helicopter, with either *Over the Rainbow* or the *Star Wars* theme blasting from an in-chopper sound system; he owns an island called Dumpling in Long Island Sound, which not only boasts its own currency but tried unsuccessfully to secede from the United States; and performs his ceaselessly creative cerebral calisthenics in a refurbished textile mill overlooking the Merrimac River. As one does.

Like Thomas Edison, furthermore, Kamen is an extremely astute marketing man, a brilliant self-publicist who exploits his alleged eccentricities to telling promotional effect. The sheer amount of coverage he gets, at a time when celebrities are two a penny and there's a gadgeteer in every other garage, stands testimony to his astounding marketing acumen. Acumen, incidentally, that he hotly denies possessing, thereby adding to the aura of mystique that envelops him. If proof were needed, however, one need look no further than the frenzy that surrounded "Ginger," a.k.a. IT.

Announced in January 2001 and accompanied by an E-normous, net-propelled publicity push, Ginger was alleged to be the greatest invention since the invention of the sliced bread cliché. No one knew what IT was and the seer astutely refused to say.[12] Pundits, pontificators, and publicity-seekers had a field day with their fantasies about what IT could possibly be. IT was variously envisaged as a personal jetpack, a hydrogen-powered scooter, a dilithium crystal-driven palm pilot, and a warp-factor pooper scooper. The high-profile backers of the invention, including Jeff Bezos, Steve Jobs, and prominent venture capitalist John Doerr, added further credence to its revolutionary potential. At one stage it was actually put on sale at Amazon.com, the real company in a virtual world, thereby extending Bezos' range to infinity and beyond.[13] And, to cap it all, the marketing maestro's ghost writer parleyed a $250,000 advance from Harvard Business School Press for the scoop on the poop on the scoop, scoot, scope, or whatever IT turned out to be. The only thing anyone knew for certain was that entire cities, no less, would have to be retrofitted in order to accommodate Kamen's revolutionary invention. Seal off those sidewalks. Rip up those autoroutes. Tear down those tollbooths. Because Ginger's coming down the turnpike, powered by a perpetual motion motor that runs on hot air and hyperbole.

Naturally, the Wizard of IT denied all accusations of spin doctoring, though this didn't prevent him hiding the contraption behind a curtain on *Good Morning America* for a week prior to the official launch. Or letting it be known that John Doerr was brought on board by the tease "There's something we're working on you really oughta see." Or informing all and sundry that Christian Scientists forced a name change on the device, since they controlled the estate of Ginger Rogers, the original nomenclatural inspiration. Or indeed using his naïf, invention-is-all, not-in-it-for-the-money image to negotiate an incredible deal with extremely hard-nosed venture capitalists. Credit Suisse First Boston and Kleiner, Perkins, Caufield & Byers each paid $38 million for 7% of the company, which values it at some $550 million, an amount that'd make most pre-crash dot.coms blush.

It is striking, however, that Kamen's biggest objection to the spin doctoring accusations – like that of any good marketer – was that public expectations concerning IT would be raised so high that they could never be matched, no matter how radical the idea turned out to be.

And so it proved.

When the Segway Personal Transporter was revealed to the world in December 2001, there was a definite sense of anti-climax. It looked like a cross between a springless pogo stick and emasculated lawnmower. Granted, Kamen beat the drum energetically on behalf of his electrical-powered, gyroscopically-balanced, 12-mph transporter. He graced *Good Morning America* twice in one week; he was covered by CNN, *NBC Nightly News*, *ABC World News Tonight*, and countless local stations; he played traffic cop on *The Tonight Show* while Jay Leno, Russell Crowe, and Sting scooted round the studio; he grabbed front page headlines the world over and captured the covers of everything from *Time* and the *New Yorker* to *Woman's Wear Daily*. All told, he generated approximately $100 million worth of free publicity.[14]

Irrespective of whether it actually turns out to be an Edsel or a Model T, the Segway's status as a twenty-first century marketing icon is already secure.

At the same time, however, the Segway attracted a lot of negative comment, though that's not necessarily a bad thing, and more than a little ridicule, which is. The *Washington Post* dismissed it as the invention that runs on hype.[15] The *Economist* simply asked, "is that IT?" and reminded its readers of the Sinclair C5, an earlier revolutionary advance in transportation technology that failed miserably.[16] A spoof ad in the *Onion* outlined several salient selling points,[17] such as "Upright handlebars ergonomically designed to maximize loss of dignity" and "Can reach speeds of up to 100 mph with a special tow rope." All sorts of objections, what's more, have since been raised about its practicality, legality, likely competition, and basic marketability.

In this regard, it is striking that the Segway debate didn't finish or diminish when the prototype hit the talk shows. The conversation simply segued from "What is IT?" to "Is there a market for IT?" Everyone is a marketing expert these days, remember. So much so, that the will it/won't it succeed debate was almost as exciting as the pre-launch discussions about IT's attributes. Besuited business analysts the world over brought their self-appointed expertise to bear on the Kamen case and many a corporate coffee break was spent considering possible market segments, putative distribution strategies, potential sales volume, and precise price points. Irrespective of whether it actually turns out to be an Edsel or a Model T, the Segway's status as a twenty-first century marketing icon is already secure.[18]

Kamen, meanwhile, is working on his next top secret project, a portable, non-polluting, maintenance-free engine that runs for years on any form of fuel from kerosene to cow dung. Unlike IT, it even has a name. The Stirling Engine is named after a Scottish cleric who proposed the basic concept in 1816, though its operationalization has defeated all comers until Dean Kamen. By all accounts, mostly his own, Kamen's coming contraption is the cold fusion of the new millennium, a machine capable of alleviating the principal woes of the developing world. It will generate sufficient power to run a household, purify enough water to meet an average family's daily requirements and, if strapped to a specially adapted Segway, will solve the transportation problem for good measure. But does it have internet access?

Clearly, IT ain't over 'til the fat checks arrive. Yet, regardless of the eventual outcome – Segway saves the day or Segway sinks without trace – the most striking thing about Kamen's marketing campaign is that it is an exact replica of a stunt pulled by P.T.

Barnum 140 years previously.[19] In 1860, the master trickster unleashed "What is It?" upon an unsuspecting world. Coming just a few months after the publication of Darwin's *Origin of Species*, Barnum's "It," like that of his latter-day replicant, spawned a feeding frenzy of speculation, discussion, and controversy. Was it the missing link between man and ape? Was it related in some way to the African gorilla, discovered only a decade previously? Or was it yet another of Barnum's notorious humbugs, akin to the Feejee Mermaid, the Wooly Horse, or Joice Heth? The great man refused to say and, at a time when everyone was an expert in natural history, or held a strong opinion at least, "What is It?" became one of Barnum's three most successful presentations, alongside General Tom Thumb and Jenny Lind, the Swedish Nightingale.[20]

Is this historical parallel an accident? I don't think so. Kamen is a latter-day Barnum and, like Barnum, he's a master trickster. Actually, the "Wizard of IT" appellation is singularly appropriate, since the original wizard in L. Frank Baum's much-loved fairy tale was based on P.T. Barnum.[21]

It Takes Two To Tango

Kamen and Barnum's respective ITs, then, typify the deadpan variant of tricksterism. We are never quite sure if a trick is being played, but strongly suspect that one is. Indeed, exploiting our uncertainty is key to the trickster's success. The other major form of trickery relies on loudness, exaggeration, and ostentation. I'm-a-trickster-I-am, the character seems to say and the gaudy livery reinforces this impression (as with the fool's motley, carnival masks, Richard Branson's penchant for cross-dressing, Donald Trump's delectable three-scoops quiff).

The arts, of course, are replete with ostentatious tricksterism, be it Komar and Melamid's marketing-inflected exhibition, *America's*

Most Wanted (see Free Gift 4) or William Castle's sublime *Tingler*.[22] The latter, a 1959 B-movie starring Vincent Price, was ballyhooed by Bill Castle's proprietary "butt-buzz," a promotional stunt whereby thousands of theater seats were wired up and their gibbering incumbents given an electric shock during particularly scary scenes. The ruckus this caused was surpassed only by the reaction of Bostonian blue-rinses, who were innocently watching Audrey Hepburn in *The Nun's Story*, when a bored projectionist decided to test the newly-installed "Tingler" equipment. It worked.

Free Gift 4: The Elephant Men

Whenever we think of arts-based trickery, our natural tendency is to recall the glory days of Hollywood hoopla, when (for example) Russell Birdwell conned the country into searching for someone to play Scarlett O'Hara in *Gone With the Wind*, or indeed the immortal Marty Weiser ballyhooed *Blazing Saddles* with a special show for horses – yes, horses – which came complete with "horse d'oevres," a "horsepitality" bar, and what have you.[23]

However, the visual arts are equally prone to tricksterism (surrealism, tromp l'oeil, fakers, imposters, etc.) and the modern masters are Komar and Melamid. A pair of émigré Russian pranksters, they made an initial splash with *Color Therapeutics*, a series of 25 colored plaques that purported to cure diverse ailments if stared at for the appropriate amount of time (Drinking Problems, 3 min. 7 sec.; Impotence, 6 min. 2 sec., and so forth).[24]

More recently, the tricksters have turned their attention to the artistic potential of Indian elephants.[25] Armed with a selection of paintbrushes and pigments, the pachyderms produce canvasses that stand comparison with the Abstract Expressionism of Jackson Pollock or Willem de Kooning. What's more, the works not only bear the stamp of authenticity – each is individually signed by the artist's footprint – but are increasingly sought after by collectors. When an auction of Elephant Art was held in Christie's during March 2000 it raised $30,000. This was donated to an Elephant Academy in Thailand, which provides occupational retraining for elephants left unemployed by the collapse of the Thai timber industry.

K&M's elephant art extravaganza, fantastic as it proved, pales into insignificance beside *The People's Choice*, a masterpiece of marketing trickery.[26] In the mid-1990s the hoaxers hired Marttila & Kiley, a respected market research agency, who polled a representative sample of 1001 Americans about what they want and don't want in art, paintings in particular. The results, significant at the 95% level with a 3.2% margin of error, were used to develop two composite canvasses, *America's Most Wanted* and *America's Least Wanted*. The former was a big, bright blue landscape, featuring lakes, people, and wild animals in their natural setting. The latter was small, dark, stark, and abstract, a riot of sharp overlapping triangles. An exhibition, featuring the nation's preferred choices, subsequently toured the country; public meetings were held in towns and cities en route; the artists advertised their findings in newspaper free sheets and similar pennysavers; and the research generated an great deal of debate, discussion, and controversy, especially among the disdainful artistic community, who objected to the commodification process and the artists' complicity with the demands of the marketplace.

However, such was the interest in the exhibition – to say nothing of the publicity value – that Komar and Melamid repeated the experiment in China, Denmark, Finland, France, Iceland, Kenya, Russia, Turkey, and the Ukraine. Incredibly, the results were pretty much the same, despite vast national differences in culture, history, geography, religious belief, social structure, and economic development. Although the artists were surprised by the seeming unanimity, humankind's universal preference for blue landscapes, Noam Chomsky assuredly wasn't. "Landscapes," he observed,[27] seem a natural point of return once humanity has reached the end of its creative capacity with paint and brush . . . humans have mastered the problems of color, perspective, and representation and, that done, have pushed to the limits of color, form, and abstraction . . . maybe we've gone as far forward on this particular road as our internal wiring will allow."

Chomsky's conclusions, interestingly enough, parallel the problems of marketing in our postmodern epoch. At a time when every conceivable advertising treatment, promotional stunt, and marketing campaign has been tried several times over; at a time when marketers are driven to ever more desperate attempts to stand out from the crowd; at a time when every marketing textbook trots out the same old customer-oriented message, what could be more appropriate than returning to the pre-modern marketing era of tricksterism, playfulness, and over-the-top Barnumesquery? More pertinently perhaps, if *Blazing Saddles* is given a theatrical re-release, will the "horsepitality" bar make a comeback? I think we should be told.

Brands, too, can be egregiously tricksterish and none is more tricksterish than Tango. An orange-flavored carbonated soda, much like any other orange-flavored carbonated soda, Tango is one of the greatest post-war success stories of British branding. It is a success story based entirely on tricksterism.[28]

Tango was originally launched in the 1950s and signally failed to make a meaningful marketing mark. For thirtysomething years it languished in a nondescript mid-market position, somewhere between supermarket own-labels and the big budgeted battalions of Pepsico and Coca-Cola Great Britain, which led the field with its Fanta brand. In 1986 this marketplace mediocrity was acquired by Britvic, a soft drinks conglomerate, and six years later the Tango account was won by HHCL, an irreverent "fourth wave" advertising agency.[29] Creative first and last, HHCL decided to eschew the conventions of happy-clappy soda advertising – conviviality, community, coolness, catchy jingle – and focused instead on Tango's distinctive taste, best described as sharper and edgier than most. To symbolize this "bite," they came up with a compelling trickster figure, who featured in the TV advertising. Big, bald, bellicose, and bright

87

orange, the Tango Man crept up behind innocent bystanders and boxed them about the ears. The ads, again in contrast to soda commercial convention, had a video-verité, reality-TV quality – low rent, instant replay, excited sports commentator voice-over – and concluded with a sensational strapline: "You know when you've been Tango'd."

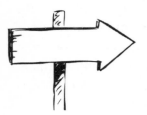

Brands, too, can be egregiously tricksterish and none is more tricksterish than Tango.

The campaign took off. Schoolchildren all over the country Tango'd each other at playtime, lunchtime, and every other time, frankly.[30] Parents were not best pleased, though the kiddy target market couldn't get enough of the Tango taste sensation. The bite indeed made other brands taste bland. However, just as the campaign was beginning to lose its impetus, a marketing miracle occurred. An unfortunate schoolkid had his eardrums punctured by an over-enthusiastic exponent of the Tango maneuver. The TV ads were banned. Sales soared even higher and, as Grant notes,[31] the brand "went from Ronald McDonald to Sid Vicious in a matter of months."

The Tease That Refreshes

One campaign does not a victory make, admittedly. But HHCL's brilliance lay in its continued adaptation and development of Tango's tricksterish brand personality. Almost every element of the long-running communications strategy played on the insouciant ethos that the first ad established. Furthermore, it tapped into the marketing savvy of the primary target market, Generation ®. Thus, the Tango Man sidled up behind senior British politicians conducting live interviews outside Parliament and effectively "placed" his product on the national evening news. Tango voodoo dolls were offered as promotional tie-ins. Letters of complaint from French students, who'd failed to see the humor in a xenophobic jibe at their great nation, were ridiculed in newspaper inserts. A direct mailshot, consisting of "postcards" purporting to be from a member of the opposite sex the recipient had "met" on holiday, all-but shattered Britain's domestic bliss.[32] Likewise, the country's stiff upper lip-ness was countered by Tango bullhorns, through which consumers were encouraged to express their innermost feelings and generally vent their rage at those around them.

The tricksterism continued, moreover, when variations on the regular flavor were introduced, though this time the advertising treatments were suitably tangential. Lemon Tango featured a new cult religion based on citrus worship. Apple Tango involved imbibers' bizarre sexual fetish for the product. Blackcurrant Tango depicted a disgruntled drinker being challenged to a fight by a belligerent employee of the customer care department. Tropical Tango centered on a preposterous parody of Lilt, the leading competitor in the category, whose benign, bouncy, beach-party commercials had been running for decades. Diet Tango was positioned as the perfect complement to unhealthy eating, thanks to the wonderful slogan, "You need it because you're weak." This was accompanied by a promotional CD consisting of nothing but the grisly sounds of "bad food" being cooked.

Best of all was the hoax public service announcement for an uncarbonated version of the beverage, launched in 1994. The "marketing director" of Tango Still solemnly warned television viewers that rogue supermarkets and convenience stores were selling a bootleg of the brand – its lack of fizz was the dead giveaway – and encouraged them to report the miscreant outlets by telephoning a special, toll-free hotline. Some 30,000 concerned citizens rang up, only to be informed that they'd been tricked as part of the new product promotion. Better yet, the ITC, Britain's advertising watchdog, was not amused and rapped the brand's knuckles for abusing the public service information format, thereby adding further fuel to the promotional flames.

Come the end of the decade, the big multinational brands were getting decidedly worried by the merry prankster and set out to frustrate its knavish tricks. They responded, as only they can, with massive marketing firepower. In 2001, Tango's British sales fell 9% by volume and 12% by value to £69 million. Set against this, the sales of Fanta, Coca-Cola's orange-flavored rival, rose by 59% to £100 million.[33] HHCL was dropped and a new advertising agency appointed. After much deliberation, CHI's debut television commercial, which aired in May 2002, revived HHCL's original 1992 slogan, "You know when you've been Tango'd." It's hard, clearly, to teach an old brand new tricks. Meantime, the nation's soda-swillers are holding their collective breath, waiting for the marketplace's verdict on the incorrigible practical joker.

Cheap Trick

The jury is currently out on Tango, but its cavalcade of cunning stunts – from the bullhornswoggle to the hoax hotline – show that marketing tricks don't have to be elaborate productions like Dean Kamen's IT, or Ty Warner's aborted Beaniegeddon or Donald Trump's remarkable real estate ruses. To the contrary, tricks can come cheap, as the classic *Blair Witch Project* – is it a snuff movie or not? – bears witness. Similarly, the recent turn to "sneaky" sales promotions, where the gregarious, round-buying barfly in the way-cool club is actually an employee of a drinks company, involves minimal expenditure on the mischievous marketers part.[34] However, the rewards can be great if the brand is embraced and adopted, even briefly, by the trend-setting in-crowd. Big budget blockbusters are unnecessary. Sneaky seeding activities are little more than twenty-first century versions of old get-em-started stunts, such as a few pump-priming pennies in a vagrant's tin cup, the removal of several cans from a supermarket's pristine display, or the applause inveigling ability of claques, plants, and analogous audience accomplices.[35] Encore. Bravo. More.

> The key to a successful trick is not its size, nor its expense. The key to the trick is the treat.

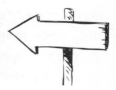

The key to a successful trick is not its size, nor its expense. The key to the trick is the treat. There must be a reward, a pay-off, a good-humored punch-line that permits the tricked to appreciate the trickery.[36] *Blair Witch* was a good movie; the sneaky drinks are free; Dean Kamen's transporter has already amused millions and doubt-less millions more before it runs out of gas, steam, guano, Energizer bunny droppings, or whatever renewable resource propels the thing. If there is no treat, the trick quickly slides from delicious to deceitful from agonizing to antagonizing, from unforgettable to unforgivable. The boundary, admittedly, is difficult to discern, as the deactivators of web-browser back buttons recently discovered. A clever ruse to extend casual browsers' visits to selected web sites, it backfired when the no-way-out effect led to accusations of E-trapment.[37] The web, indeed, is infested by all sorts of scams, from the notorious Nigerian 419 racket to the South African Reserve Bank bilk.[38] How-ever, scamming and tricksterism are not synonymous, though they can be if the trick doesn't come with a sufficiently reciprocal treat.

The Last Trump

The lesson, then, is that if you're going to confuse, confound or confute consumers, make sure there's some kind of recompense, reward, or reimbursement. As Donald Trump makes clear,[39] "You can't con people, at least not for long. You can create excitement, you can do wonderful promotion and get all kinds of press, and you can throw in a little hyperbole. But if you don't deliver the goods, people will eventually catch on." The fact of the matter is that people *like* to be tricked, as the popularity of Halloween and April Fool's Day bear witness. People *enjoy* a good hoax and have done for centuries, certainly since Benjamin Franklin's serial tomfoolery kick-started the US trickster tradition.[40] Even ivory tower-immured academicians have been known to fall for egregious pseudo-scholarly scams.

Free Gift 5: Slouching Towards *Beal Feirste*

A couple of years ago, I played a trick on marketing academicians. It was a fairly low-key trick, to be sure, but it shows that even deadly serious sectors are susceptible to practical jokes. As you already know from Lesson Three, I firmly believe that some of the greatest marketers are to be found in the arts. So, in an attempt to demonstrate this obvious if rarely acknowledged point, I wrote a lengthy academic article about "W.B. Yeats, Marketing Man." William Butler Yeats, you must appreciate, is generally regarded as one of the greatest poets of the twentieth century, possibly *the* greatest.[41] He is also widely perceived as the epitome of art-for-art's-sake estheticism, someone who was totally opposed to the cheap and tawdry vulgarity of the marketplace.[42] A perfect candidate for the trickster treatment, in other words.

The article comprised a long and learned argument, supported by copious footnotes and quotations from the master's poetic *oeuvre*, that Yeats was a marketing man manqué.[43] Actually, he really was, but that needn't detain us here. As part of the scam, which was written under a pseudonym plagiarized from Yeats's own pen names, I composed a "lost" poem by the Nobel Prize winner and concocted an elaborate back-story about its discovery. The "missing" poem addressed marketers and acknowledged the importance of the marketing profession, thereby "proving" my case about Yeats's marketing credentials. It wasn't a very good poem, I grant you, but it was very Yeatsian. Yeats has been so thoroughly studied by scholars that lists of his favorite words and expressions are readily available. It was comparatively easy, therefore, to write a Yeats-ish poem and even easier to surround it with sufficient academic apparatus to give readers pause.

The pseudonymous article eventually appeared in a learned marketing journal that I just happened to be guest editing.[44] Time passed. And then, lo and behold, a naive academician fell for it hook, line, and sinker. Scholarly propriety prevents me from revealing his name. Regrettably. Suffice to say that he hailed from the West Coast, San Francisco to be precise. Convinced that both the article and the poem were perfectly authentic, our professorial patsy went crazy trying to track down the obscure author and the non-existent university he hailed from. What's more, he wrote to world-renowned Yeatsian researchers – genuine researchers – about this marvelous missing poem. When they poured scorn on the doggerel, this only served to increase his conviction concerning its veracity!

In retrospect, I suppose I should have contacted the media at this point, since the story's combination of trickery, Yeatsianism, and West Coast flakiness would have been perfect fare for a slow news day. But as my employer might have taken a dim view of prank playing by professors – why aren't you out investigating the market for widgets? – I decided that scholarly silence was the better part of marketing valor.

As Yeats himself almost said, "I will arise and go now, and go to Innisfree gift inside."

The most enjoyable instances of all, however, transpire when the trickster is tricked, the hoaxers are hoaxed, and the trump is trumped. In 1988, while President Gorbachev was in a summit meeting with President Reagan, a New York television station hired a Gorbachev look-alike to take part in a walkabout "tour" of Manhattan. The tour attracted huge crowds, but the truly magical moment occurred when Donald Trump, of all people, descended from his golden eyrie, broke through the clamoring crowds, and, thinking the look-alike was his good friend Mikhail Gorbachev, pumped the bemused imposter's hand with gusto. My, how we laughed.[45]

Wonderful as the art of The Donald is, Dean Kamen remains the latter-day master of marketing tricksterism. His trick is perfectly attuned to today's marketing- and advertising-savvy society, insofar as his seeming innocence in promotional matters is a superb marketing ploy. It's a brilliant double-bluff. It gets people talking about the product and talking about the marketing of the product. It enjoys awesome product placement in top-rated sitcoms like *Frasier*, which spun an entire episode around the Segway (at no cost, one suspects, to the Kamen corporation). The treat is that he fools us into thinking that we know more about marketing than Kamen does, though the trick is ultimately on us. Meanwhile, the Wizard of IT attends to his magnificent pompadour (a sure giveaway, if ever there was one), polishes his denim-clad, down-home demeanor (fake naivety is the oldest trick in the book) and hides behind his hi-tech screen in Manchester, NH, doubtless counting his column inches, archiving his television appearances, and accepting advance orders for the dream machine. Segway to go.

How to Trump the Trick-or-Treat?
Do the Tango.

HOW TO EMPLOY
EXCLUSIVITY EFFECTIVELY

More Than a Filene

It's five-thirty in the morning. The crowd is already twenty strong. Cold and silent, stomping feet, coughing occasionally, sipping coffee, keeping out the chill. Two hours later, the mob has swollen to several hundred or so. Excitement is mounting. The noise is deafening. The caffeine has kicked in big time or perhaps they're imbibing freshly brewed adrenaline.

Strip lights stutter from within. An inchoate cheer goes up. A tattoo is beaten out on the doors. Faces press against plate glass. Push, push. Shove, shove. Elbow, elbow. The quarry is discernible in the distance. The thrill of the hunt. Anticipation unbound.

It's almost eight a.m. The countdown begins. *Five*. Everyone shouts in unison. *Four*. The sprinters take their marks. *Three*. Anxious glances across at their rivals. *Two*. The bolts are being withdrawn. *One*. The heavy doors start to open. *Zero*. They are flung to the wall by a tide of howling humanity.

Down the stairs. Dodge the voyeuristic camera crews. Ignore the gaggle of gloating reporters. Past the snooty, seen-it-all-before store personnel. Go! Sprint!! Faster!!! Into the basement. The bargain basement. The bridal bargain basement. The bridal, bargain-of-a-lifetime basement. Heaven can wait.

Gowns are grabbed. Others are guarded. Yet others are fought over. Property rights are asserted. I saw it first. Tugs of war transpire. Tears occur. Tears flow. Fists fly. Foul language. From demure brides-to-be. Modesty doesn't matter. Who needs changing rooms. Strip off in the middle of the store. Bra-, panty- and sneaker-clad shoppers as far as the eye can see. Allure is not an issue.

Try it on. Does it fit? Does it hell. Does it matter? Looking good. Check the price tag. $295. For a $5000 gown. Full train. French lace. Over satin. Pearl inlay. Petite bustle. Rolled up in a ball. Only $18 to clean. $20 to tailor and tweak. What a bargain. What a carry on. What came over me? Here comes the bride.

Approximately two minutes after the doors open, the excitement's over. Silence reigns. Near enough. The display racks are picked clean. Only empty clothes hangers remain. They make the ransacked racks look like dinosaur skeletons. Designer dinosaur skeletons. The wedding hunters huddle in small groups, sizing up the spoils. Occasionally gowns are discarded and quickly gobbled up by circling packs of latecomers who missed out on the kill. Till death us do part.

The media disperse, impending deadlines to meet. Store personnel stand down and let lunatic shoppers take over the retailing asylum. Barter begins. Haggle. Deals are done. Higgle. Trousseaus are traded. How much? War stories are exchanged. Have you ever seen anything like it? Bonds of connubial friendship are forged. When's the big day? It's like sex in reverse. Climax first. Foreplay later. The earth moved. The merchandise moved. Another day in paradise. All's well that ends well. Except for those that didn't get what they came for. Not to worry. There's only three months to wait for the next one.

The Wedding March

The Filene's Basement Bridal Event takes place four times per year.[1] In February, May, August, and November, the world-famous Boston store buys in 800 or so bridal gowns especially for the occasion, usually end of lines or the previous season's designs. Price wise, they range from $750 to $7500, though they are all sold on the day for $249. And sell they do. In the blink of an eye, since the supply of stock doesn't even begin to meet demand. Financially, the store makes next to nothing out of the event. But publicity-wise, it is a goldmine. Frantic, frenzied, fighting shoppers are always good for a news segment or two, a headline or several, especially when demure brides-to-be are slugging it out.

The event, in other words, has become an event with a capital E. It attracts bargain hunters from all over the country. It attracts more tourists than any other Boston landmark, bar Faneuil Hall. It attracts the media, and media reports on the media. It vies with Harrods' January sale as the most celebrated contest in the retailing calendar. It is also one of the shortest and most intense. It is an extreme sport for shopaholics. It is loss leading in excelsis. In many ways it is an intensified version of Filene's automatic mark-down policy, whereby goods are progressively reduced in price and finally given away, which places consumers on the horns of a delicious dilemma.[2] Buy or wait? Pay or delay? Spend now or forever hold your piece of plastic.

Filene's, of course, is not unique in this regard. Sales events are a staple of commercial life. Get it now. Only five remaining. Offer ends Friday. Final few days. Limited time only. Better buy now. Last gas for 500 miles. The list is endless. The very ubiquity of such imprecations, however, attests to their effectiveness. As Cialdini shows in his influential book, *Influence*, going, going, gone tactics are predicated on the psychology of rarity. "Opportunities," he

97

observes,[3] "seem more valuable to us when they are less available." Numerous scientific studies, involving everything from cookies and censorship to romantic attachments and grade point averages, convincingly demonstrate that things become much more attractive when they are scarce and getting scarcer.[4] Nothing sells like elusive exclusives. *Exclusivity*, the second element of the TEASE framework, is an exceptionally powerful marketing precept.

Everything Must Go

This rarity ruse may be one of the oldest arrows in marketing's well-filled quiver. But it never fails to hit the spot. Exclusivity is standard practice in the auto industry, as would-be buyers of Miatas, Harleys, Honda Odysseys, and Ford T-Birds know only too well.[5] It is used by everyone from Wall Street brokers, with an IPO to pass off, to

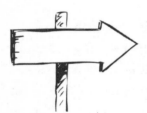

Numerous scientific studies convincingly demonstrate that things become much more attractive when they are scarce and getting scarcer.

the chocolate consiglieries at Cadbury's, whose creme eggs are strictly rationed and highly seasonal. It supplied the basic premise of the Estée Lauder cosmetics empire, the eponymous founder of which posed as a grande dame of distinction and discernment. It straddles the B2C and B2B divide, since it is the foundation stone of the collectibles business (love that Franklin Mint limited edition) and is routinely used by retail buyers, who extort enormous slotting allowances from suppliers desperate to get their products on the supermarkets' strictly limited shelf space (pay and display, partner).

Exclusivity, likewise, is employed by the very best and the very worst in the marketing business. Disney regularly releases choice items from its back catalogue of classic children's movies and withdraws them equally quickly.[6] Meantime, the dirty denizens of stocks and bonds "boiler rooms" bamboozle their marks with breathless now-or-never sales pitches.[7] Indeed, as sales pitches go, "last orders, please" is much more effective than "have it your way." Psychological studies show that people are much more motivated by the thought of losing something than by the thought of gaining something of equal value.[8] Or, as Joni Mitchell reminds us in *Big Yellow Taxi*, ". . . you don't know what you've got till it's gone."

Be that as it may, there are two main components of Exclusivity-based marketing strategies: Exiguousness and Evanescence. The former involves restrictions on *the amount* of merchandise that is available, whereas the latter refers to restrictions on *the time* it's available for. Ideally, exiguousness and evanescence should be used in combination, as the Filene's Basement Bridal Event brilliantly illustrates (800 gowns in two minutes). The Christmas shopping frenzy, where stores are rapidly running out of merchandise and time is running short, is another institutionalized version of the same, as indeed is eBay.[9] Fine art auctions (going, going, gone) and the peerless patter of flea market merchants (hurry, while stocks last) are equally exiguously evanescent.

In practice, however, one or the other tends to predominate, though the outcome is still a foregone conclusion. When it comes to Evanescence, for example, the "happy hour," that timeless tavern standby where drinks are cheap, time is tight, and drinkers tighter still, never fails to drum up custom. Cialdini, similarly, tells a cautionary tale of vacuum cleaner salespersons, who are specifically instructed to inform customers that it's now or never if they want that special deal on the machine. It's company policy not to call back, because there are just so many people to see, you see. The

carefully concocted "looks," seasons, and to-die-for ephemera of the fashion industry are also as evanescent as they come. On a macro-scale, moreover, the rapid depletion of the earth's resources, coupled with the lack of clean water, fresh air, and fossil fuels, indicate that evanescence is here to stay.[10]

The KKK Took My Donut Away

However, one doesn't need to agonize about the fate of the planet or rail against the principle of planned obsolescence – a principle that applies to almost everything except itself – since evanescence operates at the most mundane level. Consider Krispy Kreme. A 225-strong chain of delicious donut retailers, currently on roll out, Krispy Kreme is a southern culinary institution, second only to deep-fried banana and peanut butter sandwiches.[11] Its gorgeously glazed, melt-in-the-mouth, quasi-cotton-candy comestibles may be high in calorific content, but they are considerably higher in customer estimation. The Krispy Kreme Klan of donut lovers thinks nothing of driving 10-15 miles to the nearest outlet and the lines outside the stores have to be seen to be believed. Wall Street has also fallen in line, thanks to the corporation's rapidly growing sales and healthy profits. Revenue rose to $395 million in fiscal 2002, a 31% increase on the year before, meanwhile profits rose 79% to $26 million.

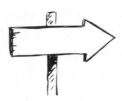

Eat your sclerotic heart out, Pavlov.

Impressive though this is, Krispy Kreme's success is not based on a big marketing budget or expensive advertising campaign. To the contrary, the chain relies entirely on word of mouth recommendation ("so good, they should be illegal," said one celebrity sheriff in Arizona),[12] coupled with free giveaways at new store openings (which never fail to draw a crowd) and highly effective retail atmospherics (consumers can watch the mouth-watering donuts being made).

Its popularity, rather, is primarily predicated on the ultimate evanescent sales pitch: get-em-while-they're-hot! A large neon sign – Hot Donuts Now! – is illuminated when a new batch of Krispy Kremes is being rustled up. And, like the proverbial moths to a flame, a swarm of slavering consumers never fails to respond to the flick of the switch. Eat your sclerotic heart out, Pavlov.

Exiguology 101

To be sure, Krispy Kreme's appeal is partly attributable to exiguousness, the second element of Exclusivity marketing. Many states have yet to be invaded by the delightful donut dealer and those that have already surrendered are rather less than saturated. Thus, the absolute number of Krispy Kreme consuming opportunities is still fairly limited. Compared to many fast food franchises, Krispy Kremes remain few and far between. As a konsequence, they have considerable kulinary kachet . . .

Sorry, I'm getting karried away. Let me move swiftly on. Krispy Kreme may rank higher on evanescence than exiguousness, but the latter remains a timeless marketing maneuver. The allure of the Hermès Birkin, discussed in Lesson One, rests firmly on scarcity, on unattainability, on strictly limited stocks. Cartier, Tiffany, Prada, Manolo Blahnik, Philip Patek, Louis Vuitton, Moët & Chandon, and the entire luxury goods trade is predicated on the same premise, as is the rapid rise of so-called cult brands like Razor scooters, Velvonia scents, Vertu cellphones, Bill Amberg baby-bouncers, and

Adidas's "I Signed" selection of extra-exclusive sneakers (limited editions of 100 pairs, individually autographed by A-list celebrities).[13]

Top-of-the-range designer submarines, which come fitted with every modern convenience and necessary luxuries – such as large picture windows, elegant passenger cabins, and well-stocked galleys – are also available from a strictly limited number of upscale nautical dealerships.[14] Prices range from $4.5 million to $20 million. Whatever happened to run silent, run cheap?

Deluxe U-boats notwithstanding, the all-time master of exiguousness – with just a soupçon of evanescence – is the peerless de Beers. Named after the two brothers who sold the original Kimberly mine for a pittance, de Beers is the diamond's best friend.

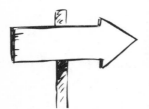

De Beers was able to take tormenting the customer to its ultimate like-it-or-lump-it limit.

Appearances to the contrary, diamonds are not particularly rare. They are widely scattered throughout the earth's surface, as massive latter-day strikes in the Canadian Shield show. Diamonds, moreover, are of no practical worth, drill bits, glass-cutters, record styluses, and the orthodontic enhancement of celebrities excepted. Thanks to de Beers' de facto monopoly, however, diamonds are one of the world's most precious commodities. A mere decade ago, de Beers controlled 80% of the $6 billion diamond trade. By carefully adjusting the supply and dealing ruthlessly with rogue producers – usually by flooding the market, depressing the price, and forcing the renegade back into line – the de Beers-controlled cartel ensured that diamonds retained their high status status.[15]

Despite their ubiquity, diamonds have always been highly prized. The myths and legends surrounding certain named stones are, well, mythical and legendary. Nevertheless, diamonds' contemporary cachet is almost entirely due to de Beers. Such is the strength of the cartel that, until recently, de Beers was able to take tormenting the customer to its ultimate like-it-or-lump-it limit. Ten times a year, the Diamond Trading Company (DTC), a de Beers subsidiary that deals in roughs (uncut diamonds), holds "sights" in London's Hatton Garden. A very select group of accredited traders, retailers, and middlemen, known as "sightholders," is invited to attend, where they are permitted to view an assortment of roughs assembled by DTC. The precise mix of "stones," "shapes," and "cleavages" is at the discretion of DTC, depending on the wares de Beers wants to dispose of. If sightholders are unhappy with the offering, they are made to wait, often for hours, before a salesman descends to discuss it with them. If they are still unhappy, DTC has the ultimate sanction of "deselection," the removal of their treasured sightholder status.

Apparently, this selling process is known by DTC insiders as "feeding the ducks," whereby diamond-buying ducklings are fed with whatever de Beers decides to throw at them. As Hart wryly notes,[16] it must be "the only transaction in the world where a man may arrive to spend $200 million without knowing what he's getting." It's not so much a case of buyer beware as buyer be grateful.

Dude, Where's My Cartel?

Feeding the ducks is all fine and dandy, but the existence of the aspiring *Anatidae* depends on another aspect of de Beers' exiguousness. Namely, its magisterial manipulation of demand.[17] Prior to the Second World War, the market for diamonds was looking decidedly rocky. The discovery of new sources of supply, combined with the aftershocks of the Great Depression, which forced many newly

103

impoverished investors to sell off family heirlooms, gave rise to a glut of diamonds that, if not quite as big as the Ritz, was certainly closer to a mountain than a molehill. De Beers responded with what is generally considered, if the myths and legends of the advertising business are to be believed, as one of the greatest slogans of all time.[18] A diamond is forever. The campaign, devised in April 1947 by hotshot W.J. Ayer copywriter Frances Gerety, effectively transformed the diamond market. Beforehand, they were widely regarded as an investment, to be bought and sold when the price is right. Afterward, diamonds became a totemic keepsake, an integral part of the matrimonial process, something special that is given, prized, and kept for ever and a day.

In the sixty-six years since Gerety's stroke of genius, the same alluring message has been repeated, reinforced, and regularly refreshed. To the tune of $200 million per annum. The recent millennial transition, for example, brought forth a perfect diamond pitch, "show her you'll love her for the next thousand years." This increased retail sales by 44%, from $5 to $7 billion.[19] So successful has the company's ongoing campaign been, that it is hard to imagine that diamonds were once regarded as investments, or heirlooms at most, and that matrimony did not automatically involve the exchange of a de Beers-derived diamond. Their transmogrification of the market is such that more than 85% of American women possess at least one piece of diamond jewelry and, even in Japan, where the traditional wedding ceremony comprised the ancient Shinto rite of drinking rice wine from a wooden bowl, a diamond engagement ring is worn by four fifths of brides to be.

In keeping with the evanescence precept, however, the cartel's time may be up. The recent diamond discoveries in Canada, and Australia's emergence as a major player in the precious stones market, has meant that de Beers' share of world trade is steadily slipping. The company's difficulties have been compounded by the "blood diamonds" scandal – an unsavory trade in roughs from war torn states in West Africa – which has attracted the ire of anti-capitalist protesters like Naomi Klein.[20] Fearful that such developments may undermine diamonds' hard-won cachet, let alone lower the price to commodity levels, the company is abandoning its monopolistic practices and relinquishing its role as "market custodian." The de Beers brand, painstakingly built on decades of expensive advertising, is being exploited big time. A $400 million joint venture with LVMH, the luxury brands conglomerate, was announced in early 2001. Over the next five years, the partners will develop a worldwide chain of de Beers flagship stores. The duck-feeding times have yet to be announced.

Cult Culling

Although evanescence and exiguousness are powerful sales accelerators, especially when used in combination, they are very difficult to manage and maintain. By its very nature, evanescence imposes a temporal limit on sales potential and flouting the time's-up contract

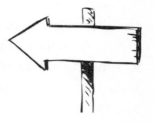

> Once everyone has it, or drives it, or drinks it, or is wearing it, or whatever the end is nigh.

can be disastrous, as Ty Warner discovered when Beaniegeddon backfired. Exiguousness, similarly, is extremely sensitive to sales volume. It rapidly dissipates as more and more goods are made available. Once everyone has it, or drives it, or drinks it, or is wearing it, or whatever, the end is nigh. Companies are thus caught between the desire for growth – driven in part by the demands of investors and the prevailing precept of stakeholder value – and seriously denuding the cachet of the brand or product. The rise and demise of Tommy Hilfiger,[21] which went from zero to hero to has-been in quick succession, is an object lesson in how "to die for" soon becomes "wouldn't be seen dead in." Lexus, likewise, is starting to lose its hitherto maxclusive reputation as sales sail ever upward and ubiquity all-but beckons. Krispy Kreme will face the same dilemma if its store opening campaign continues at the same rampaging pace. When competitors respond, as they will, with McKrispies, "Where's the Kreme?" knocking campaigns, and suchlike, the slippery slope will get slippier and slippier.

To be sure, cult companies are well aware of the growth-means-death dilemma and are cognizant that abandoning exiguousness can cause corporate evanescence. Jonathan Drew, the visionary behind Acid Cigars, captures this perfectly when he says, "The day I go mass market, I'm out of business." His wine-, oil- and herb-flavored stogies are only sold in 500 stores nationwide and if he wants to stay in business it has to stay that way. "When people are in a store, they'll buy a $150 box, because they don't know if they'll see one again for another three months," he notes.[22] If something is too easy to get hold of, it loses its allure. In many ways, the allure derives from the fact that it is difficult to get hold of. Studies of painful group initiation practices, such as frat house hazing, consistently show that "persons who go through a great deal of trouble and pain to attain something tend to value it more highly than persons who attain the same thing with the minimum of effort."[23]

The adoration that many people feel toward cult brands is thus not simply due to the allure of the object, but to the fact that they struggle to get hold of the object in the first place. The best way to generate customer loyalty, then, is not to pander to their every need, as the conventional marketing model suggests, but to deny them

106

what they desire and make life difficult for them. You're doing them a favor. They'll love you for it. They want to be left wanting. Trust me. As noted in Lesson One, in a world of abundance, scarcity is scarce and the singular is multiple. The creation of seeming sellers' markets and the maintenance of "temporary monopolies" are crucial aspects of marketing success at a time of brand oversupply and image equivalence.[24]

> Marketers take a terrible risk if they make their merchandise too available, since that destroys what made it attractive in the first place.

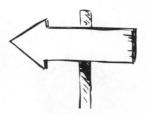

Customers, of course, don't see it that way. In *Luxury Fever*, Robert H. Frank shows that contemporary consumers are captivated by deliciously desirable objects, the rarer the better.[25] Owning them indicates that the possessors rank among the lucky few, the tasteful, the successful, the discerning elite. Far from wanting to be left wanting, consumers want them right away. What's more, as they are well aware that marketers are trained to respond to consumers' wants, they won't be told otherwise, much less take no for an answer. Marketers are thus hoist by their own petard, whereby the ideology of customer-is-king requires them to attend to the sovereign and respond instantly to their every whim. This militates against maintaining the exiguously evanescent approach that Exclusivity demands.

At the same time, marketers of much sought-after brands take a terrible risk if they make their merchandise too available, since that destroys what made it attractive in the first place. An intransigent stance is difficult to sustain, admittedly, if only on account of the tremendous internal and external pressures to grow the business. But it is vitally necessary to hold the line, to resist the pressure, to appreciate that you have to deprive customers of what they want in order to give them what they want. You know it makes sense.

To be sure, restraint can be disastrously abandoned for a number of reasons besides the growth-is-good imperative (see Free Gift 6). In Gucci's case, the disaster was largely self-inflicted, due to uncontrolled dilution of a once-lustrous brand. In American Express's case it was primarily attributable to the ferocity of the competition, though corporate hubris played a part there too.

Free Gift 6: Two Cautionary Tales

Gucci, Gucci, Goo

If ever a sublime brand went to rack and ruin, that brand was surely Gucci. It didn't so much go to hell in a hand cart as go to hell in a Hummer, a fully loaded one at that. As is well known, the fabled luxury goods manufacturer dates from 1906, when Guccio Gucci abandoned hotel bell-hopping for the rather more lucrative world of leather luggage. He set up a small workshop in Florence, his home town, concocted a totally spurious medieval heritage – saddler to kings, etc. – and gradually built up a reputation for exceptionally high quality wares. In 1932 he invented the famous snaffle loafer. Six years later, Gucci opened a store on Via Condotti, Rome's ultra-fashionable shopping street. Another followed on Fifth Avenue in 1953, and come the early 60s the distinctive double-G logo was being sported by stars of stage and screen. The jet set came ready wrapped in Gucci's signature red and green webbing. It was top of the top of the range. The brand bespoke style, taste, refinement. It had cachet to spare.[26]

Then things started to go wrong. When Guccio died in 1953 his two sons, Aldo and Rudolpho, and their two sons, Paulo and Maurizio, became embroiled in a prolonged power struggle over the ownership and direction of the family business. This led to a wanton disregard for Gucci's carefully nurtured brand image. During the 1970s and 1980s all sorts of dubious licensing deals were entered into. The brand presence proliferated. The logo appeared on everything from baseball caps to sweat pants. Counterfeit green- and red-webbed merchandise materialized in street markets throughout the developing world, and, to add insult to injury, sprouted on cheapjack stalls outside the company's flagship stores. The Gucci logo even appeared, in what was surely the marketing nadir, on rolls of "luxury" toilet tissue.

Being flushed down the branding pan is one thing, murder and mayhem is another matter entirely. Just when things couldn't get worse for Gucci, they did. Further rounds of internecine warfare involving contested wills, hostile takeovers, and, ultimately, the 1995 assassination of Maurizio by hitpersons in the pay of his estranged wife, left the renowned brand reeling, its reputation in ruins.

Ironically the revival started at about the same time, thanks to the back-to-core-principles philosophy of new CEO, Domenico de Sole (appointed in 1994) and the eye-catching apparel collections of chief designer Tom Ford (appointed creative director, also 1994). More ironically still, the salacious publicity surrounding Maurizio's slaying helped move things along, since it imbued the beleaguered brand with a frisson of decadence, danger, drama.[27] De Sole terminated inappropriate licensing deals, closed substandard stores the world over, cracked down on counterfeiters, revamped the entire Gucci range, boosted the advertising spend considerably, broadened the group's brand portfolio through judicious acquisitions (YSL, Sergio Rossi, Balenciaga, Bottega Veneta, etc.), and, notwithstanding the post 9/11 downturn affecting the entire luxury goods trade, has succeeded in getting the company back on top.[28] "Exclusivity," he notes,[29] "is what drives profitability. Sales alone are meaningless. If I want to sell more it's very simple. We have hundreds of requests from people who want to sell Gucci. I could open another 2000 doors in one hour and sales would double. But then I will have no profits. If you look . . . the better brands . . . really understand exclusivity – Louis Vuitton, Chanel, Prada to a certain extent, and so on and so forth."

Expression is the Better Part of Value

American Express is czar of all the charge cards, with a long and noble lineage. The company was founded in the mid-nineteenth century as a freight handling operation and gradually evolved into a financial service provider for elite American expatriates and Grand Tour-taking patricians. Money orders, travelers checks, bank deposits, automobile rentals, passport and visa applications, shipping services for personal effects, and an array of other tiresome but necessary functions were performed for a select segment of American society. American Express effectively owned the category of "foreign travel" and, as the travel industry burgeoned in the second half of the twentieth century, American Express burgeoned with it.[30]

Although American Express wasn't the first financial services provider to launch a charge card – Diners Club and several "single service" offerings got there beforehand – the 1958 introduction of American Express's "universal" card was a defining moment. It was universal insofar as it could be used for a wide range of travel- and entertainment-related services and was accepted in a huge number of travel- and entertainment-related service outlets. The Amex launch legitimized, and effectively established, an entire industry.

Prestige was paramount, at least initially. The card was only offered to well-heeled individuals, such as senior executives of blue chip companies, and the key to the pitch was exclusivity. Prospects were invited to become "members" of an elite group, akin to a private country club. They were the discerning few who were sufficiently creditworthy to carry the card and sufficiently sagacious not to leave home without it. Naturally, the initial membership fee reflected this privileged positioning.[31]

It hardly bears repeating that the card was a raging success, with half a million issued in the first year alone. So popular did it prove that, as the prestige of the original green card gradually declined through increased availability (22 million members by 1985), the elitist pitch worked again with both the gold and platinum cards (issued in 1966 and 1984 respectively). Indeed, if there is one sure thing in marketing, above and beyond the fact that sex sells, it is that appeals to human vanity, egotism, and sense of self-worth represent the royal road to riches. The early years of the Amex card comprise a prime example of this approach at work.

If there is one other sure thing in marketing, it is that success spawns competitors. And so it was with Amex. The BankAmerica card was launched in 1966 and renamed VISA eleven years later. MasterCard also appeared in 1966, although it was known as the Interbank card until 1979. By the late 1980s, moreover, all manner of co-branded (ATT, GE, Ford, etc.), affinity (Caritas, Sierra Club, and so forth) and no-fee discount cards (e.g. Discover) had muscled in on Amex territory.[32] Things worsened with the economic recession of the early 1990s, when many began to question the high fees and "unnecessary" benefits that American Express offered. The company itself had become arrogant and out of touch, having fallen for its own positioning. The prince of plastic had feet of clay.[33] VISA and MasterCard, meanwhile, steadily closed the cachet gap with Premier and Preferred Customer cards of their own. They were much more widely accepted, what's more, on account of the massive banking consortia that stood behind the brands. As a result, Amex's share of the US credit/charge card market slumped from 26% in 1984 to 19% in 1993.[34]

Although the privileges of membership had been trumped by "everywhere you want to be," American Express remained a force to be reckoned with.[35] It says much for the appeal of exclusivity that the product's patent competitive disadvantages – high membership fee, no revolving credit, unpopular with retailers due to its above average discount fee – were counteracted by the cash value of cachet and the vestigial éclat of the card.

Be that at it may, the fight-back began in 1993, with the appointment of new CEO Harvey Golub. Extraneous activities were disposed of (publishing, stockbroking); revolving credit and cutting edge smart cards were issued (Blue, Centurion); new markets were tackled with vigor (international, small business); co-branding alliances were entered into (NatWest, Credit Lyonnais); exclusive online banking operations were developed (Financial Direct); and the prestige of the brand was re-emphasized by a renewed commitment to consistently clever advertising (people and their stuff, Seinfeld spots, etc.). If not quite doing nicely, Amex has reclaimed its once exclusive "Do you know me?" territory.[36]

Regardless of the causes, the good news is that recovery is not impossible. Provided, of course, the following Twelve Step Program of Cachet Recuperation is rigidly adhered to:

- Step One – Reduce production.
- Step Two – Restrict distribution.
- Step Three – Raise prices.
- Step Four – Redouble communications.
- Step Five – Rearrange the range.
- Step Six – Refuse to compromise on quality.
- Step Seven – Rebuff customers, since waiting makes them want.
- Step Eight – Remind competitors, as dramatically as possible, that the brand is back.
- Step Nine – Rejoice in renewed growth.
- Step Ten – Remain flexible, because conditions can and will change.
- Step Eleven – Remember the Alamo, what made the brand great in the first place.
- Step Twelve – Return to Step One when things go awry.

Further details, naturally, are available to the discerning few, at enormous expense, for a short time only.[37]

Faster Pussycat, Kill, Kill

Rather than conclude this chapter on a mercenary note, let me wrap things up with an uplifting tale from the – dead metaphors alert! – urban jungle, concrete canyons, and mean streets of New York City.[38] In the immediate aftermath of 9/11, you may recall, there were widespread fears of bioterrorism. This led to a dramatic run on gas masks, torch batteries, bottled water, wind-up radios, Cipro stocks, and canaries. Yes, canaries. Pet stores throughout Manhattan reported that the creatures were flying off the shelves, canary prices were going through the roof, and that the birds couldn't be had for love nor money. This sudden demand, sadly, had nothing to do with the fact that hitherto hard-hearted New Yorkers were finally getting in touch with the inner ornithologist. It reflected, rather, the old coal miners' trick of using canaries as an avian indicator of impending gas attack. If they give up the ghost and fall off the perch, it's time to break out the oxygen mask, remove the rapidly stiffening cadaver, make a beeline for the nearest animal companion emporium, and wait patiently for them to throw the switch. Hot Canaries Now!

How to Employ Exclusivity Effectively?
Exiguous Evanescence Works Every Time.

HOW TO AMPLIFY

Sultan of Spin

A couple of years back, a sensational story splashed across the front pages of Britain's daily newspapers. It was also covered in most of that day's television and newspaper bulletins and dissected in the Sunday supplements as well. The story claimed that a work by the country's most famous living artist, Damien Hirst, had been thrown into an art gallery's garbage.[1] A contract cleaner, Emmanuel Asare, mistook it for trash and treated it accordingly. The work in question was an installation piece consisting of empty Budweiser bottles, crushed Marlboro packs, overflowing ashtrays, cold coffee cups, congealed paint brushes, crumpled sheets of paper, an artist's smock and beret, a half-full glass of wine, and Chinese takeaway chopsticks. Entitled *Untitled*, it depicted the daily life of a working artist. A tortured artist, naturally. A grievously misunderstood artist. A you-know-what artist.

All's well that ends well, however. Fortunately, the garbage hadn't been removed and, even more fortunately, the gallery owners had taken Polaroids of the magisterial artwork, assembled the night before by the maestro. They retrieved the precious artifact from the dumpster and, with the aid of the fortuitous photos, were able to reassemble the masterpiece. Relief was unbounded, not only in the

115

art world, but also in contract cleaning circles, since Emmanuel Asare almost lost his job over the incident.

Some steely-hearted art critics, it is true, quickly dismissed the near disaster. The incident, they claimed, was concocted to publicize the opening of a new art gallery, Eyestorm, which just happened to sell limited editions of Damien Hirst's work.[2] However, no one in Eyestorm's marketing department owned up to the dirty deed. To the contrary, they rubbished the suggestion that it was a cheap publicity stunt, based on the general public's perception that most modern art is rubbish and only fit for the trash can.

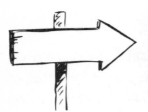

Damien Hirst's place in the artistic canon has yet to be determined, but he certainly deserves a place in the pantheon of marketing practice.

Yet, despite the affronted protestations, most media coverage focused on the fact that it was "obviously" a publicity stunt, the latest in a long line of headline-grabbing antics by the clown prince of BritArt, Damien Hirst.[3] These discussions, however, merely added to the storm of publicity surrounding the storm of publicity surrounding Eyestorm. Intentional or not, it was brilliantly effective. It generated thousands of pounds worth of press coverage for the price of a Budweiser, a packet of Marlboros, a bottle of wine, and a Chinese takeaway meal. Unless, of course, product placement was going on as well, thereby adding an additional revenue stream . . .

Art for Mart's Sake

Damien Hirst's place in the artistic canon has yet to be determined, but he certainly deserves a place in the pantheon of marketing practice. Without question, he is one of the most astute marketing talents on the face of the earth. The son of a used car dealer, Hirst's career to date has been marked by his unerring eye for the main marketing chance.[4] He first attracted attention as a 23-year-old student at Gold-smith's College, when he curated a show in a disused warehouse in the east end of London. Not only did this open a new channel of dis-tribution for young artists unable to break into the traditional gallery circuit, but it opened up the art world to this irrepressible atten-tion-seeker. He caused a stir with his sensational tiger shark in a vat of formaldehyde; he sawed various barnyard animals in half and displayed the grisly results in pristine vitrines; he filled gleaming display racks with disgusting cigarette ends, multi-colored pills, and assorted medical requisites; he produced a video installation of tele-vision commercials for headache remedies, which played at ear-split-ting, migraine-inducing, hit-the-mute-button volume; and he placed the complete contents of a gynecologist's office in a water-filled tank and stocked it with tropical fish.

There's much more to Hirst, however, than expensive pieces of offensive installation art.[5] On the contrary, his installations are akin to the loss-leaders of haute couture fashion houses. They are designed to disgust, provoke, attract attention, and stimulate sales of the artist's more mundane but money-spinning Spin Art and Dot Art. In the case of the former, buckets of paint are thrown onto rap-idly-spinning disks, whereas the latter are regular grids of multi-colored spots made out of ordinary household emulsion. Both are produced in factory-like conditions by squads of low-paid assis-tants and, as they fetch approximately $75,000 apiece, Hirst's profit margins are as stratospheric as his reputation.

Damien Hirst is by no means the only marketing-savvy artist, nor was he the first to appreciate the importance of self-promotion. Jeff Koons and Mark Kostabi, to name but two marketing-oriented pub-licity-seekers, were the Don Kings and Doug Kellehers of the New

York art scene in the greed-is-good 1980s. And they were mere foot-notes in the arts marketing textbook written by that well-known Coke bottle aficionado, Brillo Box assembler, Campbell's Soup sup-per, and sometime shoe salesman, Andy Warhol. Warhol, in turn, was inspired by Salvador Dali, who was influenced by the Surreal-ists, who were indebted to Marcel Duchamp, who installed the idea of installation art and provoked the outrage that Damien Hirst is currently recycling.[6]

Hirst, nevertheless, epitomizes what Seabrook has termed the "nobrow" mentality, the marketing-is-all ethos that characterizes the contemporary art world.[7] The old idea of art for art's sake, where serious artists disdained the money-grubbing machinations of the marketplace, has been replaced by the belief that art is a business like any other. Artists not only allude to commercial culture in their artworks – as Warhol did, as Koons and Kostabi did, as the amazing Art Guys do[8] – but they are complicit in the commodification of their output. These days, accusations of "selling out" don't refer to reneg-ing on the struggling artist stereotype. They simply mean that stocks need replenishing.

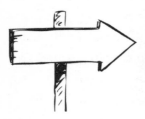

"If you make great fucking art, then fuck them. Fuck what they want. They'll buy what you fucking give them."

While Seabrook's argument has merit – there's no doubt that the art world is more marketing oriented than hitherto – it doesn't go far enough. It fails to appreciate that creative artists are at the cut-ting edge of marketing. It's not that artists have become more aware of marketing's importance, or are less concerned about its contami-nating effects than before, or can discuss a marketing plan with museum curators and exhibition directors. The point is that creative artists like Damien Hirst are more astute marketers than the denizens of many mainstream marketing departments. True, they are untutored in the ways, whys, whats, and wherefores of 4Ps marketing. However, it is this very lack of indoctrination that renders them so effective. Customer orientation, for example, rarely enters into the equation. As Damien Hirst tartly observed when an interviewer raised the customer specter, "If you make great fucking art, then fuck them. Fuck what they want. They'll buy what you fucking give them. If you're great, they'll buy it. If you're making great art, you don't have to think about the punters."[9]

In this regard, Hirst's trash-talking, trash-selling, and, more recently, extraterrestrial trash-trafficking antics contain a lesson that is germane to the contemporary marketing condition.[10] We live, as noted previously, in a world where every organization is marketing oriented, where everyone is marketing literate, where everyone is familiar with the latest management buzzword. We live in a world where the top shelves of bookstores groan under the weight of execuporn, glossy magazines extolling the virtues of celebrity CEOs and analogous corporate centerfolds. We live in a world where marketing campaigns are extremely expensive to mount and much less effective than ever before, due to the plethora of competing marketing campaigns, all professionally developed, precisely formulated and perfectly executed.

Testing, Testing, One, Two

The question, then, is how, in such congested circumstances, does one stand out from the crowd? The answer is to *Amplify*. That is, to ensure that your hot product or cool service is talked about and, more importantly, that the talking about is talked about.[11] Above all else, Hirst's *Untitled* was a media event, whereby the media reports on the reports of the media. The same is true of Beanie Babies, *Blair Witch Project*, Filene's Basement Bridal Event, Donald Trump's trumpeting and Dean Kamen's sublime Segway. Such products aren't so much famous for being famous, as Boorstin famously put it,[12] but are marketed on the basis of their marketing. That is to say, the marketing campaign *itself* becomes the focus of attention, analysis, and, ideally, appreciation, which further amplifies the amplification. The

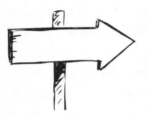

Nowadays it's not enough to make an excellent product and market it excellently. The excellent marketing must be excellently marketed as well.

central element in the TEASE framework, Amplification is vitally necessary in a world of incessant commercial chatter, where everyone is talking at once and no one can hear clearly. So much so that a marketing campaign doesn't actually exist these days unless it is mass mediated. No spin, no sale.

Lest there is any confusion, let me make it absolutely clear that Amplification is more than a fancy word for "viral" or "buzz" marketing. Viral marketing aims to get people talking up the latest cool band, hot movie, snazzy accessory, 'mazing website, or incredible telecommunications gizmo. It works by word of mouse, the distribution of free samples, and good old-fashioned face-to-face communication.

Amplification, by contrast, pertains to the marketing of the marketing: The fact, for example, that buzz marketing is being buzz marketed in *Business Week* and the *Harvard Business Review* or that Seth Godin's best-selling book on viral marketing is itself an exemplar of viral marketing.[13] Nowadays it's not enough to make an excellent product and market it excellently. The excellent marketing must be excellently marketed as well.

An excellent example of excellent marketing excellently marketed is the recent "Wassup" campaign by Budweiser. As everyone is well aware, these multiple-award-winning ads featured a bunch of beer-swilling slackers, who greeted each other with the inchoate inter-rogative "Wassup?" an utterance accompanied by much rolling of eyes and lolling of tongues. Wassup quickly became the call of the couch potato worldwide and the advertisers, DDB, capitalized on the phenomenon with a series of ads within ads, featuring wassup WASP wannabes watched with incredulity by the original Bud-imbib-ing sofa surfers. The wassup phenomenon itself became the focus of the wassup advertising campaign and this, in turn, spawned much media discussion of the wassup phenomenon, the advertising cam-paign, the advertising agency concerned, and, eventually, the media interest in the media interest. Thus, the extra-advertising origins of the ad, the fact that it began as a three-minute short by experimen-tal film-maker, Charles Stone (who actually – gasp! – appears in the ads), became marketing grist to the media mill, as did the inevitable spoofs, the wassup websites, and the celebrities who joined in the Bud-bonding fun.[14]

Ghost Writers in the Sky

In the annals of advertising slogans, "Wassup" may not call down the years like "Does she or doesn't she?" "I'd walk a mile for a Camel," or "Good to the Last Drop." Nevertheless, it is sure to feature in future books about the best ads of the twenty-first century. Books, indeed, are another noteworthy way of amplifying marketing. Many long-running campaigns and high-profile products have been immortalized between the covers of coffee-table texts – Guinness, Volkswagen, Got Milk, Pepsi, Sears, and Barbie, amongst others,[15] though Absolut is the absolute apotheosis of this brand buzzing genre (see Free Gift 7). Books, moreover, can be used as amplifying devices in themselves. Bulgari, the Italian luxury goods brand, recently commissioned the bestselling author and former advertising executive Fay Weldon to write a thriller set in the sponsoring organization. The resultant book, *The Bulgari Connection*, attracted a lot of attention, especially when it was denounced by deeply offended literati.[16] Happily, there's nothing like an outraged esthete to guarantee acres of free publicity and a suitably apocalyptic quote. Every organization should have one on retainer.

Free Gift 7: Absolut Amplification

Absolut, the celebrated Swedish vodka, is blessed with not one but two brand biographies, to say nothing of numerous honorable mentions in management textbooks and journal articles.[17] It has been amplified beyond ear-splitting to an aural sphere ordinarily occupied by a dog whistles, bat lures, Limp Bizkit buffs, and Nine Inch Nails nuts. Nevertheless, its success has been so dramatic that the Absolut case simply cannot be ignored. Its US sales rose from 20,000 cases in 1981 to 4 million cases twenty years later, making Absolut the #1 imported vodka and #3 vodka brand overall.[18]

The wonder of Absolut, aside from the sheer imagination of the magazine ads themselves, is that its campaign runs completely counter to best practice guidelines found in most marketing primers. Absolut's triumph in the marketplace of marketing campaigns is primarily due to the fact that it dared to be different and dared to be seen to be different. Absolut is living proof – 80% proof to be precise – of the old marketing aphorism, which I've just invented, "ask not what marketing can do for art but what art can do for marketing."

As Richard Lewis explains in *Absolut Book*, the story of the long-running advertising campaign, the brand's distinctively shaped bottle and innovative two-word strapline were never researched, pre-tested, or subject to any form of customer approval.[19] To the contrary, what little initial consumer feedback there was, was almost entirely negative. Back in 1979, apparently, Americans didn't associate Sweden with vodka, or anything else for that matter. The see-through, label-less bottle wouldn't stand out on the shelves of liquor stores, so they said, and it was the wrong shape as well. The proposed advertising slogan was way too obscure, what's more, and deeply pretentious to boot. But the advertising agency, TWBA, and the US importer, Carillion, pressed ahead regardless.

The rest, as they say, is history. More than 600 variations on the Absolut Whatever treatment have appeared in glossy magazines worldwide, with the noteworthy exception of Sweden, where alcohol advertising is banned. The bottle is the hero of the campaign. All the ads emphasize the bottle, or the silhouette of the bottle, or even the absence of the bottle, which is filled in, as it were, by the viewer. Variations include the celebrated cityscapes, where the perceived character of a place is perfectly encapsulated (in Absolut San Francisco, the bottle is wreathed in fog; Absolut L.A. features a bottle-shaped swimming pool; Absolut New York comprises a satellite photograph of Manhattan, complete with suitably reshaped Central Park).

Equally successful is the much-anticipated Christmas special for *New York* magazine, which has ranged from multilingual, microchip-activated seasons greetings, through musical renditions of the nation's favorite Christmas carols, to plastic snowstorms, where the flakes are suspended in replica Absolut bottles. Shaken and stirred is the brand's abiding byword, particularly when it comes to spectaculars like Absolut Centrefold (a déshabillé bottle that appeared in *Playboy*), and outdoor, tall-wall, stop-the-traffic superbillboards (the one in Dallas incorporates a working waterfall, LA's is constructed from the publicity photos of wannabe movie stars, New York's consists of a fully furnished studio apartment firmly attached to the three story sign).

Above and beyond these so-called unicates, Absolut advertising is best known for the art and artists series. This commenced in 1984 when Andy Warhol ran into Michel Roux, Carillon's CEO, and expressed his admiration for the bottle's esthetics. On impulse, Roux asked Warhol to paint its portrait, paid the Pop Art panjandrum $65,000 for the privilege and, against the better advice of both Carillon colleagues and advertising agency executives, insisted that Absolut Warhol be used as part of the series, even though it broke with the brand's well-established advertising template. It was an instant success. It revolutionized the relationship between art and advertising. It was extended to other leading artists and exponents of analogous artforms including fashion designers, photographers, moviemakers, cartoonists, actors, poets, novelists, and so on. It quickly became a badge of honor for well-established and up-and-coming creatives alike. Absolut Haring, Absolut Schnabel, Absolut Ruscha, Absolut Galliano, Absolut Newton, Absolut Marilyn, Absolut Rosebud, Absolut Hirst, et al. All have been amplified by Absolut and all have amplified Absolut in return. Sköl.

Of course, it's not strictly necessary to devote an entire book to the brand. A passing mention is sometimes sufficient. The dramatic revival of Hush Puppies casual footwear not only featured in the first chapter of *The Tipping Point*, Malcolm Gladwell's book on buzz marketing that was buzzed to the top of the best-sellers list, but it was mentioned with approval in many of the associated reviews.[20] Similarly, there is no doubt that Stew Leonard's, a tiny, two-store grocery chain in New England, owed its reputation for outstanding customer care to the favorable treatment it received in Peters and Waterman's 1982 blockbuster, *In Search of Excellence*. To this very day, Stew Leonard is lionized in popular management publications, his incarceration for fraud notwithstanding.[21]

Business school case studies are yet another interesting amplification option. Academicians are suckers for the inside story and, better yet, they'll swallow virtually anything you decide to tell them. The words "shooting," "fish," and "barrel" spring immediately to mind. If you're really desperate, however, I know of an unscrupulous Irish scholar who's prepared to amplify almost any half-baked brand for a very small consideration. Granted, his books don't sell very well – I gather he's giving free gifts in a pathetic attempt to move the merchandise – but, hey, you get what you pay for.[22]

Be that as it may, by far the most common form of bibliographic boosterism is the executive Autobiography. A CEO isn't a CEO these days unless he or she has spawned a ghost-written autobiography or several. Jack Welch, Steve Jobs, Michael Dell, Richard Branson, Anita Roddick, Martha Stewart, Howard Schultz, Ted Turner, Jurgen Schrempp, Robert Goizetta, Giovanni Agnelli, Jim Cramer, and countless others are cognizant of the corporate amplification that accompanies additions to the literary genre pioneered by P.T. Barnum.

Such texts, in truth, are often terribly stereotyped. Almost without exception, they comprise minor variations on the Horatio Algeresque, rags-to-riches, American Dream archetype, sometimes with an against-the-odds subplot (dyslexic, orphan, sociopath, occasionally all three). Nevertheless, they perform an important amplifying function. In addition to their general profile-raising purpose, they are good for employee morale, inasmuch as the team behind the great leader unfailingly receives a favorable mention. They go down well on Wall Street as well, since the fantastic financiers behind the IPO or whatever generally get their backs well and truly scratched between the pages of the breathless bestseller. They also endow the author with the aura of celebritude – the books invariably include photos of the CEO hobnobbing with politicians, movie stars, and other high-profile executives – which never goes amiss when lucrative directorships, consultancies, and speaking engagements are up for grabs.[23]

The Midden Persuaders

Commonplace though they are, biographies of business executives and their brands – do they come to resemble each other, I wonder? – are only one form of Amplification and a fairly specialized one at that. A much cheaper, if rather riskier, amplifying method is *Affront*. Whether it be Benetton, or Diesel, or Calvin Klein, or FCUK, there's nothing like a little outrage to attract attention. It can turn a tiny advertising spend into a megabudget marketing monster.

It has been estimated, for example, that Benetton's infamous advertising campaign featuring fornicating horses, terrorist attacks, dying AIDS victims, and, most frighteningly of all, a full-frontal photo of Luciano Benetton in his birthday suit, stimulated $100 million worth of free publicity. On a miniscule advertising spend of $5.6 million.[24]

When Calvin Klein mortified middle America with his notorious kiddy porn campaign of 1995, the ensuing moral panic – precipitated by the dubious *Details* centerfold in particular – was worth its weight in gold. Ill-gotten gold perhaps, but gold all the same.[25]

Similarly, the almost-offensively acronymed British outfitter French Connection UK saw its sales increase by 40%, and its share price more than double, in the aftermath of a gratuitous "fcuk fashion" billboard campaign.[26] The entire cost was recouped by the sale of identically emblazoned T-shirts and when the Advertising Standards Authority officially censured the company, it replied with another blast of bad-assed billboard bile: "fcuk advertising."

There's nothing like a little outrage to attract attention. It can turn a tiny advertising spend into a megabudget marketing monster.

Affront is not for everyone, I grant you. It is especially common among foul-mouthed fashion forwarders, desperate-for-an-image dot.com companies, shock-em-and-soak-em showbiz barkers, and, lest we forget, innumerable not-for-profit organizations, who routinely hold donors to ransom with heart-rending images of illness, injury, and impoverishment.

Affront, nevertheless, is a very powerful way of amplifying a marketing campaign. It gets people talking about the advertising, often in hushed, they've-gone-too-far-this-time tones. It gets us watching out for the next appalling installment, albeit behind can't-bear-to-look hands and between can't-bear-not-to-look fingers. Above all, it gets the moral majority into a lather, which makes it even more appealing to the intended target market. Eminem is endearing to his fans because he offends everyone else. Damien Hirst's Dot Art sells by the gallon on account of his bad boy image. Wearing a "fcuk advertising" T-shirt is not particularly smart, but smart doesn't sell as many T-shirts as cool.

Affront, then, bestows a rebellious air of attractive insouciance on the I-fought-the-law malefactor behind the campaign. Whether we like it or not, affront gives an enormous bang for the buck. In every sense of the expression. This is especially the case if the miscreant marketer goes beyond what's socially acceptable and gets banned for his or her trouble. As the previously mentioned Tango fandango perfectly demonstrates, being banned is good for business. There's nothing like a little censorship, or the threat of censorship, to set the tongues wagging, the media mouthing off, and, most importantly perhaps, the cash registers ringing. As any self-respecting rap artist, exotic dancer, penniless author, nu-metal combo, low-budget movie maker, and strapped-for-cash advertising executive will attest, an interdict, embargo, or official proscription of some kind can be a blessing in disguise. When the Sex Pistols were banned in 1977, their record rocketed to the top of the charts. The

127

Satanic Verses fatwa made Salman Rushdie a household name and an icon of free speech. *Sensation*, a shocking art exhibition featuring Damien Hirst, drew enormous crowds in New York, crowds that swelled considerably when Mayor Rudy Giuliani expressed his outrage and threatened to close the show down.[27]

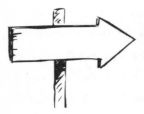

When a product is banned, it receives an additional boost from the scarcity effect. It's hard to get hold of and more attractive as a consequence.

A ban, in many ways is the ideal outcome of affront-based marketing campaigns. The killjoys are happy because the offensive artifact has been removed from view. The marketing or PR agency is happy on account of the coverage that they would otherwise have had to pay for. And the client is happy, thanks to the radical, rebellious, revolutionary reputation it enjoys thereafter. Sedition sells!

When a product is banned, moreover, it receives an additional boost from the scarcity effect, noted in Lesson Five. It's hard to get hold of and more attractive as a consequence. Intriguingly, the psychological literature shows that suppressing something does more than increase demand due to its rarity.[28] It also makes people much more favorably disposed toward the censored object. When, to cite a seemingly trivial example, phosphate detergents were banned in Dade County, Florida, the inhabitants of that distinguished district not only stocked up on scarce supplies of the precious powders, but they believed them to be superior products thereafter. They got clothes cleaner, performed better in cold water, and even poured easier than non-phosphate alternatives. Analogously, when Procter & Gamble decided to end its couponing practices in upper New York

State, supermarket shoppers were up in arms at the unilateral removal of their inalienable retail rights, even though less than one percent of the coupons actually got redeemed prior to P&G's decision. The threat was lifted and a higher rate of redemption resulted, until the infraction was forgotten about and a state of happy apathy prevailed once more.

In a similar vein, one of America's most loved reproduction paintings, *September Morn*, which adorned millions of walls before the Second World War, was impressed on the national consciousness thanks to a carefully orchestrated outcry.[29] The superlative publicist Harry Reichenbach was retained by a retail store and asked to help shift excess stocks of the unpopular print. Luckily it depicted a lightly draped woman, happily splashing at the edge of a lake. Ever ahead of the shockvertising curve, Harry leapt into action. He anonymously telephoned the then guardian of American public morals, Anthony Comstock, complaining bitterly about the bawdy reproduction on shameless display in the said store window. The offended official rushed to the scene of the crime, where Reichenbach had recruited a group of grubby adolescents, pre-paid to snicker on cue and point lasciviously at the diaphanously dressed bathing beauty. Comstock went bananas, a ban was imposed, sales soared, and a much-admired American icon was born. Granted, *September Morn* never adorned as many domestic walls or motel rooms as Tretchikoff's "deeply mysterious" *Green Lady*. However, even Damien Hirst at his most outrageous doesn't hold a candle to the amplifier's amplifier, Harry Reichenbach.

Battle of the Brands

Affront may be the amplifier's ultimate weapon, but it isn't normally necessary to go that far. Indeed, many organizations with a wholesome reputation to uphold – Hershey, Heinz, Hasbro, Hooters, and so on – are understandably leery of affront-based amplification. *Antagonism*, however, is an equally effective alternative.[30] A stand up row rarely fails to draw a crowd and rarely fails to deliver manna from media heaven. The history of modern marketing is replete with logo-a-logo loggerheads, most of which benefited both brand-name brawlers. "Every brand," as Ries and Ries rightly note,[31] "needs an enemy." Coke versus Pepsi, Avis versus Hertz, McDonald's versus Burger King, Virgin versus British Airways, Nike versus Adidas, Boeing versus Airbus, Budweiser versus Miller, *Time* versus *Newsweek*, Sears versus Penney's, Wal-Mart versus K-Mart, Disney versus Dreamworks, FedEx versus UPS, Kodak versus Fuji, Philips versus Sony, Christie's versus Sotheby's, IBM versus Apple, Dell versus Gateway, Pampers versus Huggies, Crest versus Colgate, Duracell versus Energizer. It keeps going and going.

Corporate grappling, remember, is a fantastic spectator sport, with considerable entertainment value. Who can forget Ted Turner's offer to go fifteen three-minute rounds with Rupert Murdoch in Las Vegas? Or Herb Kelleher's "Malice in Dallas," when he arm-wrestled a rival CEO for the right to use a contested advertising slogan? Or, for that matter, the commercial confrontation between Pizza Hut and Papa John's which ended up in court? Litigation has a built-in sizzle factor that astute amplifiers stand ever ready to exploit. I await Dean Kamen's, The Donald's, and Ty Warner's respective writs with eager anticipation.

You Hawking to Me?

Antagonized amplification, of course, doesn't just come in brand-to-brand form. An affray with third parties can prove equally effective. FCUK doesn't diss other fashion retailers; as a rule, it picks fights with the advertising watchdog. Red Bull, the Austrian energy drink, only really took off in Germany when public health officials controversially outlawed the brand on account of its dubious ingredients.[32] The Citroën Picasso, a mini-minivan, outraged the French artistic establishment by its misappropriation of the maestro's moniker and attracted more than 10,000 advance orders on the back of the much-publicized spat.[33] When Jonathan Franzen, best-selling author of *The Corrections*, spurned the literary industry's premier amplification opportunity, Oprah's Book Club Choice, the resultant cascade of how-dare-he hostility proved a more than adequate recompense.[34] Franzen's "snub" hit the headlines worldwide and garnered more hold-the-front-page publicity than even an Oprah endorsement could have delivered.

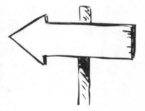

The media have their own agenda and are understandably reluctant to recycle the corporate press releases that inundate them day and daily.

As the *Corrections* kerfuffle illustrates, amplification can be unpredictable and difficult to control. The media have their own agenda and are understandably reluctant to recycle the corporate press releases that inundate them day and daily. Amplification, indeed, can go disastrously wrong, as Cadbury-Schweppes recently discovered in India, when an advertising campaign for its Temptations chocolate bar drew impolitic parallels between the too-good-to-share product and the disputed, war-torn region of Kashmir.[35] Opium perfume, similarly, felt the full ire of incandescent French feminists with a prurient promotion predicated on "porno chic".

Free Gift 8: Opium, Alas

The land of the Folies Bergères and Marquis de Sade isn't exactly renowned for its chastity, especially in marketing matters. Naked models, glamorous models, and naked glamorous models adorn every other advertising campaign. And the ones in between. Of late, however, the carnal competition is such that marketers are being pushed into ever more questionable sexual practices. Or depicting them at least. Known as "porno chic," this involves objectionable images of women in sexually degrading positions.[36] One of the most depraved showed the supermodel Sophie Dahl splayed on a velvet rug, completely naked except for some costume jewelry and sadistic stiletto heels. Open-mouthed, open-legged, and openly in a state of self-induced erotic rapture, the ad for Opium perfume provoked a prodigious hue and cry. It was defaced by affronted consumers; the French government threatened to alter the laws on censorship if marketers like YSL didn't clean up their act; and a group of feminist activists, *Chiennes de Garde*, was founded to fight the industry's inherent androcentrism.[37]

Faced with this reaction, YSL's marketing maestro Tom Ford drew attention to its esthetic qualities. The ad, he claimed, was inspired by a Delacroix painting and was the work of top photographer, Steven Meisel. What's more, he rhapsodized about its contemporary allusions to the alabaster odalisques, femmes fatales, and undulating nudes of the history of art. The public wasn't convinced, however, since surveys showed that 70% of French consumers were offended by such images. So much for *Ooh La La*.

The case for the ad is questionable, of course, but the saga suggests that YSL was engaged in what can be termed Atavistic Amplification. Ford's elaborate references to the past are a promotional front for Opium's attempt to turn the clock back to the marketing shock tactics that made its name in 1977, when the scandalous brand was first launched.

In addition to Atavism, Affront, and Antagonism, there are several other forms of Amplification. Auto-Amplification, for example, refers to marketing tactics that are primarily designed to enthuse employees and organizational stakeholders, but which "leak out" into the media. Epitomized by the rah-rah activities of Sam Walton and Doug Kelleher, this is not so much "management by walking about" as management by swaggering, swanking, strutting, and shouting about.

Conversely, it is perfectly possible to amplify through Absence. That is to say, the avoidance of amplification is form of amplification in itself. It involves keeping a low profile, adopting a minimalist approach to marketing, and ensuring that the understatement is (quietly) talked about. It screams, in effect, that the company's not screaming. It is practiced by extra exclusive brands like Guerlain cosmetics, Jimmy Choo shoes, and Tanner Krole luggage, as well as more mainstream minimalists like Muji.

Yet another variant is Ancillary Amplification, where the marketing of the marketing comes from the participation of a third party or intermediary. Armani is a perfect case in point, insofar as the brand is brilliantly amplified by movie stars and celebrities, who wear the designer's low-key ensembles to high profile media extravaganzas like the Oscars and Golden Globes. As amplification goes, you can't get much louder than that. It goes all the way up to eleven.

A final, and arguably the most insidious, form of the phenomenon is Autographic Amplification. This brings consumers on board as brand barkers by getting them to write about the product and/or its marketing. It is well known from psychological studies of brainwashing that when people write something down about themselves, they are more inclined to believe it. They become what they describe. Hence the popularity of 25-words-or-less contests in the 1950s, corporate chat-rooms and interactive websites in the 1990s, and the current fad for text message-based marketing competitions.[38] Far from being trivial promotional gimmicks, as they are sometimes considered to be, Autographic forms of Amplification are one of the most powerful ways of inculcating long-term customer loyalty in our marketing-saturated age.

At the same time, the sheer power of today's publicity machine produces outcomes that are paradoxical at best and perverse at worst. Thus the publicity surrounding the Enron-Andersen scandal has led to a sharp increase in the uptake of college accountancy courses,[39] which are now seen as "creative, even sexy." Winona Ryder's famously light-fingered trip to Saks Fifth Avenue not only boosted consumer demand for the unsuccessfully purloined merchandise, Marc Jacobs in particular, but increased movie producers' demand for the hitherto (ar)resting actress.[40] Sales of Michael Jackson's back catalogue spiked suddenly after the metamorphic moonwalker's astonishing appearance in a notorious, no-holds-barred television documentary, *Living With Michael Jackson*.[41]

However, even Wacko's wetnursing prowess pales beside the immortal Treacy and Wiersema imbroglio. Sales of their barnstorming management book, *The Discipline of Market Leaders*, took off when news broke that the authors had spent an estimated $250,000 in an attempt to hype it on to the bestseller lists.[42]

Quick, get me the Capstone marketing department. I've just had a great idea . . .

How to Amplify?
Sorry, I Can't Hear You.

HOW TO SELL SHAM SECRETS

Look Mom, No Captivity

If you go down to the woods today, you're sure of a big surprise. Especially if those woods are ninety miles south of Vilnius, the capital of Lithuania. There, in a forest clearing, lies the Soviet Sculpture Garden, brainchild of local mushroom mogul, Viliumas Malinauskas. Colloquially known as "Stalin World," it is a theme park dedicated to the horrors of the Soviet era.[1] Sixty-six statues of ex-Communist leaders, formerly scattered throughout the towns and cities of the Russian satellite prior to independence in 1991, have been brought together in a 30-acre forest park. Here, a 10-foot high bronze of Uncle Joe Stalin; over there, a 12-foot tall replica of Lenin in pink marble; round the corner, a monumental concrete bust of Karl Marx. Statues of lesser Lithuanian lights are interspersed between the Communist era superheroes, their crimes listed on plaques beneath the plinths. "The effect," one observer notes,[2] "is alternately moving, eerie, and comic."

Developed at the cost of $1 million, Stalin World is a bizarre hybrid of Busch Gardens and the Gulag Archipelago. The attraction is surrounded by insurmountable razor wire; wooden watchtowers, complete with "guards," are interspersed along the perimeter; martial music blasts incessantly from loudspeakers; a cattle truck, akin to those that transported 360,000 Lithuanians during Stalin's infamous purges, sits by the main entrance; a museum made of recycled planks from Siberian labor camps contains a display of Communist artifacts, as well as lists of the dead and disappeared. When it opened on April 1, 2001, a Joe Stalin look-alike offered the first visitors complimentary shots of vodka, a Lenin impersonator rustled up snacks in the log-cabin restaurant, and posters containing communist era propaganda – "There's no happier youth in the world than Soviet youth!" – were sprinkled around the facility. Future plans include free visitor transport from Vilnius in the fearful cattle truck tumbrels, floodlights for nighttime viewing, and, in the fullness of time no doubt, *Great Escape*-style jailbreak experiences. All it needs is a smattering of secret policemen, surveillance equipment, and coded dossiers on the visitors to make the day complete. Fun for all the family.

Stalin World attracts 200,000 visitors per annum, at $2.50 a head. It also attracts a great deal of criticism, especially from the 60,000 Lithuanian survivors of Stalin's death camps. For them, the Soviet Sculpture Garden is a grotesque attempt to profit from human depravity and suffering. Malinauskas, nevertheless, remains unmoved. A former wrestler, whose father disappeared during the Red Terror, he maintains that people need to be constantly reminded of the bad old days. Otherwise nostalgia for communism will render the former regime acceptable to those who have forgotten, or never knew, its depredations. The fact that he makes a tidy profit from his grisly tourist attraction is neither here nor there.

Disnifying Dealey

Depraved as Stalin World undoubtedly is, Soviet depravity is no match for true blue American depravity. Six million people per year visit Dealey Plaza, Dallas, where they can experience the dubious delights of driving past the infamous book depository in a Lincoln Continental convertible limousine. The ride comes complete with pre-recorded rifle shots and a high-speed dash to Parkland Memorial Hospital.[3] Board games, bumper stickers, coffee mugs, commemorative videos, T-shirts, fridge magnets, "authentic" autopsy pictures, and associated assassinabilia are also available as Kennedy keepsakes. When added to the innumerable books, movies, and forthcoming fortieth anniversary "celebrations," there is no doubt that JFK is the # 1 brand in the conspiracy business. Just as the Soviets backed down during the Cuban missile crisis, so too Stalin World can't compete with the likes of Kennedyland. With Disney on our side, what's more, we can sleep easy in our beds. At the first sign of trouble, Mickey and his minions will march on Moscow, whistling a merry tune.

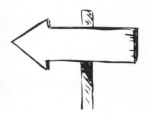

Don't look now, but mystery mongers, riddle retailers, puzzle purveyors, twister truckers, and top secret sellers are all around you.

Operation Anastasia may be some way off, but the Dallas thanathon is just one morbid show among many. As Pipes cogently explains, a vast market has developed around the "theys," "thems," and "its" of the conspiracy-industrial complex.[4] Roswell, Watergate, Oklahoma City, Schaw, TWA flight 800, the Knights Templar, and many, many more are grist to the mill of enigmapreneurs, those who exploit our love of secrets, mysteries, and puzzles to make a fast buck or several.[5] *Secrecy* is the fourth component of the TEASE framework. It makes itself felt in numerous cloak-and-dagger marketing campaigns. Don't look now, but mystery mongers, riddle

137

retailers, puzzle purveyors, twister truckers, and top secret sellers are all around you.

Lee Jeans, for instance, recently reignited interest in its somewhat stodgy brand by means of a cryptic, net-based, undercover operation.[6] A bunch of big time web surfers was e-mailed three video clips which looked like ghastly dating service postings. Such was their check-it-out cheesiness that the clip recipients immediately forwarded them to their buddy lists, address books, and just about anyone else they could think of. The web went wild with who-are-these-scumbags speculation and, after letting the rumors simmer for a few months, Lee finally revealed that the three cyber Casanovas were fictional creations, concocted for an online computer game. In order to play the game at an advanced level, participants had to get hold of the "secret code" – in reality, product identification numbers – from various pairs of Lee jeans conveniently stashed at a nearby store. Thousands agreed. Sales rose 20%. The market is out there. Everything is connected.

Geeks Bearing Grifts

Highly successful as riddle-me-Lee proved to be, the conundrummer extraordinary is peerless Steven Spielberg. His 2001 movie *Artificial Intelligence* was promoted in a highly inventive, if artificially intelligent, way. It began with a fake name inserted into the credits of a trailer. An AOL search on the name led the curious to a labyrinth of lunatic web sites, the discovery of a murder, a body of evidence and ever more mysterious goings on, completely divorced from the narrative of the movie itself. The deeper they probed, the more captivating it became.[7]

Although *AI* is not widely regarded as Spielberg's finest hour – it grossed a disappointing $79 million at the US box office – the accompanying promotional campaign was a masterpiece of conspiratorial marketing. It was perfectly pitched at the online gaming community, as an immediate off-the-dial reaction bore witness. It was webhead heaven. Nerdvana, no less.

Yet another twist on the intriguing trailer genre hit the Cineplex screens in summer 2002. *Luckystar* looked for all the world like a cryptic cross between *The Sixth Sense*, *Ocean's Eleven,* and *Conspiracy Theory*. Starring rising actor Benicio del Toro, it depicted the "luckiest man in the world" driving around LA destroying the evidence that explained his inexplicable success on the stock market, at gaming tables, and even with stoplight sequences. Nighttime car chases, botched covert operations, and stealth helicopters suddenly going haywire all added to the stylish trailer's intrigue.

Far from coming soon, however, *Luckystar* never actually arrived. Although it oozed big-budget-Hollywood-blockbuster production values, and seemed like a sure fire box office sensation, it turned out to be a commercial for the Mercedes SL500 convertible. It was an extremely expensive commercial, to be sure, directed by A-list auteur Michael Mann. It generated much date debate over whether it was a "real" movie or not. Indeed, it is probably being made – for real – by an opportunistic movie studio. But, as teaser ads go, the *Luckystar* riddle ranks with the very best of them.[8]

Curious, Colorado

Marvelously mysterious marketing, it must be stressed, is not confined to fashion, films, or flash cars, nor is it anything new. Hoaxes, humbugs, and the exploitation of humankind's innate curiosity have long been part of the marketer's armory. Lester Wunderman, for instance, tells a wonderful tale of his pioneering days in direct mail, when he stumbled on the "Gold Box of Colorado."

Rightly or wrongly, direct mail is often regarded as the bottom feeder of marketing pond life and, way back in 1975, one of

Wunderman's clients felt that a shift upscale was called for.[9] After careful consideration, the Columbia LP Record Club decided that in order to significantly increase subscriber numbers it should mount an expensive TV advertising campaign.

Hoaxes, humbugs, and the exploitation of humankind's innate curiosity have long been part of the marketer's armory.

Understandably miffed by the media giant's assumption that advertising is always best, Wunderman challenged the agency, McCann-Erickson, to a subscriptions shoot out. And so it came to pass that the country was divided into three sectors: one received the McCann-Erickson brand-building, no-response-required television treatment, a second was placed in the capable hands of our direct mail maestro, and a third control sector was left to manage without any additional marketing intervention.

Wunderman's trump card, which came to him during a Colorado ski trip, involved placing a seemingly innocuous yellow bar at the bottom of each direct mail coupon. When tie-in advertising revealed that this secret gold box contained buried treasure – a free LP record of the subscriber's choice – the response exceeded all expectations. Wunderman's thirteen test markets increased uptake by 80%, compared to McCann-Erickson's 20%, and cost considerably less, to boot. The following year, gold boxes were embossed on all Columbia's direct mailings. A national treasure hunt transpired and subscriptions soared. So efficacious did it prove that Wunderman subsequently adapted the same tactic to other clients and other countries, all equally successfully. To this very day, variants on the gold box are in widespread use, as anyone who logs on to Amazon.com will quickly discover.[10]

Secrecy Sells

Irrespective of the extent and prehistory of mysterious marketing, the essential point is that it is predicated on Secrecy. Intrigue, enigma, inscrutability, hidden agendas, strange-but-true, riddle-me-ree, believe-it-or-not, and the entire supermarket tabloid ethos of Bigfoot assassinated JFK and escaped in a black helicopter piloted by Elvis bin Laden, are part and parcel of the twenty-first century consumer psyche. True, the so-called "paranoid style" of American politics and society dates from the founding of the republic.[11] However, it has become particularly prevalent in recent years, primarily on account of the internet. Various statistics are quoted about the extent of such conspiratorial beliefs – 56% of the American population believe in a JFK plot, for example[12] – though rumor has it that the statistics themselves are a conspiracy, concocted by a statistics-cooking cabal in the dirty tricks department of the CIA. Promise not to tell anyone.

Free Gift 9: One For The Money

Although JFK is the conspiracy brand leader, many aficionados maintain that the King is, well, the King. Dead or not, murdered or not, residing in or around Kalamazoo, Michigan, or not, Elvis Presley is still hot, still rockin', still as magically mysterious as ever. Granted, the second coming of 2001 signally failed to materialize – as numerous numerologists anticipated[13] – however the twenty-fifth anniversary of his untimely demise convincingly demonstrated that Elvis's body may have left the building but his soul is shakin', rattlin', and rollin' on.

In the frenzy surrounding the once and future King, it is sometimes forgotten that he owed almost everything to the Emperor of Enigma, the Sovereign of Suspense, the Impresario of Intrigue, Colonel Tom Parker. Nowadays, Parker is widely regarded as a Machiavellian figure, who ruthlessly manipulated the greatest musical talent of the post-war era.[14] The Colonel, so the legend goes, channeled Elvis's raw energy into a series of tacky Hollywood movies, which got tackier and tackier through time. He immured him in the tawdry glitter of Las Vegas, in order to accommodate his own gambling habit. He refused to let Presley tour outside the United States, on account of the fact that he, himself, was an illegal alien. He sacked incomparable songwriters Lieber and Stoller, then encouraged his charge to record a series of embarrassingly sentimental, hopelessly schmaltzy albums. He not only opposed Elvis's classic comeback concert in 1968, where the King reclaimed his rock 'n' roll crown, but tried to turn it into a saccharine Christmas Special. In the early months of 1977, moreover, he imposed a punishing schedule of personal appearances on the addled, unwell superstar. And, to cap it all, he siphoned off the bulk of Elvis's career earnings, leaving him a comparative pauper by the time he died on August 16.

Although the criticisms of the Colonel are almost entirely justified – he was a hound dog, no question – it is also true to say that without Parker, Presley would have been a flash in the pan.[15] It was Parker's marketing genius that built Presley into one of the greatest, arguably *the* greatest, brand names in the history of popular music. When the Colonel took Elvis under his wing, there were many other equally talented singers and musicians who were forging the hillbilly-blues hybrid that became rock and roll. Abundance abounded. Functional equivalence prevailed. There was very little to choose between them. But whereas most of these pioneers quickly disappeared into the where-are-they-now abyss, Parker ensured that Elvis enjoyed a long and lucrative career. By the time of his death in 1977, the king had sold some 400 million albums and posthumous sales have more than surpassed that figure. Twenty-five years after Presley's undignified demise, the Elvis brand still performs extremely well in the musical marketplace, as the recent #1 album (of #1s), bears witness.

To be sure, the opprobrium heaped on the Colonel is partly attributable to the intimidating persona he adopted; partly due to the crassness of his behavior in the aftermath of the King's demise; and partly to a feeling that Parker somehow stumbled on a golden goose and feathered his nest thereafter. He lucked out, in other words. Luck, however, had little or nothing to do with it. The Colonel was one of the most astute marketing men of his day.[16] Long before he met Elvis Presley, he had steered Eddie Arnold and Hank Snow to national musical prominence. He was a virtuoso advance man for the Royal American Shows, a huge traveling circus, where he devised all sorts of creative promotional stunts to draw Depression Era audiences (marriage ceremonies on the Ferris Wheel, for example). He was one of the first showmen to attract commercial sponsorship (by persuading Kroger to underwrite the Grand Ole Opry's wartime tours) and proved equally adept in the political marketing sphere (three grateful state governors made an honorary "colonel" of him). Even during his infamous period as a Floridian dog-catcher, the Colonel exhibited an incredible flair for fund raising, animal adoption schemes, and decidedly dubious, pocket-filling sidelines.[17]

Yet for all his shady maneuvers and corny carny contrivances, Colonel Parker possessed incomparable promotional éclat. His Presleymarketing strategy was predicated on the marketeasing principles that absence makes the heart grow fonder, that unattainability increases desire, that denial engenders devotion, that overexposure is fatal, that mystery maketh megabucks.[18] Accordingly, he strictly rationed Elvis's appearances, he carefully limited the amount of recorded material that was available, he repeatedly removed the King from circulation, most notably during his two-year sojourn in the Army, and he always ensured that his customers – fans and record company executives alike – were left begging for more. Between 1960 and 1968, the Colonel had Elvis make three movies a year, each one accompanied by a soundtrack album, each one heavily promoted and each one immediately followed by a four-month period of secret seclusion, in order to build up the audience's anticipation again. Indeed, Presley's live shows were based on the exact same premise. They consisted of short, sharp sets; the innumerable warm-up acts served to heighten audience expectations; the king teased and tantalized his fans by deploying or withholding his trademark wiggle; and, during his first telecast in 1958, the entire country held its breath waiting for Elvis to unleash the Pelvis on prime time.[19]

Far from espousing the principles of customer-orientation, Colonel Tom Parker turned his product into the ultimate unattainable, a forbidden musical fruit that appeared intermittently, intriguingly, intoxicatingly. Elvis may have crooned "Don't Be Cruel," but the Colonel ignored his imprecations. He treated the King's customers mean and he kept the King's customers keen. He appreciated that secrecy is the secret of success.

Thankyouverymuch.

From a marketing perspective, the important thing is not whether there is really an enigma wrapped in a riddle, or conspiracies about conspiracy statistics, but the brute fact that mysteries move merchandise. Most marketing textbooks, I grant you, fail to disclose this

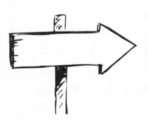

Mysteries move merchandise.

fundamental point. I have yet to find a discussion of teaser campaigns, much less recommendations on riddling, in mainstream marketing texts. This is suspicious in itself, I'm sure you agree.[20]

Many companies, fortunately, ignore the marketing textbooks

and happily tap into consumers' conspiratorial imaginings. Consider the "secret" recipes that help purvey all sorts of comestibles, such as Coca-Cola, Heinz Ketchup, Kellogg's Frosties, Mrs Field's Cookies, Brach's Chocolate Cherries, Gray Poupon Mustard, and many more.[21] Consider the cosmetics industry (the secret of youthfulness), the proprietary medicines business (the secret of good health), and the tourist trade (secret hideaways a specialty).[22] Consider the gift-giving business, which is predicated on secrets, surprises, and agonizingly delayed gratification, as are gift-rich occasions like Christmas, birthdays, and St. Valentine's Day.[23] Consider management consultancy, where every Tom, Dick, and Harry claims to possess the secret of corporate success, but no-one actually does (bar yours truly, naturally).[24] Consider also the alleged "trade secrets" of jewelers, auto shops, TV repairmen, computer trouble-shooters, and suchlike. Almost without exception, they exploit the arcana of their calling, the fact that very few people in today's hi-tech society really know how these things work, let alone how to repair them, in order to make a mint. Many do so unscrupulously, as Blumberg's classic dissection of the Predatory Society sadly demonstrates.[25] However, the simple fact of the matter is that secrecy sells.[269] Always has. Always will.

Finger Lickin' Dude

Of all the sellers of secrecy, none was more successful than Harland Sanders. The founder of Kentucky Fried Chicken, Sanders retailed riddles like they were going out of style. He discovered the "secret blend of eleven herbs and spices" that propelled his organization to culinary immortality. He came up with a clandestine method of cooking chicken and parleyed the concept into one of the largest fast food franchises of all time. He concocted the quirky Colonel Sanders persona – a grinning, goateed southern gentleman – that features to this very day on every bucket of KFC comestibles. And, he himself was one of the most curious figures ever to grace the commercial stage. His bizarre life is worthy of a place in Ripley's Believe-It-Or-Not. He truly was a marketing man of mystery.[27]

Recipient of the Horatio Alger Award in 1965, Harland Sanders is a paradigm of the American dream. On the surface at least. He was born on a small farm just outside Henryville, Kentucky, on September 9, 1890. His father, a butcher by profession, died when Harland was only five years old. In order to make ends meet, his mother went to work in a distant tomato-canning factory and often found it difficult to get home at nights. So Harland was left to bring up his younger brother and sister. He learnt to cook and clean. He cut school of take care of his kin. And, when his mother subsequently remarried, a tyrannical stepfather forced the boy to hit the road at the tender age of twelve, his meager possessions in a cardboard suitcase.

For the next forty years or so, he drifted from job to job. Railroad engineer, insurance salesman, personal injuries attorney, ferry boat operator, acetylene lamp manufacturer, chamber of commerce chairman, Michelin Tires sales representative, gas station proprietor. You name it, he did it; sometimes successfully, oftentimes not. The turning point, however, transpired when he opened a family restaurant next to his gas station in Corbin, Kentucky, which abutted the busy US25. The restaurant proved very popular – it earned Harland an Honorary Colonel's commission in 1949 – and its signature fried chicken was lauded by acclaimed inter-war food critic Duncan Himes, amongst others.

Cooking chicken, unfortunately, was a slow, wasteful, and messy business. It caused countless headaches for those who wished to prepare it on a commercial basis. Nevertheless, with the aid of newly invented pressure cookers – and innumerable failed experiments – Sanders developed a method of pre-frying chicken that not only retained the meat's taste and texture but enabled it to be prepared quickly to order. Hot, tasty, and secretly spiced, the Colonel's chicken was an instant hit. Business boomed and he spent furlough at the 1952 National Restaurant Association annual convention in Chicago, where he encountered Pete Harman, the owner of a small restaurant in Salt Lake City. They hit it off, the idea of franchising the secret recipe was floated, and by the end of that year Colonel Sanders' Kentucky Fried Chicken was up and running, with Pete Harman as the first franchisee.

Sanders was 65 years old when opportunity finally called and the Colonel greeted it like a long-lost friend. He visited almost every roadside restaurant in the south, selling fried chicken franchises like they were going out of fashion. Although business was very slow to start – franchises were frequently given away – Harland was a nothing if not able salesman. Aided and abetted by Dave Thomas, who went on to fame and fortune as the founder of Wendy's, Sanders' secret recipe became the talking point of the restaurant business.[28] The fifties, to be sure, was the golden age of fast food franchising; expansion was rapid and, thanks to the Colonel's promotional flair, Kentucky Fried Chicken expanded faster than most.[29] By the early sixties, the chain boasted 300 outlets, international expansion had started, the franchises were virtually selling themselves, and the 75-year-old decided to follow suit. He sold the corporation for $2million in 1964, the new owners turned his one-man-band into a thriving multinational and, with the aid of the Colonel as a celebrity spokesperson, KFC went from strength to strength. When the chain was acquired by Heublein in 1971, Sanders' empire had spread into 48 states and contained more than 3,000 outlets. He was world famous; a Hollywood biopic was produced; he was a friend of presidents and pop stars alike; a museum devoted to Kentucky's "most famous citizen" was opened in Corbin; he died a hero in 1980, at the age of ninety, and was awarded a state funeral. Hail to the chef.

Revealed – the Secret of the Secret Spices!

So far, so Horatio Alger. However, for all his apparent adherence to the American ideal, there was a dark side to Harland Sanders. He was a mass of contradictions, a marketing enigma made flesh. He had a volcanic temper, yet his outbursts were often staged for effect. He affected aw-shucks cornballisms, yet was a highly educated man. He deplored the demon drink, yet they say he resorted to bootlegging during Prohibition. He was a born again Christian, yet cursed like a particularly irate trooper. He was a champion of family values, yet his lechery was legendary. He shot and seriously wounded a competitor in Corbin, yet was acquitted of the crime. He was a generous giver to medical causes, yet he fell for every quack medicine doing the rounds. He was unfailingly charming to customers, yet treated his employees abominably. He sold the company for a princely sum – and made a fortune from his ambassadorial role – yet he publicly excoriated the new owners and their products on numerous occasions. And he championed a no-nonsense, super-efficient approach to business, yet as a life-long freemason and sucker for the supernatural, he made crucial executive decisions on the say-so of palm readers, astrologists, and conspiracy theorists.

Such irreconcilables, ironically, added to rather than detracted from Sanders' marketing mystique. His evident inconsistencies intrigued people and the rumors that swirled around the Colonel meant that there was often something to talk about. For all his faults, staged or otherwise, the finger licker supreme ensured that there was always plenty to discuss, debate, and dumbfound. He was a master of the publicity stunt and photo opportunity. From his earliest days as a Michelin tire salesman, when he provoked the dealers of cheaper brands into pump-em-til-they-burst competitions, to the Democratic Party Convention in 1972, when every delegate was given a free, distinctively-liveried bucket of his fried chicken and a huge coast-to-coast television audience witnessed a master-stroke of product placement, the Colonel had an unerring eye for the main marketing chance.[30] He revolutionized the family restaurant business with printed rather than waitress-recited menus. He publicized his first backwoods filling station by – believe it or not – offering a midwifery service (presumably, the world's first word-of-uterus marketing campaign). He used a distinctive white Cadillac at all times, even when he didn't have enough money to fill the tank with gas. He sold the KFC concept to prospective franchisees by an egregious *Gone With the Wind* routine, whereby his wife dressed as Scarlett O'Hara and he did a passable Rhett Butler.

> For all his faults, the finger licker supreme ensured that there was always plenty to discuss, debate, and dumbfound.

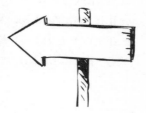

In the early days of television, what's more, Sanders appeared on innumerable talk and game shows and thereby demonstrated that "there was a strong streak of ham in the chicken king." For example, he appeared on Johnny Carson with a box allegedly containing his $2 million for the sale of the company. He staged a fight with a fried chicken rival on Merv Griffin and, naturally, carried the day. His "finger lickin' good" expression became a national catchphrase in 1965, perfect fodder for cartoonists, stand up comedians and newspaper headline writers. He founded and lectured at the KFC university, where he inducted novice franchisees into the secrets of his patented preparatory process, if not the secrets of his signature mixture of herbs and spices. In other words, he sold them on the *existence* of a secret and, having done so, was able to charge huge premiums for what were inexpensive, everyday ingredients. An investigation by Poundstone in 1983 revealed that the "secret" KFC recipe consisted of nothing but salt, pepper, and monosodium glutamate.[31] The secret of the secret ingredients is that there are no secret ingredients. The *real* secret of KFC is that the Colonel was a showman supreme and marketeaser extraordinary.

Hey, Presto!

Secrecy, then, is a powerful marketing mechanism. It not only attracts prospective purchasers, as the US Air Force is currently demonstrating with its "Can you Keep a Secret?" recruiting campaign (complete with images of Stealth bombers), but it can work equally well in Internal Marketing situations. According to the management bestseller *Built to Last*, the secret corporate protocols of Disney, P&G, IBM, McKinsey, Nordstrom, and so forth, help cultivate the

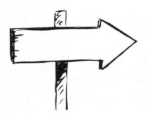

But what, I hear you ask, is the secret of secrecy? How does it work?

cult-like culture that such organizations enjoy.[32] Devotion to duty, never say die attitudes, and absolute commitment to the company cause are a consequence of their curiosity-led induction procedures. As layer after layer of corporate arcana are revealed, adepts become more and more convinced that the company's belief system is worth believing in, the best in the business. Internal Marketing, it seems, is less about selling customer centricity within organizations as revealing that the company's secret weapon is its commitment to customers. Customer orientation isn't the secret of corporate success, secrecy is the key to inculcating customer orientation (or any other organizational aspiration). Thus does a platitude become a principle.

But what, I hear you ask, is the secret of secrecy? How does it work? Well, that's my little secret and, sadly, I'm sworn to secrecy on the subject.[33] Suffice it to say that Secrecy involves *Strangeness* and Strangeness expedites *Seduction*. Secrecy doesn't necessitate a written document, like Coke's secret formula locked in the legendary Atlanta strongbox, nor an inviolate ritual, such as the apparel salesperson's trade secret, whereby the most expensive outfits are always shown first.[34] Strangeness is often quite sufficient. Something unusual, something anomalous, something atypical can serve to attract attention, prick people's curiosity, get them wondering what's going on and, most importantly, get them talking about it to others, who then proceed to do likewise. Bafflement burgeons. Intrigue accelerates. Perplexity proliferates.

In this regard, Cialdini convincingly shows how the simple act of looking up at a tall building quickly attracts a crowd of fascinated rubber-neckers.[35] Don't jump! The sainted Harry Reichenbach – he of the blessed *September Morn* imbroglio – transformed an unpopular pet store into a thriving establishment by the equally simple act of placing a tank of water in the show window and stocking it with "invisible fish" (a hidden pump rippled the surface from time to time, thereby convincing skeptical onlookers).[36] Nike, no less, is doing a twenty-first century version of the same with its discombobulating billboards, print ads, and window displays for Presto sneakers. Two Presto-shod adolescents lie comatose in a backyard, one sprawled on a lounger, the other splayed on the decking. Exhausted from overexertion? Sleeping off last night's party? Poisoned by a peace and quiet loving neighbor? Trespassers on private property who paid the ultimate price? Who knows. Click on nike-presto.com to find out more.[37]

Strangeness is one way of getting around TiVo touting television viewers – make the ads so cryptic that consumers will want to record and replay them – but intrigue can work internally as well. Mike Daisy's hilarious expose of life in the customer care cubicles of Amazon.com reveals that Jeff Bezos' internal marketing includes extremely strange, well-nigh surreal, employee get-togethers called All Hands Meetings.[38] Bezos not only intrigues his customers through secret boxes, as we have seen, he also builds corporate commitment through meaningful meaninglessness. He understands, perhaps intuitively, that secrecy and strangeness help increase the involvement of purchasers and partners alike. Indeed, if Nike's beguiling Presto puzzle is any indication, future years may be beset by ever more curious, ever more mysterious, ever more suspenseful, ever more surprising marketing campaigns. It might even get to the *really* strange stage where marketing books start including unannounced chapters, akin to hidden tracks on CDs, which serve no purpose other than to tease innocent readers and tempt reviewers into amplifying the insertions in a suitably cryptic manner.

Surely not. Reviewers aren't so easily tricked. Are they?

A much more likely scenario is that epitomized by Britney Spears' sublime Pepsi commercial prior to the 2001 Oscars, itself a monument to who'll-be-the-lucky-winner style anticipation, intrigue, and feverish speculation. Teaser ads, featuring lovestruck admirers watching teaser ads for Britney's forthcoming Pepsi commercial, were trailed for several weeks beforehand. The spectacular commercial itself, furthermore, climaxed with the unanticipated appearance of periodic Pepsi pitcher, vaunted Viagra volunteer, and sometime US senator, Bob Dole, who was shown watching the commercial while clutching a can of the invigorating fluid and making notes with a (presumably) well-leaded pencil. Oops, I endorsed it again.

Seduction Production

As Britney brilliantly demonstrates – and countless "sex sells" messages attest – seduction is an integral part of the marketing process. For many conventionally-minded marketers, admittedly, the key to success involves establishing long-term, mutually satisfying, serially monogamous relationships with customers.[39] Loyalty, ideally life-long loyalty, is the ultimate marketing objective. Now, this is all very well. Endearing, even. However, it is based on the mistaken assumption that both parties feel the same way about each other. Unfortunately, customers don't love marketers as a rule, let alone honor and obey them.[40] They are aware of our obsequious wiles, self-serving pseudo-abasement, and decidedly dubious declarations

> Customers don't love marketers as a rule, let alone honor and obey them.

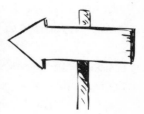

of undying love. They consider us pests at best and poisonous at worst. The question, therefore, is how can we turn the tables and make them love us, want us, need us? It isn't by throwing ourselves at their feet, or showering them with free gifts, though that can work in the short term. We have to make our putative partners fall for us – truly, madly, deeply – despite their natural reservations. They have to be seduced. They want to be seduced. They yearn to be seduced. They desperately desire to be seduced.

There's much more to seduction than secrecy and strangeness, I grant you. Nevertheless, as countless books and articles on the art of making out attest, secrecy, curiosity, intrigue, fascination, and so forth are integral to amorous endeavors (Free Gift 10). Establishing

153

patterns of hope and despair; increasing desire, dashing expectations; sowing the seeds of confusion; bringing guile to bear on the victim; playing the he-loves-me, he-loves-me-not coquette; blowing alternately hot and cold, and generally inducing an aura of mystery, enigma, and enchantment are part and parcel of the seduction production process.

Free Gift 10: Alluring Marketing

Seduction, so they say, is a four-stage process. It can be applied to everything from carnal encounters to election campaigns. Wild Bill Clinton had it in spades. Sad Al Gore hadn't. It is a process that is especially astutely practiced by the hoarse whisperers of Madison Avenue, those who stoop ever lower to insinuate themselves into the consumer's unconscious. The four stages are: (1) stirring interest and desire; (2) creating pleasure and confusion; (3) deepening the effect; and (4) moving in for the kill.[41]

Stage One: Stirring Interest and Desire. It is essential, according to expert seductioneers, to study the prey carefully and identify those who are likely to be susceptible to your particular charms. They should be approached obliquely, instead of head on (as it were), because being too direct stirs up resistance, which is difficult to overcome. Once the target is lulled into a false sense of security and vaguely intrigued by your presence, their interest should be stirred. Obviousness, again, must be avoided at all costs. Mixed signals – tough and tender, primal and poetic, hot and cold – suggest depth, prick the victim's curiosity, and sow the seeds of confusion. An enigmatic aura starts to wrap itself around you as the object is drawn into your orbit.

Stage Two: Creating Pleasure and Confusion. At the end of stage one, remember, they are nibbling at, rather than swallowing, the bait. Desire must be further stirred by insinuation, ambiguity, and hints of wonderful things to come. They must be made sufficiently curious to overcome their understandable doubts and anxieties. It is necessary to create suspense, punctuated with sufficient surprises to keep them in your thrall. Once people know what to expect, or can anticipate the next move, your spell over them is broken. Familiarity and overexposure, likewise, are fatal, though flattery always works a treat. No one can resist sweet nothings, especially when they are followed by nothing. That is, a calculated absence. The alternation of exciting presence and cool distance accentuates the intrigue that the intended is now feeling. Blowing hot and cold, melding interest and indifference, combining chastity and crudity serve to cloud their emotions and render them unable to distinguish between illusion and reality.

Stage Three: Deepening the Effect. Once they've swallowed the bait, the catch must be firmly hooked. Doubts still abound at this stage. Motives are questioned. A dramatic gesture is often called for. A declaration of undying love. A request to vote Republican. A sure-fire sales pitch that has been practiced and polished. The moment must be seized, even at the risk of looking foolish. And why? Because failure to act raises legitimate concerns about your lack of commitment. Even if the action fails or is misunderstood, it shows how far you are willing to go to win their love. However, if the ground has been properly prepared – alternating ambiguity, anxiety, anticipation, et al. – the big gesture can engage their emotions, over-whelm all objections and effect the engineered union.

Stage Four: Move In for the Kill. Reeling them in is an art it itself. The intended is at the point of surrender. Now is the time to strategi-cally withdraw. Inflict pain. Play hard to get. Instigate a break up, swiftly followed by a joyous rapprochement. Do it again. Create a void that they can fill with their overactive imaginings. The ensuing highs and lows dramatically increase their desire, drive them to anguished distraction, and turn them to putty in your hands. Once they are completely under your spell, take a final step back. They will start chasing you. The tables are turned. The pursuer is being pur-sued and, since they are doing the pursuing, you are in control of the situation. You hold the whip hand. They can have you, but only on your terms. They'll love you for it. The deal is signed. The vote is cast. The boudoir beckons. Another one bites the dust.

Despite what the CRM cabal contend, pursuing one's intended victim, meeting their every heart's desire, and generally abasing yourself before them, is *not* the way to make consumers fall head over heels in love with you. True, it can and does work. But only at a superficial level. The tables have to be turned at some stage. The pursued must become the pursuer. This is best achieved when their interest has been roused and desire is starting to stir. A strategic withdrawal of one's affections, coupled with a studied air of seeming indifference, is often sufficient to throw them off balance and precipitate them headlong into the seducer's welcoming web. Holding out rather than holding on is the key to success.[42]

Marketing, in short, is about seduction not servitude. Consumers will appreciate your offerings more if they have to chase after them or are forced to endure an adorably agonizing wait. Cuddling, cosseting, and caring for customers works. And works very well. But coaxing, cajoling, and conniving works better. Tease, tempt, tantalize. Flirt, philander, flatter. Bait, beguile, bewitch. Let's get it on, baby. Oh yeah.

Naturally, I'd love to tell you more and there's so much more to tell. Regrettably, it's time for my strategic withdrawal . . .

How to Sell Sham Secrets?
My Lips Are Sealed.

HOW TO ENTERTAIN WHEN ENTERTAINMENT IS EVERYWHERE

I Sell the Body Electric

Learned historians of marketing spend many a happy hour debating the origins of their calling. For some, it dates from the mid-1950s, when Drucker, Levitt, and latterly Kotler turned traditional thinking on its head by placing the customer at the center of the commercial universe. For others, marketing emerged in the nineteenth century, when mass production necessitated mass consumption and marketing developed as a necessary bridge between the two. For yet others, marketing's origins go back to the very dawn of time, when goods were bartered in the ancient Greek agora, trade formed the basis of Mesopotamian civilization, and flint axe heads were circulated over thousands of miles in late Paleolithic times.[1]

All of these arguments have merit. They hinge, however, on the precise meaning of the word "marketing" – is it a philosophy, an industry, another word for exchange? – and, consequently, academicians' chances of reaching agreement are slim, verging on emaciated. Yet regardless of when and where marketing originated, a significant turning point occurred in or around 1770, when James

Graham, a young Scottish physician, met the one and only Benjamin Franklin in Philadelphia.[2]

Now Benjamin Franklin, as Blaine McCormick shows, was the father of modern management thought.[3] But Graham was much more concerned with Franklin's practical bent, his electrical experiments in particular. Like many of his contemporaries, most notably Christian A. Kratzenstein, Graham was convinced of electricity's therapeutic potential.[4] Unlike Kratzenstein and Co., however, Graham threw off the shackles of scientific detachment and treated these therapeutic possibilities theatrically, dramatically, energetically. He added entertainment to electricity and sold the intoxicating mixture.

After his fateful meeting with Franklin, Graham repaired to Western Europe, where he spent several years on the road perfecting his electrotherapies. Eventually this so-called "superquack" settled in a fashionable part of London and proceeded to open his celebrated Temple of Health and Hymen. This Elysium of eroticism was an early example of what Pine and Gilmore[5] term "the experience economy." Established in 1780, the Temple comprised a vast multi-media spectacle centered on Graham's daily lectures, which were devoted to sexual dysfunction and the remedial powers of electricity. Scantily clad Goddesses of Health helped demonstrate the good doctor's theories; various forms of electrical therapy were placed on public display; and, at the end of each "lecture," a massive galvanic shock was administered to the entire audience, via conductors beneath the seat cushions. One hundred and eighty years before William Castle's butt-buzz, Graham was doing a *Tingler* on his customers.

158

Be that as it may, the Temple's piece de resistance was the "Celestial State Bed." Purportedly reserved for the treatment of infertility, this comprised a giant, gently vibrating divan, constantly wafted by relaxing music and musk-enriched incense.[6] By all accounts, mainly Graham's, the bed was a thing of beauty. It perched on mirrored pillars. It was elaborately carved with figurines in appropriately carnal postures. It came emblazoned with the pro-creative motto, "be fruitful, multiply, and replenish the earth." At £50 per session, I grant you, this early example of the experience economy wasn't exactly an economical experience, particularly for those

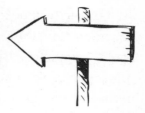

> This early example of the experience economy wasn't exactly an economical experience

prepared to pay £500 extra to have the drapes drawn. Nevertheless, even if the celestial bed was reserved for the fortunate few, Graham's pre-modern pleasure dome proved enormously popular with peeping toms and prurient puritans alike.

The superquack, naturally, didn't confine himself to the Temple's takings. He supplemented the box office with a private consultancy practice, which attracted up to 200 patients per day. The quackster also sold a selection of impotence-alleviating medicaments, princi-pally Graham's Solar & Imperial Pills, rumored to be extracted from sunbeams. He was not afraid to advertise his acumen either. On the contrary, he was a brilliant barker, who excelled in over the top sales pitches, blatant to the point of baloney hyperbole, and promises that could only be kept by means of divine intervention. Centuries before anti-advertising advertising – Image is Nothing, etc. – Graham paro-died the shameless excesses of panacea peddlers, of which he was a prime example. Sadly, his exuberance was exceeded by his extrava-gance and he died a penniless wretch in 1794.[7]

For all his financial failings, James Graham fully understood the final element of the TEASE framework, *Entertainment*. Graham was an entertainer, an entertainer with added electricity. An electrotainer.

159

Nowadays, of course, electricity is generally regarded as inconsequential, mundane, a boring utility that we take for granted. Except when the supply is interrupted, as the unhappy inhabitants of the Sunshine State know only too well. In the eighteenth and nineteenth centuries, however, electricity was miraculous, amazing, and endlessly entertaining.[8] Electrotaining, no less.

Electricity, indeed, is a wonderful metaphor for marketing. What began as something incredible, something exciting, something that could completely transform an organization, has become pedestrian, pervasive, plodding, plain. There are numerous exceptions, naturally, as the present book shows. Nevertheless, marketing's latter-day obsession with customer orientation – and the ever-increasing servility that followed in its wake – has all-but emasculated a once-effervescent endeavor.

What can be done? Well, we could do a lot worse than look back to the glory days when marketing was exciting, when electricity was exciting, when electrotainment was the order of the day.

Call Thomas Edison.

Electric Kool-Aid Acid Test Market

Thomas Alva Edison is generally considered to be one of the greatest inventors that ever lived. Certainly, his record of 1073 US patents and several key discoveries in decidedly divergent fields – photography, telegraphy, telephony, electric light, motion pictures, recorded music, and more – is unsurpassed and unsurpassable.[9] What is less fully appreciated about the Wizard of Menlo Park is that he was a very astute marketer.[10] Like his twenty-first century descendent, Dean Kamen, Thomas Edison was well aware that commercialization is crucial. He didn't invent for invention's sake, unlike many tinkerers, fiddlers, experimenters, and gifted amateurs. He invented in order to sell the fruits of his labor. From an early age,[11] he determined "not to undertake inventions unless there was a definite market demand for them." When there wasn't a market demand, moreover, he set out to create one. Edison played the press like a virtuoso; he was a master of the publicity stunt; he was quite content to stir up controversy if it served his promotional purposes; he frequently claimed to have cracked insoluble problems, when he had done nothing of the sort;

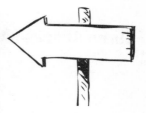

Thomas Edison didn't invent for invention's sake.
He invented in order to sell the fruits of his labor.

and he exploited his carefully nurtured image as an uber-inventor to attract investors, outmaneuver competitors, generate favorable publicity, acquire the most gifted employees, and, not least, move his brand name merchandise (Edison lamps, Edison phonographs, Edison electric current, etc.).[12]

Nowhere is Edison's marketing savvy better illustrated than in the electric light imbroglio of the 1880s.[13] Most people are familiar with the great scientist's painstaking development of the light bulb – 6,000 experiments with every conceivable filament – but it is sometimes forgotten that a well-established and deeply entrenched competitor already existed. Gaslight, contrary to contemporary perception, was no pushover. Nevertheless, Edison rose to the challenge magnificently, if rather unethically. A series of snazzy publicity stunts, such as the illumination of luxury steamships, residential suburbs and, in September 1882, large parts of Lower Manhattan, ensured a favorable press for the wizard's system. This was accompanied by a systematic knocking campaign against gas lighting. From his first breathless boast about electric light, which decimated the share prices of gas manufacturers and distributors, to an endless

161

stream of pamphlets attacking the safety record of his principal rival, Edison tormented the gas industry at every possible opportunity. Anti-gas newspaper articles were produced; reports of explosions or fires were collected, collated and circulated; and rumors of gaslight's allegedly injurious effects on eyesight, health, and beauty were brought to the attention of all and sundry.[14]

Three Shocks and You're Out

Brilliant as he was, there is something deeply ironic about Thomas Edison, Marketing Man. He himself was an electrotainer extraordinaire – "very much in the mold of his countryman P.T. Barnum," according to a recent biographer[15] – but he often failed to see the entertainment potential of his electrical contraptions. The phonograph, for example, was originally marketed as a piece of office equipment, ideal for dictation, stenography, and record keeping, as well as sober-sided educational uses such as elocution lessons, rote learning, and foreign language acquisition. Unsurprisingly, it flatlined until such times as several disgruntled investors reconfigured Edison's phonograph as a "nickel in the slot" singing machine and amusement parlors sprang up to exhibit his musical marvel. Similarly, the maestro's first moving picture machine, the kinetoscope, was a flash in the peep show pan, largely on account of the free software, so to speak, that came with it. Short films of horse shoeing, hair cutting, highland dancing, and so on were not exactly what the "sporting crowd" wanted to see. It was not until enterprising competitors substituted saucier alternatives, such as *Serpentine Dancers*, *How Girls Undress*, and *Little Egypt*, that the penny dropped and the penny arcade market really took off.[16]

Thomas Edison, to put it bluntly, was blind to his inventions' true value – their entertainment value – just as today's marketers are blind to the true character of their calling. Or myopic, at least.

Happily, not everyone was as short-sighted as Edison. As Nasaw rightly notes, by far the best early advertisements for electricity were the urban entertainment districts, the glittering Great White Ways that burgeoned in the 1890s.[17] Equally important were the breathtaking World's Fairs in Chicago, Omaha, Buffalo, et al., which dazzled all comers with their fabulous floodlit fantasias.[18] Most

> Amusement parks that began as a means of generating traffic for electric streetcar companies, but gradually took on an incandescent life of their own.

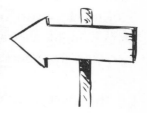

electrotaining of all, however, were the amusement parks that began as a means of generating traffic for electric streetcar companies, but gradually took on an incandescent life of their own.[19] The first and most famous of these was established at Coney Island in 1897, when promoter George Tilyou corralled a collection of unrelated rides into Steeplechase Park and charged admission at the entrance. Six years later the "Electric Eden" known as Luna Park joined the fray. It not only surpassed Steeplechase but established a template that was replicated the world over.[20]

Luna Lunacy

Built by a pair of former Tilyou employees, Frederic Thompson and Skip Dundy, Luna was an architectural riot of towers, turrets, columns, and domes. It was like nothing else that ever existed, an Arabian-themed fantasyland, a palace of play, a world apart,[21] "where all was artifice, extravagance, and excess." The centerpiece was "A Trip to the Moon," an interactive illusion that transported visitors to another world, as did "20,000 Leagues Under the Sea," "The

163

Dragon's Cage," and a number of national tableaux – Eskimo Village, Irish Hamlet, Japanese Garden, Venetian Canals and more besides. To this terrestrial and extraterrestrial array, the owners added an assemblage of live animal acts, such as stunt elephants sliding down shoot-the-chutes and thoroughbred horses leaping into tubs of water, as well as diverse disaster extravaganzas. A four story apartment block burnt several times daily; Vesuvius erupted and Pompeii fell with clockwork precision; several famous floods were reenacted; and, at night, the entire park was illuminated by 250,000 electric lights, an incandescent display that was visible thirty miles out to sea.

The effect was stunning. Luna was designed to overwhelm and it did. It immersed customers in a collective phantasmagoria. Contemporary commentators were completely lost for words. Maxim Gorky, the notoriously gloomy Russian writer, perhaps came closest to capturing the hallucinogenic nighttime scene when he described[22] Luna as "A fantastic city all of fire suddenly rises from the ocean into the sky. Thousands of ruddy sparks glimmer in the darkness, limning in fine, sensitive outline on the black background of the sky, shapely towers of miraculous castles, palaces, and temples. Golden gossamer threads tremble in the air. They intertwine in transparent, flaming patterns, which flutter and melt away in love with their own beauty mirrored in the waters. Fabulous and beyond conceiving, ineffably beautiful, is this fiery scintillation."

In Luna, everything was exotic, bizarre, and unrestrained. Trick seats and sidewalks flung visitors to the ground; electric prods and ticklers kept people on their toes; helter skelters and switchbacks helped overcome Victorian inhibitions; and freak shows satisfied consumers' appetite for the bestial and grotesque. Innocuous it wasn't; never more so than when Topsy, a sadly addled elephant, had to be terminated with extreme prejudice. Not a man to look a gift attraction in the mouth, Frederic Thompson electrocuted the deranged pachyderm before an excited crowd, though it took several grisly attempts to dispatch poor demented Dumbo.[23]

Although it was almost impossible to top topping Topsy, Luna's early box office was beyond the owners' wildest dreams. Their entire investment was recouped in three months. More than 4 million people visited the park in its first year and numbers rapidly rose thereafter. Such was the popularity of Thompson and Dundy's operation that it quickly attracted competitors. In 1904, an even larger version of Luna, Dreamland, opened on an adjacent site. Its buildings were bigger; it boasted 1 million electric lights; it offered even more spectacular shows, such as "The Creation" and "Fighting the Flames"; and it trumped Luna's national tableaux with a "Lilliputian Village" containing 300 diminutive inhabitants.[24]

Dreamland's initial capital expenditure, however, far exceeded Luna's and the gate receipts, good though they were, simply couldn't support the operating costs of what was, in truth, an egregious imi-

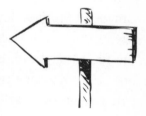

Several lions escaped the Dreamland nightmare and ran through the streets of Coney Island, their manes ghastly collars of fire.

tation, a shameless copy, a Luna-alike. Its end, nevertheless, was more spectacular than even Maxim Gorky's fervid imaginings. On May 27, 1911, a pot of tar was ignited by an electrical short at the "Hell's Gate" ride. The entire park was engulfed, the flames rose hundreds of feet into the night sky, and scores of circus animals died a death more agonizing than anything Topsy endured. Several lions escaped the Dreamland nightmare and ran through the streets of Coney Island, their manes ghastly collars of fire. Paradoxically, if unsurprisingly, the disaster further added to the attraction. The next day's crowds were bigger than ever. Almost all of New York turned out to see the immolated amusements, the flambéed City of Flame.

Dreamland was never rebuilt. Luna languished after the deaths of Dundy and Thompson, eventually closing in 1946. Steeplechase staggered on, surviving fires, economic depression, world wars, and massive social and cultural change, until it too essentially shut up shop in the 1960s. However, the pyrotechnic insanitarium that was Coney Island still lives.[25] Apart from Disney's recently announced aspiration to do a Times Square on the run-down resort,[26] Luna's legacy is evident in every single theme restaurant, festival mall, heritage park, flagship store, amusement arcade, and "edutainment" complex. As a chronicler of Coney observes,[27] "Amusement parks . . . pioneered merchandising techniques that designers of shopping malls would later adopt: dramatizing objects of desire, elevating goods and attractions to fetishes, they made spending a pageant." Niketown, ESPN Zone, Faneuil Hall, Harborplace, Dollywood, American Girl, Sony Meretron, Busch Gardens, Planet Hollywood, Universal Studios, Rainforest Café, Wisconsin Dells, Mall of America, Irvine Entertainment Center, Stalin World, Six Flags, Legoland, and the brand new Bob Bullock "experience" in Austin (see Free Gift 11) are contemporary reminders of the electric cornucopia that captivated consumers at the start of the twentieth century.[28]

Free Gift 11: Texas Tingler

Huge screen. Deep seats. Dolby surround-sound, with extra THX. The lights go down. The audience settles. The *mise-en-scène* unfolds. Sagebrush. Tumbleweed. Big sky. Whistling wind. Distant horizon. Deep in the heart of Texas. The Lone Star state. John Wayne country. Where men are men and longhorns horny.

A rocky outcrop looms into view. A tell-tale rattle. A rattle that's getting louder and louder. There's a snake about. An ornery snake. An extremely ornery snake. An extremely ornery snake in a state where everything is bigger than big. I'm rattled. You're rattled. We're all rattled.

It strikes! The audience lets out a roar and leaps from their padded seats as one!! They've been bitten in the butt by a big ornery rattler!!! Lucky there's plenty of people to suck out each others' poison. Or not, as the case might be . . .

Remember *The Tingler*? Remember Luna's personal prods? Remember the Temple of Health and Hymen? Well, they're back, they're buzzin', they're buzzin' butts in Austin, TX. But not at a suburban cineplex or downtown theater. They're buzzin' butts in the newly-opened Bob Bullock Texas State History Museum, already the biggest tourist attraction in town and one of the hottest tickets in the state. Clearly, they like that kind of thing down south.

The Texas Spirit theater is the money-spinning centerpiece of the Bob Bullock Museum.[29] Its "rumble" seated auditorium, coupled with a state-of-the-art audiovisual presentation on the privations that faced pioneers and frontierspeople, helps generate the $5 million to $8 million per annum that the museum needs to remain profitable. There's much more to Bob Bullock than the rumble seats, admittedly – fascinating tableaux on the Caddo Indians, the expeditions of La Salle, the rise and fall of Indianola, for example – but without the Texas Spirit experience, or the accompanying corporate sponsorships, or the beautifully appointed museum shop, the institution would find it difficult to keep the wolves from the door. Since the traditionally tight-fisted Texas Legislature insists that the Bullock pays for itself, the only way to go is the Great White Way, the Electrotaining way, the Marketease way, the Texan Tingler way.

Bob Bullock's rumblers, needless to say, have attracted a lot of antipathy. The Texas Spirit experience has been condemned by both outraged esthetes and offended antiquarians as a hokey travesty of the state's distinguished history, an affront against museums' time-honored mandate to move and inspire. Elevation, edification, and exultation have been sacrificed on the altar of ersatz. "There's been some criticism, sure," says Rick Crawford, executive director of the Texas State Preservation Board, the agency responsible for the Bullock.[30] "But while the Texas Spirit theater may be kind of theme-parky, it tells a good story."

It does indeed. And it's not the only one. The museum business is big business. There are an estimated 30,000 competing institutions in the US alone and, although visitor figures have increased from 485 million in 1989 to approximately 850 million today, the fight for footfall is getting fiercer and fiercer.[31] If not quite red in tooth and claw, it's rapidly reverting to the law of the jungle.

Contemporary museums, as is the case in so many product categories, are required to stand out from the identikit crowd. Consequently the days of dusty displays, hallowed halls, and sepulchral silence are long gone. Nowadays, it's all about blockbuster exhibitions, knock-em-dead buildings, museum-brand merchandise, and destination retail stores to sell the tie-ins in.[32] The curatorial cabal is being forced to dance to the marketers' tune and, while some dowagers' dance-floor contortions are not a pretty sight, the footwork of some museum directors is mighty impressive. Tom Krens, the Ray Kroc of the McGuggenheim, is a particularly nifty mover, as was the Metropolitan Museum of Art's swivel-hipped hip-hopper, Thomas Hoving.[33] It may be some time before Bob Bullock boogies on down, but at least he's got his tinglers to fall back on.

Reminders they may be, but that is all they are. It's hard, when strolling through Times Square or hanging out in Irvine's Entertainment Center, to avoid the feeling that something is missing, that there is a shortage of excitement, edginess, electricity. For all the esthetic appeal of such settings, the environment is singularly sterile, ingratiatingly insipid, decidedly disappointing. Definitely not Luna. It's just like any other edutainment complex, nice but dim. It's just like marketing itself, a once dynamic now dead corporate battery.

So, how and where can we get a marketing recharge? Where else but our latter-day Luna, the city that was built on juice, Las Vegas.

The Las Resort

The Frankenstein's monster of western civilization, assembled from bits and pieces of Coney Island and Atlantic City, activated by cheap hydroelectricity from nearby Hoover Dam, and amped up on illicit substances from the Mob's bulging medical bag, Las Vegas puts Sodom and Gomorrah to shame.[34] Like Luna, it glows in the distance, the night sky ablaze with its beckoning attractions. Like Luna, it is a neon saturnalia, Dante's inferno with strip lights and spots. Like Luna, it is New Year's Eve all year round, with added chutzpah and extra thermal units. Like Luna, it offers concentrated and caricatured versions of other places, from Venice and Paris to Monaco and Polynesia. Like Luna, it is a stunning sight, even to generations jaded by countless Hollywood blockbusters, stadium rock spectaculars, and over-the-top Olympics opening ceremonies. Like Luna, it reduces cultural commentators to embarrassed silence, as they try to articulate the *genius loci* of Glitter Gulch, explain the semiotics of the Strip, and account for the strange attraction of this inhospitable hospitality suite.[35]

Clearly, I would do well to call a halt before adding to the rapidly accumulating pile of academic evocations of Sin City. My aim, however, is not to capture the fear and loathing that permeate this epitome of electrifying entertainment. My intention, rather, is to learn from Las Vegas and its lessons are twofold. The first of these involves Excess. For all its faults, Vegas flaunts its flirtatiousness. Vegas takes pride in its tackiness. Vegas boasts of its bamboozling abilities. Vegas makes a virtue of its vices. It is the epicenter of entrapment, the apotheosis of imposture, the acme of agonizing near misses and might have beens. It is a place where hype springs eternal, pipe dreams are permitted, and castles in the air are constantly under construction. These flying fortresses, admittedly, may be hewn from the finest polypropylene, but Las Vegas is the *locus classicus* of tormentation. It is *Temptation Island* times ten. It is the world headquarters of heightened expectations. It is the citadel of casino-beating secrets, schemes, and scams.

Above all, Las Vegas is a place of shameless selling, profligate promotions, immoderate merchandising, and hyperbolic hucksterism. It represents marketing in the raw. Marketing, may I remind you,

Las Vegas is a place of shameless selling, profligate promotions, immoderate merchandising, and hyperbolic hucksterism. It represents marketing in the raw.

isn't about respectability, or reliability, or reticence, or restraint. Marketing is brash, marketing is vulgar, marketing is crass, marketing is up front, in your face, beyond your wildest dreams. A little ain't enough and too much is impossible. Despite the best intentions of do-gooding, well-meaning, hand-wringing, have-it-your-way customer huggers, the bottom line is that marketing is exaggerated, excessive, exuberant, extraordinary, energetic, electrifying, extrovert. We forget this at our peril.

Contemporary marketing, to be sure, suffers from a surfeit of more-ness, as noted in Lesson One. But there's "more" and there's MORE. There's more of the same – same products, same performance, same positioning, same 3Cs, 4Ps, 7Ss, same research procedures, same old customer service – and there's more-more-more. Marketing needs more more-more-more. It needs excitement, it needs extravagance, it needs excess. It needs extra excess, extreme excess, excess excess. It needs the likes of Larry nothing-suc-ceeds-like-excess Ellison.

Free Gift 12: There's Something About Larry

As adverts go, "IBM SQL/DS & DB2. DBMS now on PC," is not a thing of beauty. Compared to "We try harder," "The king of beers," or "Kills Bugs Dead," it doesn't so much trip off the tongue as stick firmly in the craw. Nevertheless, Oracle's arcane advertisement in an obscure computer trade magazine had almost as much impact as Apple's seminal *1984* ad, which was broadcast nine months earlier and cost several hundred thousand dollars more. In terms of bang per buck, Oracle's oracular announcement was a clap of thunder compared to Apple's champagne cork.[36]

Whatever its esthetic merits, Oracle's 1984 claim to have IBM's relational database available on PC is entirely typical of the organization and its charismatic founder, Larry Ellison. The claim was incredible, unbelievable, improbable, and utterly untrue. But, my, what an impact his ad had. It catapulted Ellison's then tiny corporation to the forefront of nerdygeek consciousness, a position that it has subsequently refused to relinquish. Oracle is one of the largest software companies in the world – it vies with you-know-what for top spot – and Larry Ellison is one of America's wealthiest people (ninth on the current *Forbes'* 400, down from third in 2001).

Larry's possessions are legendary. Houses, yachts, planes, cars, koi, art, et al. Larry's passions are legendary. Four marriages, sexual harassment suits, allegedly enough arm candy to OD Diabetics Anonymous. Larry's powers of persuasion are legendary. He put the IT into titivate, the BS into brash, the con into silicon.[37]

Enigmatic, exciting, electrifying, and economical with the truth, Larry Ellison is a marketer of genius. He took an IBM discard, the relational database, and built up a world-beating organization. His original product was significantly inferior to that of Oracle's principal competitor, Relational Technology Inc. It had more bugs than a Discovery Channel documentary. Yet Ellison sold his infested software again, and again, and again. In so doing, he turned Oracle into the McDonald's of its sector. Dunkin Data, so to speak.

Oracle's triumph, then, had nothing to do with the technological superiority of its database. Nor, for that matter, was it a function of the company's customer centricity. To the contrary, Ellison treated his customers abominably, especially in the early days.[38] He exaggerated the properties of Oracle's product. He misled consumers about the compatibility, portability, and connectivity of his system. He sold what is euphemistically known as "vaporware," products that don't exist and will likely never exist. He dissimulated, shall we say, about his background, his business, his backers, and more besides. Oracle's after sales service wasn't so much non-existent as a form of grief counseling, where customers didn't actually get their problems solved but somehow learnt to live with the disappearance of their data. Indeed, when the SEC filed a complaint against Ellison's organization, in September 1993, it reported that "Oracle double-billed customers for products, double-billed customers for technical support services, invoiced customers for work that was never performed, failed to credit customers for product returns, booked revenues that were contingent, and prematurely recognized revenue." But, apart from all that, the company got a clean bill of health.[39]

Larry's marketing élan doesn't stop at customer gouging. Hell no. When it comes to Oracle's competitors, Ellison is completely ruthless. It is not enough, he declares, to defeat the competition, they must be destroyed, dispatched, dismembered, and their disemboweled cadavers hung out to dry. Oracle's "attack ads" are the stuff of cybersplatter legend. They depict competitors as – variously – dead meat, "kills" on a jet fighter's fuselage, deep sea divers with Larry's foot on the airline, and a blazing biplane being shot down by the fearsome F-15 that is Oracle. When the market share of Ingres, a powerful early competitor that had the temerity to make an excellent product, was finally surpassed by Ellison's swashbucklers, he told his troops[40]: "I want them on their knees. Begging for mercy. Pleading for their lives. Confessing their every sin . . . Kill, kill, kill." On another occasion,[41] he showed a slide of the Ingres HQ at an Oracle sales conference and announced, "We're going to run them out of business and buy that building, which we're going to bulldoze. After that we'll salt the earth. Then we'll go after their families." All good clean fun, don't you know.

Unsavory perhaps, over the top unquestionably, but such shenanigans must be set against Larry Ellison's chutzpah, charisma, cheek, and charm. Yes, he's a complete rogue and a serial dissimulator, for good measure. Yet his boundless ebullience, incredible enthusiasm, unflagging energy, and sheer effrontery are difficult to argue against. He is smart, he is snazzy, he is snappy, he is sharp. He is unstoppable, impossible, incorrigible, unpredictable. He is, as they say, a force of nature. Above all, he is the out-and-out antithesis of Steamboat Bill Gates.

In this regard, it's hard to dislike someone who bought a fully-armed MiG fighter in order to strafe the Steamboat in his Redmond redoubt. Or passed himself off on Oprah as a poor, misunderstood multi-billionaire. Or who calls special company conferences in order to consider "The Excitement Factor," ways and means of injecting razzamatazz, hullabaloo, and abracadabra into Oracle's product and service offerings. Or who responded to vaporware accusations with, "You know, it's true. We don't actually have any software. This year we sold a billion dollars' worth of stuff and we never delivered anything. It's a really great business."[42]

Being liked, admittedly, isn't everything in marketing. But as every salesman knows, it is impossible to do well without basic likeability.[43] Larry is likable. Larry is remarkable. Larry is excitable. As his biographer, quoting a disgruntled ex-employee with no love lost for the main man,[44] judiciously observes, "He gets enthusiastic. He's wildly enthusiastic. I mean, it's infectious. He's just like, whoa. When he's into something, man, there's energy around it. And he drags people along in his wake."

Larry Ellison is the personification of marketease.

Important as excess is, there is an equal and opposite issue, another scintillating lesson to be learnt from Vegas's scintillating skein. And that concerns Ennui. The energetic ebullience of the place must be set against constantly creeping apathy. Obsolescence is instant. Boredom soon sets in. For most people, one visit is enough. More than enough. A miasma of monotony quickly envelops even the most astounding attraction. Been there, done that, didn't buy the T-shirt, kind of thing.[45]

Show business isn't slow business. Change is constant. Next is now. Now is then. Yesterday is history.

These days, every business is in show business, or so the spokespersons for the entertainment economy remind us.[46] However, show business isn't slow business. Change is constant. Next is now. Now is then. Yesterday is history. The velocity of vapidity is rapidly increasing. The developers of Las Vegan venues – and themed environments generally – are thus caught on an extremely expensive treadmill, where each facility must eclipse all that has gone before, in the full knowledge that it too will be eclipsed almost instantaneously. Fifteen minutes of fame is a lifetime these days. In a two-minute culture, tedium sets in after twenty-five seconds.

The lesson for marketing is clear. Exaggeration, exuberance, excess, and so on are vitally necessary. But they are very short lived. They need a constant infusion of excitement, energy, electrotainment. When the supply is cut off, things go flat very quickly.

Analogously, marketers are laboring under the delusion that they have identified eternal commercial verities, customer-oriented tablets of stone that are inviolate, inveterate, invincible, inalienable. But marketing is just as mutable as any other element of the entertainment economy. Marketing, sadly, has become monotonous. It refuses to change its tune. It no longer electrifies.

Electricity, in conclusion, is the perfect metaphor for marketing. Once dramatic, dangerous, and dazzling, it is now safe, sorry, and sad. The electrical Elysium sold by superquack Graham has deteriorated into Disney's Electrical Parade, led by Donald Duck and his unthreatening toon goons. Goofy has a lot to answer for. It's time, I fear, for Mickey's Topsy treatment.

How to Entertain When Entertainment is Everywhere?
Electrify. Electrifly. Electrifry.

NOW THAT'S WHAT I CALL MARKETING #2

Trickery, Exclusivity, Amplification, Secrecy, Entertainment. TEASE, for one. Trump, Evanescence, Affront, Seduction, Electricity. TEASE, for two. Tango, eBay, Absolut, Saunders, Ellison. TEASE, for three. Tingler, Exiguousness, Antagonism, Surprise, Excess. TEASE, for four. Tom Sawyer, Estée Lauder, Armani's Army, Stalin World, Edison and on. TEASE, for five.

Had it up to here with TEASE yet? Time to ease up on TEASE, you think? Anyone for No TEASE Please? In the preface I promised you a terminological cold turkey, a bracing buzzword detox, a Totally Stressless Acronym Excision Exercise (whoops, those caps look familiar). And, as someone with my customers' best interest at heart, I have not only endeavored to deliver on my promise but Also Totally Exceed Subscribers' Expectations (it's congenital, dammit!).

Candelabra in the Wind

Still, I suspect you've had too much TEASE for the meantime and, in order to let you catch your breath before we push on into the final, bring-it-all-together-sure-there-are-limitations-but-it's-still-worth-considering section, another musical interlude is called for.

You may recall that when we last trebled our clefs and swashed our semiquavers, the late great Lillian Russell was being interred with appropriate pomp and circumstance. You may not be aware, however, that just as the American Beauty was being buried, another marketing-minded musical prodigy began picking out his first tune on the family piano. The place was West Allis, Wisconsin. The tune was "Yes, We Have No Bananas." The 3-year-old pianist was Wladziu Valentino Liberace.[1] The third issue of an unhappy marriage between Salvatore Liberace, a former cornet soloist for John Philip Sousa, and Frances Zuchowski, the matriarch of a mom and pop grocery store, Liberace magnificently melded his mother's moneymaking acumen with his father's musical talent. Such was his gift, indeed, that he completely eclipsed the local music teachers before his seventh birthday. At eight, he met the great Polish virtuoso, Paderewski, who declared that the boy would one day take his place. By the age of eleven, he was winning national piano competitions, even though he was one of the youngest finalists. Three years later, "Walter" gave his first public recital at the Wisconsin College of Music. Not long after, in an attempt to puncture the whiz kid's rapidly inflating musical ego, his teacher entered the teenage sensation in a particularly demanding competition at the Athenaeum in Milwaukee. He won. Hands down. And received rapturous press notices, as well.

The climax of Liberace's classical career occurred on January 16, 1940, when the precocious twenty-year-old played the Liszt A Major Concerto with the Chicago Symphony Orchestra at the Pabst Theater. It was a triumph. But it was already too late. Walter had long kept the wolf from the door – and paid for his piano lessons – by playing popular music in local restaurants, nightspots, supper clubs, and the like. His father heartily disapproved, but it gave the wunderkind an outlet for his innate showmanship, which was evident from his high school days when he dressed up, produced plays, and generally acted the dandy. Liberace's musical epiphany, however, occurred in 1939, six months prior to the Pabst Theater performance. He had completed an all-classical set to an appreciative audience in La Crosse, Michigan, when calls went up for an encore. Play "Three

Little Fishies," shouted a slightly sozzled sophisticate and the performer readily complied. However, he played the then popular novelty number in the style of Johann Sebastian Bach. The audience went wild; it captured the front page of the local newspaper; the accompanying headline, "Three Little Fishies Swim in a Sea of Classics," was picked up by the wire services; and the piscatorian pianist was rewarded with considerable national coverage. It was Liberace's first publicity coup. It wasn't his last.

Walter had found his musical gimmick – sorry, USP – and every recital thereafter featured an encore of audience requests played after the manner of a musical titan: Chopin covers "Chopsticks," Brahms' rendition of "Mairzy Dotes," Liszt's interpretation of "Tea for Two" and so on. Liberace, admittedly, wasn't the first to combine classical and popular in this way. The blind pianist, Alec Templeton, had previously made a career out of something very similar and, of course, Disney's *Fantasia* hit the movie theaters around about the same time. However, as far as the ambitious 21-year-old was concerned, the Chicago Symphony Orchestra couldn't compete with Paderewskian versions of "Home on the Range," Beethovenesque renderings of "Deep in the Heart of Texas," and Tchaikovskyish takes on "Tiptoe Through the Tulips." They paid a lot better, too.

Karaoke Classics

Over the next five or six years, Liberace honed his cabaret act in clubs and watering holes throughout the Midwest and the Eastern Seaboard. He also found another musical gimmick. Inspired by the success of vaudevillians who did impressions of Rudy Vallee, Bing Crosby, and Morton Downey, while miming to their hit records, Walter developed what can only be described as classical karaoke. This involved playing along, note for note, with recordings of virtuoso pianists, such as Arthur Rubinstein, Vladimir Horowitz, and Jose

Iturbi. Hokey though it now seems, Liberace's "finger syncing" was an enormous hit with wartime audiences and it rapidly propelled the young man to fame, glory, and prodigious prosperity.

Well, that's not strictly true, because Liberace's most remarkable gimmick was himself. He was a superb self-marketer. According to his latest biographer,[2] indeed, he was "the greatest showman of the twentieth century," a veritable "public relations genius." In 1984, furthermore, the *Los Angeles Times* described him as the "sharpest showman since P.T. Barnum."

Forty years prior to the *Times'* encomium, however, young Wally was still polishing his product, perfecting his pitch, burnishing his brand, and creating his customer base. Despite appearances, Liberace didn't give his customers what they wanted, since most had never seen anything like it before. On the contrary, he gave them something completely different, something strikingly original that was at the same time reassuringly familiar, a cheesy yet charming combination of classics and pop. Likewise, the wisecracks, the ad libs, the inter-tune patter, the mamma's boy shtick, the wry refusal to take himself seriously, and his absolute determination to give his all yet leave people begging for more, were gradually brought together during the 1940s.

His marketing campaign commenced round about the same time. He came up with the iconic candelabra after seeing a 1944 biopic of Chopin, *A Song to Remember*, starring Cornel Wilde. He acquired the largest and most expensive Blüthner piano in the United States and transported it from venue to venue. He developed a comprehensive press pack containing all sorts of off-beat story ideas, from the proper pronunciation of his name (Liber-Ah-Chee), though recipes for apple pie (small town mama's boy makes good), to the logistics of transporting his instrument (the latter generated copious column inches). And, in an action then unheard of by a musical artiste, he undertook a massive direct marketing campaign to the owners and managers of entertainments auditoria across the USA. Fortune favors the brave, because one of his fliers dropped on the doorstep of Maxine Lewis, proprietor of the Last Frontier casino in Las Vegas. If ever a venue and performer were perfectly matched, it was Liberace and Las Vegas. They grew in gaudiness together.

In between stints at the Last Frontier, Liberace worked up and down the west coast. Thanks to his increasingly polished act, he was starting to attract significant attention. He played a command performance at the White House in 1950 and fronted a national beer advertising campaign the following year. However, his big break occurred at 7.30 p.m. on February 3, 1952, when *The Liberace Show* first aired on Los Angeles' Channel 13. Although only 15 minutes long, the show was an immediate hit. This led to a summer guest spot on NBC's *Dinah Shore Show* and, although network television seemed a natural step for the pianist, a contract never materialized. His act was considered too radical for mainstream American audiences. Accordingly, Liberace pioneered the independent production route, when he signed a contract with Guild Films for a series of half-hour shows (initially 13, eventually 177). They were sold to myriad local stations and used to fill in the gaps between network programs. It was an extremely hard sell, in truth, since there was nothing else quite like *The Liberace Show*. Although it was essentially the entertainer's cabaret act writ large, the show's "striking juxtaposition of high style and hokeyness, polish and error, urbanity and provincialism" made it difficult to market to conservative station managers.[3]

If *The Liberace Show* was slow to sell to wary television stations, it was a big hit with audiences and sponsors. The latter were especially grateful because Walter was a natural and gifted pitchperson. He eagerly incorporated the sponsor's product into his act, especially so when it was a mortician or manufacturer of toilet tissue; he made himself available for associated promotional duties, such as product launches and new store openings; he made limited edition recordings for the companies concerned and shilled them simultaneously. During one such show, sponsored by the Citizens National Bank, he announced that anyone who opened a new account would receive a free Liberace record. Next day, the lengthy lines led many to conclude that a run on the bank had commenced. So gifted a marketer was Liberace, that his much-admired Hollywood mansion – the one with the famous piano-shaped swimming pool – was built entirely by endorsing organizations. His fleet of glamorous automobiles was also supplied by grateful sponsors. Both served as signature promotional devices, along with the candelabra and Blüthner, and were thus a consequence of and contribution to his marketing-friendly aura. As Pyron observes,[4] "He liked selling things. He liked advertising. He liked making money. He liked spending money. He promoted himself shamelessly, but he promoted his sponsors with equal commitment."

A sublime combination of show and business, Liberace's stock rocketed in the mid-fifties. He was attracting huge television audiences, selling prodigious quantities of chart-topping albums, and being puffed from here to eternity by the mass media. Front cover stories were legion; he guested on countless TV shows; his ingratiating accent, stage persona, and uncertain sexuality became national talking points; and, most importantly perhaps, the great showman's personal appearances shattered all existing box office records.[5] He knocked 'em dead wherever he went. The tickets themselves were to die for; never more so than when the guardians of high culture lambasted the low-brow upstart, who dared dilute the classics with his mawkish shtick. This was the era of Abstract Expressionism, Jack Kerouac, and American high modernism, remember.[6] For avant-garde intellectuals, Liberace represented the abyssal depths of Mid-Western vulgarity. But as the free-spending money-spinner famously quipped in response to a scathing review, "I laughed all the way to the bank."

Bewitched, Bothered, and Bewildered

The laughing didn't last, unfortunately. Like every performer, Liberace's fortune waxed and waned, and waxed again. By the late fifties, his hitherto illustrious career had crashed ignominiously to earth. It was driven down by allegations concerning his sexual orientation, a successful, if damaging, lawsuit against an English newspaper that mocked his masculinity, and an ill-judged attempt to modify his stage persona with a more manly mien. Come the swinging sixties, however, Liberace successfully reclaimed his camp crown. A series of triumphant talk show appearances, coupled with the hard graft of non-stop touring, restored his sorely tarnished reputation. He immediately capitalized on his new-found marketability with a line of men's clothing, a sprinkling of antique stores, a couple of cookery books, a profitable real estate operation, and a chain of theme motels, each boasting a mannequin dressed in one of his extravagant stage outfits. He even started selling commemorative concert programs, complete with adverts for Blüthner pianos, priceless antiques, and his latest recordings. The program, in effect, was a product that sold the product and the product's products prior to the product's product-promoting performances. Or something like that.

Be that as it may, the seventies saw another slide in Liberace's fluctuating fortunes, largely because his Mr Showbiz excesses were out of tune with the anti-capitalist ethos of the oil-crisis afflicted decade. The great man, admittedly, continued to bedazzle in Vegas. His staggering stage shows piled outlandishness on hyperbole, with additional helpings of sensationalism. In 1973, he came on stage in a $35,000 mink coat and trumped this with a virgin fox cape valued at $300,000. "How do I know it's a virgin?" he asked the audience rhetorically. "It takes one to know one!" Yet, for all his grand entrances, glittering costumes and hyperventilated Vegasisms – "wait while I slip into something more spectacular" – the showman was making a spectacle of himself. A particularly cruel *Rolling Stone* article denounced the "Church of Liberace," as well as his (entirely plausible) claim that showbusiness was a manifestation of the religious impulse, something that was inherently exotic, mysterious, inalienable, and escapist.[7]

Denunciation, to be sure, always pays dividends at the box office. *Rolling Stone*'s 1981 attack notwithstanding, the greed is good decade was made for Liberace's brand of excess, ostentation, and glorious vulgarity. Indeed, he was never more popular than during the mid-1980s. He played at the Academy Awards ceremony. He entertained the Reagan White House. He stormed the talk show circuit. He wrapped the radicals on *Saturday Night Live* around his bejeweled little finger. He undertook concert tours that again broke all box office records. He opened the Liberace Museum in Las Vegas, still the conurbation's third biggest tourist attraction.[8] He charmed even his sternest high-brow critics, all of whom capitulated to the unstoppable showman. He died on February 4, 1987, at the peak of his profession. He left them begging for more.

Brand Ambition

Liberace may have embodied the hedonistic materialism of the 1980s, but he wasn't the only one. If anything, Mr Showbiz had to play second fiddle to another hard-working Italian-American, a marketing genius whose brand ambition bestrode the late twentieth century and who also traded on a memorable, one-word stage name. Madonna. Born in the summer of 1958, just as her fellow Mid-Westerner was at the peak of his pianistic powers, Madonna Louise Ciccone lies on a direct line of descent from Liberace and

Lillian Russell. As the great showman's biographer notes, of all the performers that have been compared to Liberace, Madonna comes closest.[9] In addition to similar family circumstances, prodigious work ethic, gender-bending stage persona, partiality to religious iconography, and unerring ability to put on a knock 'em dead stage show, both Liberace and Madonna owed their success as much to marketing ability as musical ability.[10]

Madonna, in fact, owes *more* to marketing than Liberace ever did, since her musical talents are modest, some say miniscule. As the artist freely admits in *Truth or Dare*, a back-stage rockumentary of her 1990 Blond Ambition tour, she is a limited singer, an average dancer, and a competent lyricist, at most. Such self-deprecation, to be sure, shouldn't be taken at face value, especially in a movie whose very title questions its veracity. But whereas Liberace was a musical prodigy and marketer first class, Madonna is a very capable musician and marketer of genius. So sublime a marketer is she that the material girl purports to be much less musically gifted than she actually is in order to make her rise to fame appear even more remarkable, even more mythical, even more in keeping with the anything-is-possible American archetype.

Like a VP

Yet, for all her strategic self-effacement – musically at least – the simple fact of the matter is that Madonna is an artist of Brobdignagian ability. Her artistic abilities, indeed, were apparent at a very early age. She stood out as a high school cheerleader, made waves as an amateur actress, and shocked all and sundry with her Lolitadonna stage presence. She entered the University of Michigan on a dance scholarship; dropped out after eighteen months, despite good grades; made her way to New York, with the legendary $35 in her pocket and a duffel bag filled with tights and tutus; joined the highly regarded Pearl Lang dance troupe; and generally made ends meet with a succession of service sector McJobs, occasional nude modeling assignments, tacky porno movie parts, and, in keeping with the classic rags-to-riches schema, spells of penniless scavenging in Hell's Kitchen garbage cans.[11]

Ever reluctant to remain on the slow train to fame, Madonna abandoned the hard station of modern dance for the fast track that is rock music. She started as a drummer, graduated to Liberace-like lip syncing in diverse dives and insalubrious nightspots, moved on up to lead vocalist and lyricist in several small-time bands, and, after catching the eye of several A&R executives, signed a low-budget, two-single deal with Sire Records. Her first record, "Everybody," was the dance floor sensation of 1982. The follow-up, "Burning Up," was a minor hit thanks to the intercession of MTV, which had started showing dance videos, a medium Madonna quickly mastered. However, it was "Holiday," a song rejected by several established stars, that really got the Madonna machine moving. It dominated the charts from Thanksgiving thru New Year 1983, helped make her debut album a Christmas best-seller, and was quickly followed by "Lucky Star," the first of her fifteen top five singles. The self-titled album went on to sell more than nine million copies worldwide. It was so successful that Warner Brothers held back the release of her second album until the demand for *Madonna* was sated.

Lucky as "Lucky Star" proved to be, the star's luck was really in on September 14, 1984, when she stole the show at the inaugural MTV Video Music Awards. Perched on top of a giant wedding cake, while wearing a striking combination of white bustier, tulle veil, strings of pearls, and trademark Boy Toy belt buckle, the cheeky cherub launched into the title track from her forthcoming album, *Like a Virgin*. As she writhed across the stage in a most unladylike manner, it was clear that a star was being born, or suffering from severe labor pains, at least. The single went straight to # 1 and stayed there for the next six weeks. The Madonna "look" took off; an entire generation of teenage girls rallied to her provocative flag; and a new word, "wannabe" (as in wannabe Madonna), entered the American-English language. Within a year, the arriviste artiste had graced the cover of *Time*, made a hit movie, *Desperately Seeking Susan*, and released the sublime "Material Girl" video, an affectionate pastiche of Marilyn Monroe's unforgettable performance in *Gentlemen Prefer Blondes*. She also pitched the academy into a frenzy of theorizing as starstruck scholars and postmodern philosophers struggled to explain the perplexing Madonna phenomenon. More to the point perhaps, Macy's devoted an entire department to Madonna-look merchandise – cut off gloves, crop tops, rubber bangles, lacy leggings, long scarves, Boy-Toy belts, "Virgin" emblazoned T-shirts, etc. – and many other retailers followed suit.[12]

Who's That CEO?

Although Madonna mania has slackened somewhat since the heady days of 1984, her staying power is as remarkable as her dramatic ascent. Initially dismissed as a cut price Cyndi Lauper, the Cabbage Patch Doll of pop, Madonna has had more hit singles than any other recording artist, bar The Beatles and Elvis Presley. A series of chart-topping albums, a series of sold out tours, a series of no-holds-barred videos, a series of movie roles (ranging from excellent to abysmal), a series of stage performances (critically panned but big box office), and a series of short-lived looks and personae (sex kitten, gay icon, Barbie doll, Earth Mother) have kept the singer at the forefront of popular culture.

In this regard, it is often said that Madonna's mutability is the secret of her success. Reinvention, certainly, is a career-spanning leitmotif. Each new model, however, is recognizably the same old mutable Madonna. As such, it is analogous to FMCG marketers'

187

periodic refreshment of an established brand image or long-running advertising campaign. Like many superstars and entertainment icons, Madonna only ever plays herself, regardless of the role.

Of course, the role Madonna plays best of all is lead marketer. Almost every commentator on the Madonna phenomenon, from fellow entertainer to cloistered academician, acknowledges her promotional genius. According to one captivated chronicler of her capitalistic machinations,[13] she is nothing less than "a spiritual heir to Barnum." Even Michael Jackson,[14] himself no slouch in the self-publicity stakes, readily bows to her marketing prowess, "I don't get it. What is it about her? She's not a great dancer or singer. She does know how to market herself. That must be it."

The important thing to "get" about Madonna is that she is first and foremost a businessperson. Her personal fortune is estimated at $6 billion. She runs a multi-million dollar record label, Maverick, and controls a plethora of subsidiaries dedicated to songwriting, publishing, merchandising, and much, much more. She keeps a very close eye on the bottom line; her frugality is legendary; and, from the earliest days of her career, she has immersed herself in the practicalities of corporate life. For artistic purposes, admittedly, she denies her status as a music industry mogul. She spurned an invitation to speak at Harvard Business School, for instance, and famously refused to contribute to a *Fortune* cover story. She also gives corporate sponsors the run around, as Pepsi discovered to its cost. Indeed, she occasionally waxes lyrical about the "innocent days before I became an empire." But the fact of the matter is that Madonna has been an empire from day one. A marketing-oriented empire.

Madonna marketing, however, isn't predicated on conventional precepts of customer centricity.[15] To the contrary, she treats her audience abominably and they love her for it. Her stage persona during the Drowned World tour of 2001 was profane and contemptuous by turns. Her inter-song patter eschewed "love you all" showbiz platitudes for "fuck you, motherfuckers" and analogous customer-isn't-king marketing epigrams. With the exception of "Holiday," she refused to play any of her greatest hits, preferring to focus on more recent, less audience-friendly, material. The show ended, not with several hot rockin', hand wavin', lighter holdin' encores, or hard earned curtain calls, but with a giant screen video clip informing the audience that "she ain't comin back, so go on, piss off." Bearing in mind that the tour was her first in nine years, a period when her career sank to its lowest commercial ebb, Madonna's "forget the customer" stance was bold, bordering on suicidal. As *Vanity Fair* rightly observed,[16] "Drowned World . . . stood in direct opposition to the scientifically designed, focus-grouped extravaganzas that in our day pass for pop concerts."

Madonna, then, attracts customers by refusing to pander to them, by refusing to listen to them, by tantalizing, tormenting, and teasing them unmercifully, by playing hard to get, by making them work for it, beg for it, abase themselves before her. From the very outset of her career she has resisted giving encores, preferring to leave the audience baying for more. She tours comparatively rarely – only five major tours in twenty years – and, when she does, the number of dates is strictly limited (20 for the Girlie Show, 29 on Blonde Ambition, 48 during Drowned World, etc.). Her sets, at ninety minutes or thereabouts, are relatively short, though what they lack in length and longueurs, they compensate for in excitement and spectacle. The upshot of this strategy, however, is that her shows are instant sell-outs, which reduces the need for associated promotional expenditure; her ticket prices are premium-plus, the highest in the industry by far, and, despite the enormous staging costs, her tours are extremely profitable.[17]

Papa Don't Pitch

If her brand ambition is voracious, Madonna's marketing strategy is outrageous. When it comes to offensive tactics, she is a five star general. She is a serial controversialist, a sensationalist supreme. From her schoolyard exhibitionism, through the Pope's threat to excommunicate her for blasphemy, to the scandal over her early nude photographs, which mysteriously appeared simultaneously in *Playboy* and *Penthouse*, Madonna has mastered the fine art of scandalmongering. She is the Warren Buffet of the shock market, a broker of blue blue chips. She is acutely aware that sex sells, shock sells, and shocking sex sells best of all.

In November 1990, for example, she engineered an MTV ban on her semi-pornographic video "Justify My Love" and, thanks to the subsequent publicity, proceeded to sell 400,000 copies of the $9.99 videotape, released just in time for Christmas. The year before that, she pulled the wool over Pepsi Cola's eyes by making a commercial for the soft drink giant featuring her new single, "Like A Prayer." At the same time, she made a second, non-corporate version, purportedly to promote a greatest hits package, *The Immaculate Collection*. Ever mindful of her sponsor responsibilities, the second take included images of inter-racial sex, priestly perversion, and the KKK for good measure. The ensuing outcry persuaded Pepsi to withdraw its support for the chanteuse, which further fanned the flames and, as if that weren't enough, Madonna got to keep the corporation's $5 million check. Show business ain't schmo business, that's for sure.

Yet for all her calculated controversies, premeditated provocations, and hate-the-media-but-ready-for-my-close-up fits of anti-paparazzi pique, the marketing maestro stumbled in the early 1990s and almost fell into where-are-they-now oblivion. The "Justify" scandal, the gratuitous *Sex* book, a risible quasi-porno movie, *Body of Evidence*, and a disastrous appearance on *David Letterman*, where her foul-mouthed rant prompted Paul Shaffer to observe that the Material Girl has got no material,[18] led many to believe that Madonna had finally gone too far. *Erotica*, the album that all the premeditated provocation was designed to promote, sold less than two million copies, the worst of her career. Her 1993 art house movie, *Dangerous Game*, was laughed off the screen and grossed a dismal $60,000 at the box office. She was seriously overexposed, both literally and figuratively. Her ability to shock was no longer working, as consumers became wise to, and bored with, her create-a-rumpus-buy-the-record marketing maneuvers. In desperately seeking salacity, she lost her ability to seduce. Madonna, above all else, is a seductress supreme. As a parade of picked up and quickly discarded professional stepping-stones readily reveals, she tantalized, teased, and tormented her way to the top. Her appeal to the wannabes, according to one astute observer, lay in the fact that she introduced a whole new generation to two age-old activities, dressing up and sexual teasing. "Nobody under forty," he noted in 1985,[19] "has teased anyone sexually in the US for something like 20 years." Ten years later, unfortunately, Madonna had forgotten how to flirt. She had become an embarrassing pest, a dirty-talking stalker, a sleazy sales representative whose clients were inured to her pornographic patter.

Don't Buy for Me Argentina

Like Liberace, however, Madonna responded to this mid-career slump by working harder than ever. She went back to her roots and, in effect, got retro. The Girlie Tour, a Lillian Russell-like burlesque – all plush velvet, high camp, and Barnum and Bailey – was rapturously received. This was swiftly followed by *Bedtime Stories*, featuring the retro hit singles "Secret" and "Take A Bow"; *Something to Remember*, a career retrospective of Madonna's best ballads; and

Evita, the big-budget movie of a 1980s stage show set in the 1950s. The retro turn continued with her new age comeback album, *Ray of Light*; "Beautiful Stranger," from the hit sixties spy spoof *Austin Powers*; "American Pie," a successful revival of Don McLean's 1971 classic; and *Music*, an affectionate nod to the good old days of disco with a dash of country and western. Even the Drowned World tour of 2001 was a weird retro-futuristic fusion of punk, disco, geisha, and Ghetto Fabulous, all based on a 1962 science fiction novel by J.G. Ballard, which was itself based on the four alchemic elements: earth, air, fire, and water. The cabbala has superseded Roman Catholicism as the foundation of Madonna's belief system. Appropriately, the strain of cabbalism she espouses, as expounded by former insurance salesman Rabbi Philip Berg, maintains that only the things achieved through hard work are properly appreciated.

Madonna may have made the transition from material girl to ethereal girl, but for our present purposes her true significance lies in her managerial girl side. Notwithstanding the mid-career hiatus, brought on by overexposure, she is a marketer nonpareil. As she recently observed about her spectacular, if infrequent, world tours:[20] "I don't see the point of doing a show unless you mind-boggle the senses. It's about theater and drama and surprise and suspense." Liberace, Lillian Russell, and Patrick Sarsfield Gilmore would surely agree.

HOW TO DO A HARRY POTTER

JKR and the Beanstalk

It's the old, old, rags to riches story, familiar from countless soap operas, chick flicks, fairy tales, and glossy magazines. A struggling author and single mother, who lives in a freezing garret, suffers from clinical depression and has hardly a bean to her name, somehow manages to write a literary masterpiece in a café, over coffee, while her daughter gently sleeps. The opus, however, goes unnoticed by perfidious publishing houses and the rejection slips pour in. Just as she is about to admit defeat and return to her McJob in the typing pool, an astute agent spots the gleam of gold in a tottering pile of textual discards. He leaps into action, negotiates a near-vanity deal with a prestigious publishing house, and the book is eventually issued with nary a sniff of pre-publicity or Sunday supplement hoopla. However, the public loves it, word gets around, sales take off and it climbs to the top of the charts. A bidding war for the American rights breaks out, a six-figure advance is extracted, the book slays them in the States and the rest of the world follows suit. The sequel eclipses the original; the sequel's sequel eclipses the sequel; and the sequel's sequel's sequel stops the world in its orbit, a total eclipse of the market. The once impoverished author is not only loved and lauded, she lives happily ever after.

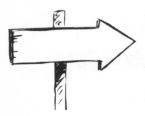

The sequel's sequel's sequel stops the world in its orbit, a total eclipse of the market.

Such a scenario, if pitched at a Hollywood producer, would probably be dismissed as too stereotyped, too schmaltzy, too Walt Disney for words. Yet that is exactly what happened to Joanne Kathleen Rowling, multi-millionaire author of the Harry Potter books, a series of stirring tales about a teenage wizard who attends Hogwarts, a magical boarding school.[1] Or, to be more precise, that's how her story is portrayed by the mass media. In fairness to Rowling, she goes to great lengths to explode this media-generated myth by stressing her happy childhood, normal upbringing, successful if somewhat directionless pre-Potter career, and, not least, the fact that she is deeply unsettled by the extent of her success, which has been accompanied by unwelcome side-effects, such as stalkers, loss of privacy, prurient press coverage, and so forth.[2]

Yet, for all her protestations, it is singularly appropriate that a teller of fairy stories should have her story told in fairy-story fashion. She is the Cinderella of our times, whose foot fits the glass slipper of celebrity; a twenty-first century Snow White, poisoned by the ostensibly appetizing apple of stardom; the owner of a Golden Goose that feeds on bookworms and is laying eggs with gay abandon.

To date, 180 million copies of the first four books in a seven book series have been sold, making Rowling the richest woman in

194

Great Britain with an estimated personal fortune of $400 million.[3] The books have been translated into 47 languages – only the Bible has done better – and are best-sellers in 200 countries, Britain and America in particular.[4] At one stage during his 98 week "run," Harry Potter occupied the first four positions in the *New York Times'* *Bestsellers List*. Such was his dominance, indeed, that the newspaper was forced to establish a separate list for children's literature in order to create space for Old Guard authors like John Updike, Philip Roth, and Saul Bellow.[5] In Britain, similarly, the Harry Potter titles have outsold everything under the sun, often by a factor six or seven. They have not only topped every bestseller list, bar none, but Muggles (Rowling's term for non-magical folk) are simply unable to explain or make sense of the phenomenon.[6] According to a London *Times* editorial, there has been nothing like it since the serialization of Charles Dickens's *Pickwick Papers*, when massive crowds gathered to await the appearance of each arresting episode.[7] Harry Potterism is more than a phenomenon, it is a warp factor phenomenon, a phenomenon with knobs on, a phenomenon to the third power. And then some.

Pottermania is having a significant multiplier effect on the global economy.

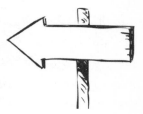

There is more to Harry Potter, however, than the staggering sales figures suggest. Pottermania is having a significant multiplier effect on the global economy. The printing industry, for instance, has been forced to work at full capacity in order to meet first day demand. Overnight delivery services are stretched to their elastic limit during new release date frenzy. The wizards of Wall Street are so taken with the wizard of Hogwarts that they have spirited the share prices of his US and UK publishers, Scholastic and Bloomsbury respectively, to unprecedented heights. A 24% sales increase in the children's book sector as a whole has been reported, thanks to Potterites' desperate desire to read something similar while waiting for the next exciting installment. In Britain, there has been a sharp rise in visitor numbers at "magical" holiday destinations, such as Tintagel, Cornwall; Knaresborough, Yorkshire; and Merlin's Castle, Carmarthen. French boarding schools report a sudden spike in applications and even Harry Potter-style spectacles are back in pre-teen fashion.[8]

Likewise, an extensive secondary literature, comprising fanzines, websites, "readers," "companions," critiques, parodies, unauthorized biographies of J.K. Rowling, etc., is developing apace.[9] Signed first editions have reached record prices at auction; one of the original cover designs sold for a whopping £85,750; a 93-word summary of the fifth book went for £28,680 at Sotheby's; they have been produced in all sorts of formats (illustrated, Braille, Latin, Ancient Greek, audiocassette, adult cover, cloth bound, large print, box sets), including a special edition to mark 100 million copies sold.[10] Counterfeits, furthermore, are a growing problem in China, where cut-price fakes went on sale before the originals, although the latter are still the most bestselling titles since Mao's little red book. Completely new episodes, such as *Harry Potter and Leopard Walk Up to Dragon*, have also been written by pseudonymous Chinese authors and attributed to J.K. Rowling.[11]

Harry for Hollywood

While it is an exaggeration to state that when Harry sneezes the economy catches cold, there is no denying the market power of the Potter bubble. The live-action movies, in particular, have raised the economic ante considerably. Warner Brothers signed an initial seven-figure, five-year, two-movie deal with Rowling in October 1998. A script of the first book was developed by Steven Cloves, ace screen-writer behind *Wonder Boys*, and after the project was spurned by Spielberg, a number of top rank directors, including Ivan Reitman, Bard Silberling, and Terry Gilliam, were auditioned by Warners. Christopher Columbus, whose previous box office smashes include the kiddy classics *Home Alone* and *Mrs Doubtfire*, finally got the nod, primarily because he promised to remain faithful to the sacred text.[12]

Shot entirely in the United Kingdom, with an all-star cast of Brit-ish thespians, *Harry Potter and the Sorcerer's Stone* was released on November 16, 2001. Despite indifferent reviews, most of which com-plained about excessive fidelity to the source material, the $125 million movie was a monster hit. It opened on an unprecedented 8,000 US screens, broke all previous box office records – first day, opening weekend, fastest to $100 million and so forth – and eventu-ally grossed $980 million worldwide, making it the second most successful movie of all time, after *Titanic*.[13] The second episode, featuring much the same cast and crew, was unleashed a year later. It too placed numberless bums on countless cinema seats (to the tune of $450 million and counting). Big screen versions of books three and four are also in the pipeline and, although forecasting the fate of feature films is fraught with difficulty, it is fair to assume that Harry Potter will be packing the megaplexes for some time to come.[14]

The movie cavalcade doesn't stop at box office takings, more-over. It also means ongoing employment for actors and technicians, subcontracted CGI work for special effects suppliers, fully occupied film studios and sound stages, healthy bottom lines for popcorn vendors and hot dog wardens, a thriving tourist trade in Harry Potter movie locations, such as Oxford University, Gloucester Cathedral, and Alnwick Castle, and, not least, lots of extra work for Warner

Brothers' legal advisors, who have been valiantly attempting to police Potter piracy, occasionally ineptly.[15]

The tie-in merchandise business is more massive still. In addition to Coca-Cola's $150 million sponsorship package, and the usual CD, video, DVD triumvirate, licenses have been granted to all manner of memorabilia manufacturers. These include Mattel, for board games and toys, Hasbro, for trading cards and candy, Electronic Arts, for video games and computer-based ancillaries, the Character Group for plastic and porcelain figurines, and Lego, for the eponymous building bricks.[16]

In total, more than 200 book-and-movie affiliated items are currently available. Toy retailers the world over have set up dedicated Harry Potter departments. It has been calculated that an outlay of

Whereas J. Alfred Prufrock famously measured out his life in coffee spoons, it is now possible for kids to spend every waking minute surrounded by Harry Potter paraphernalia.

$500 is necessary to acquire the entire range. And, whereas J. Alfred Prufrock famously measured out his life in coffee spoons, it is now possible for kids to spend every waking minute surrounded by Harry Potter paraphernalia. "Children," claim Harlow and Chittenden,[17] "can wake up on Harry Potter sheets, brush their teeth with his toothpaste, wash their hair with his shampoo, take their Harry Potter rucksack to school, use their Hedwig, Bertie Botts, and Gryffindor notebooks in class, drink their Harry Potter Colas, eat from themed lunch boxes, check the end of the school day on their Harry Potter watches, and go home to play on electronic games starring the boy hero before doing their homework on Harry Potter desk sets and curling up again in bed in pajamas emblazoned with his image to reread the novels using a Harry Potter bookmark."

All told, it has been estimated that the Harry Potter tie-in market is worth approximately $1billion.[18] Bearing in mind that: (a) the HP franchise is extendable well beyond the Rowling originals; (b) that each new installment creates additional memorabilia opportunities for characters, settings, objects etc.; (c) that each release generates renewed interest in the back catalogue of collectibles; and (d) that generations of unborn kiddy consumers will become acquainted with the Harry Potter universe as the years and possibly decades pass, it seems that the sky is the Pottermarketing limit.[19] Like the world's most admired megabrands – Apple, Barbie, Coke, Disney, Ericsson, Ford, and so forth – Harry Potter has attained iconic status. In six short years. He has become a license to print money (literally, since board games employing the Galleons, Sickles, and Knuts of Rowling's coinage are also on sale).

I Can't Believe it's Not Barnum

Iconicity notwithstanding, the most remarkable thing about the Potter texts is the way they are marketed. The books – less so the movies – have been marketeased to perfection, insofar as the hawking of Harry is predicated on unavailability, on postponement, on absence, on deferral, on tricksterism, on razzamatazz.[20] The complete anti-thesis, that is, of the conventional marketing concept. As noted in

The hawking of Harry is predicated on unavailability, on postponement, on absence, on deferral, on tricksterism, on razzamatazz.

Lessons One through Three, "modern" marketing is customer centric. It aims to make life simple for the consumer by getting the goods to market in a timely and efficient manner, so that they are available where and when they're wanted, at a price people are prepared to pay. The marketeasing approach, by contrast, deliberately eschews the here-it-is, come-and-get-it, there's-plenty-for-everyone proposition, by limiting availability, by delaying gratification, by heightening expectation, by tantalizing, teasing, tormenting the consumer, and by incessant hubba-hubba hubbub.

Harry Potter's publisher, it must be stressed, discovered "denial marketing" (as it terms marketease) by accident.[21] As sales of the first book took off – thanks largely to word-of-mouth, schoolyard conversations, internet chatroom buzz, etc. – the publisher kept running out of copies and found itself unable to meet the rapidly growing demand. These product replenishment problems, however, helped increase the book's cult following, rendering it akin to a rare Pokémon card or first day cover.

In fairness to Bloomsbury's marketers, once they recognized the power of customer tormentation, they exploited it brilliantly. Their denial marketing strategy for Book IV in particular was a masterpiece of marketease, inasmuch as it comprised a complete black-out on advance information. It started with a teaser campaign, consisting of "Harry's Back" billboards and a countdown to the rapidly approaching publication date. However, the title, length, and price were kept secret until two weeks before the big day. Review copies were withheld, author interviews were prohibited and foreign translations deferred for fear of injudicious leaks. Juicy plot details, including the death of a (minor) character and Harry's sexual awakening, were drip fed to a slavering press corps immediately prior to the launch. It was even announced, with some solemnity, that the original manuscript had been locked in a carefully guarded safe, after it was almost stolen from under a Bloomsbury executive's nose. Gasp! Shock!! *Quelle horreur*!!!

Printers and distributors, meanwhile, were required to sign strict, legally enforceable confidentially agreements. Bookstores were bound by a ruthlessly policed embargo, though they were allowed to display the tantalizing tome (in locked cages) for a brief period prior to Harry Potter "Day," July 8, 2000. Many retailers, in fact, opened at midnight to long lines of eager-beaver, pajama-wearing, broomstick-clutching, wizard's cloak-clad children, and even longer lines of no less excited publicity agents and television crews, who dutifully recorded the late-night revelry, and recorded the recordings of the late night revelry, and recorded the recordings of the recordings of the late night revelry . . .

The publisher's marketing campaign, it must be stressed, was not confined to confounding consumers. Their sadistic marketing strategy also demonstrated a darker yet undeniably potent dimension. This included dropping less than subtle hints that there weren't enough copies of the book to go around, thereby exacerbating the gotta-get-it frenzy of fans and distributors alike. Fake television footage of heavily armored security vans delivering the precious Potter cargo to online bookstores was also produced and broadcast a week prior to publication. Twenty advance copies of the top secret book were "accidentally" sold by an unnamed Wal-Mart in deepest West Virginia, though one of the "lucky" children was miraculously tracked down by the world's press and splashed across every front page worth its salt. Another copy "inexplicably" landed on the news-desk of the Scottish *Daily Record*, though it was returned, unopened, to the publisher by *DR*'s ever-ethical news hounds.[22]

In the event, of course, the *Record*'s textual telekinesis found its way to the front pages, as anticipated. The "lucky" schoolkid in West Virginia resisted the temptation to reveal salient plot points or sell her precious possession to a piratical third party. Deliveries to online bookstores were actually made the night before publication. And, as for the supposed shortage of copies, it never transpired, strangely enough. The book was ubiquitously unavoidable, available everywhere from grocery stores to roadside restaurants. Naturally, no one complained, because everyone had managed to get their hands on the precious Potter and, by the time they had finished reading the magical mystery, they'd conveniently forgotten about its magically mysterious marketing campaign.

By the time they had finished reading the magical mystery, they'd conveniently forgotten about its magically mysterious marketing campaign.

If anything, in fact, the marketing campaign was much darker than the book, itself the darkest and most frightening so far. It has been alleged, for example, that the Hogwarts' Express debacle was deliberately engineered.[23] On Harry Potter Day, the author's British book signing tour set off from a mock-up of Platform $9^3/_4$ at King's Cross Station. However, Rowling's minders couldn't control the massive media scrum, fistfights broke out amongst frustrated photographers, and some ever-faithful fans were caught up in the affray. Unfortunate perhaps, but as denial marketing goes, the acres of ensuing newspaper coverage demonstrate that it went very well indeed.

The campaign for Book IV didn't stop at denial. It was accompanied by a huge blast of marketing hot air. Press junkets, television appearances, radio interviews, newspaper spreads, book signings, online discussions, launch parties, and every other weapon in the arts marketing arsenal was pressed into Potteresque service. P.T.

Barnum himself would've been proud of the profusion of statistical superlatives. That is to say, the plethora of gee-whiz, well-I-never, *Guinness Book of World Records*-ish factoids that were disseminated by Harry's hypemeisters and which happily peppered each and every newspaper article or press report on the publishing phenomenon. So pervasive was the promotional hoopla that it precipitated a Big-Bad-Bloomsbury backlash. The Goblet of Hype, as the fourth volume was unceremoniously renamed, was loudly denounced for its shameless snake oil salesmanship, deemed an affront to the anti-commercial ethos of the literary establishment, and condemned for its connivance with the money-grubbing machinations of media conglomerates, multi-national corporations, and the capitalist conspiracy.

Even better yet, leading members of the literary establishment elbowed their way into the affray. In Britain, Anthony Holden criticized all concerned from his pulpit in the review section of the *Observer* newspaper. Harry Potter, he impatiently explained, represented a triumph of puffery over poesy. Bloomsbury, he bellowed, had resorted to advance hype worthy of Wonderbra. J.K. Rowling, he roared, couldn't write to save her life, was afflicted with a "pedestrian, ungrammatical prose style," generated less dramatic tension than an average soap opera episode, and used cloyingly sentimental storylines that were clichéd, unimaginative, and all-too predictable. What's more, she was personally responsible for the infantilization of British culture and owed her success to Bloomsbury's mendacious marketing department, with its disingenuous spin doctors, devious strategic planners, and not so hidden persuaders. Naturally, neither personal animosity nor – Heaven forbid! – professional jealousy played any part in Holden's attack on Harry Potter. To the contrary, he wished the royalties-replete author well, whilst urging her (in a sadly clichéd, unimaginative, and all-too-predictable expression) to take the money and run.[24]

Holden, moreover, wasn't alone. In the US, leading literary critic Harold Bloom poured scorn on the horror that is Harry Potter from the *Wall Street Journal*'s weighty pages and followed up with a salvo of Sidewinders in the *Harvard Business Review*.[25] So upset was the bookish behemoth that he excreted a recommended reading list of his own, *Stories and Poems for Extremely Intelligent Children of All Ages*.[26] Equally affronted was the memorably-monikered children's literature specialist, Jack Zipes, who zapped the teenage mage unmercifully.[27] The Potter Ponzi scheme, he raged, was a manifestation of the mendacious malfeasance of multi-national capital, a money-making monster that sucked young readers into its mephitic, memorabilia-lined maw, leaving none for more worthy children's authors. The Modern Language Association, likewise, devoted a special session to Harry Potter during its 2001 conference in New Orleans. As one particularly irate participant pompously announced,[28] "Rowling will have to accept that not only will children and their parents buy the action figures, but that in the global economic culture, children *are* the action figures manipulated by the giant fingers of corporate, and ultimately social and political, control." Of course, the fact that it was Harry Potter who bestowed momentary celebrity on and provided a national audience for such self-important scholarly ramblings is neither here nor there.

Harry Potter Pricked a Peck of Pickled Ps

Excellent as the literary establishment's outrage proved to be – in marketing terms, that is – the best contribution of all came from J.K. Rowling herself. Her purported hatred of the Potter publicity machine proved to be perfect publicity material. Her detestation of marketing was much publicized at the time, as were her concerns about Warner Brothers' meretricious merchandising of her marvelous creation.[29] Not only is a perfect puff for the collectibles – if JKR doesn't like them, they must be worth something! – but it is of enormous benefit to Warner Brothers when bargaining with would-be licensees. The supplicants can be tantalized with the Damocles' sword of Rowling's "disapproval," which is perfect for extracting further concessions at the negotiating table. "The idea," one skeptic observes,[30] "that she sits down and sifts through it all, I don't believe for a second. All the feedback from Warner Bros has been that any deal, any merchandising, has to be passed by her. The impression is that she has right of veto. But whether that's just a convenient excuse, I don't know. I think it suits them to use her as a get-out clause."

And it doesn't end there. The author's near nervous breakdown during the writing of the central book in the series also made the front pages, alongside her "sensational" spat with Steven Spielberg. Rowling's reputed "stalkers" have even been grist to the media mill, though one denied the trumped up charges, claiming that it was a cheap publicity stunt (clearly, he had been accidentally excluded from the promotional loop). Analogously, anti-Potter protests by Christian fundamentalists, accusations of devil worship by concerned parents, book bans imposed by straight-laced Australian librarians, and insinuations of plagiarism by unpublished authors, who "thought of it first," are all absorbed into the black PR hole that is Harry Potter.[31] It even got to the stage where newspaper reporters reported on the reporters who reported on the reputed secrets of Rowling's first, failed marriage (disreputable renegades, one and all). Others reported on the reports that Rowling had reportedly become too big for her boots and was much too grand to report to reporters. A self-sustaining feeding frenzy thus ensued – grubby hacks versus freedom of the press – as the column inches gratifyingly mounted. *Pace* Thomas Pynchon, there's nothing more newsworthy than a newswary celebrity.

Many Harry Returns

Accidental as some of it has been, the marketing of Harry Potter exemplifies the TEASE framework in action. Tricks are repeatedly played on the public (the lucky schoolkid, the precious manuscript locked in a Bloomsbury strong room). Exclusivity is actively practiced (special limited editions in Ancient Greek and Latin) or cunningly alluded to (oh no, not enough copies to go round). Amplify, amplify, amplify is the publishers' abiding byword, since everything that is even remotely newsworthy is shoveled into the media's insatiable incinerator (the shoveling is also shoveled constantly). Secrecy, similarly, is central to the whole operation, everything from the title of the fourth book to the rumor that a major character was going to be killed off in *Harry Potter and the Order of the Phoenix*. The stories themselves are mysteries, remember: a judicious mix of Tom Brown, Agatha Christie, and the Hardy Boys.

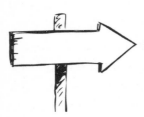

Harry Potter reminds us of the easily forgotten fact that marketing is fun.
Yes, fun!

Above all, however, the Harry Potter phenomenon is enormously entertaining. The books themselves are entertaining, especially when read for their marketing content (see Free Gift 13). The reaction of the public is entertaining, as the tribute websites, themed parties, and lines outside bookstores indicate; the reaction of the Harry-haters is entertaining, especially that of the literary establishment;[32] and, not least, the marketing campaign itself is enormously entertaining, particularly when a dash of Hollywood hoopla is added to the already impressive efforts of Scholastic and Bloomsbury.

Harry Potter reminds us of the easily forgotten fact that marketing is fun. Yes, fun!

Free Gift 13: Deconstructing Harry

The Harry Potter books are more than a marketing masterstroke, they are a marketing masterclass. They are as much *about* marketing as the outcome of marketing activity. They deal with marketing matters. They are full of marketing artifacts. They contain analyses of marketing phenomena. They provide insights into the contemporary marketing condition.

Thus, the stories refer to almost every element of the marketing mix as well as aspects of buyer behavior, environmental conditions, marketing research, and more besides. In Book IV, for example, one character is preparing a market research report on cheap continental cauldrons, most of which fail to conform to UK safety standards and must therefore be denied access to the great British market. Another aspiring importer wonders whether there is a niche in the UK market for flying carpets, the minivans of the wizarding world, only to be brusquely informed that the British will never give up their broomsticks (even though carpets were once the English conveyance of choice). Broomsticks, in fact, provide Rowling with a wonderful vehicle for exploring buyer behavior. Every phase of the purchasing process is described in detail, all the way from the consumer's desperate desire to acquire new and improved models, through the information gathering phase, where impartial consumer reports (*Which Broomstick?*) are consulted, to the heartbreak of a broomstick owner, whose pride and joy is written off in an unforeseen accident:

> He didn't argue or complain, but he wouldn't let her throw away the shattered remains of his Nimbus Two Thousand. He knew he was being stupid, knew that the Nimbus was beyond repair, but

Harry couldn't help it; he felt as though he'd lost one of his best friends.[33]

Advertising, likewise, is incorporated in the shape of huge hoardings, akin to electric scoreboards at football stadia, with constantly changing sales pitches for broomsticks ("The Bluebottle, A Broom for All the Family"), detergents ("Mrs Skowers All Purpose Magical Mess Remover – No Pain, No Stain"), and outfitters ("Gladrags Wizardwear – London, Paris, Hogsmeade"). Logistics also get a look-in, albeit in the form of Floo Powder (a magical mixture that transports wizards, Santa Claus-like, to chimneys of their choice), Portkeys (graspable objects, such as old shoes and empty cola cans, that ferry groups of holders very long distances), and the emblematic Hogwarts Express (an old-fashioned steam train that takes pupils to and from Hogwarts School of Witchcraft and Wizardry). All sorts of retail establishments are described in evocative detail (the Diagon Alley shopping "mall" figures prominently in every adventure), as are personal selling (when Harry gets fitted for his wand and uniform, for instance), promotional gimmicks (the Weasleys win a holiday to Egypt, courtesy of a newspaper competition), and, entirely appropriately, Harry Potter-ish marketing crazes (Hogwarts pupils collect Pokémonesque wizard cards, which are swapped and traded incessantly).

The books, in short, take the objects and artifacts from traditional fairy stories – cauldrons, wands, broomsticks, flying carpets, magic potions, wizard's apparel, et al. – and give them a marvelous marketing spin. Even marketease, of all things, features in the sublime form of Gilderoy Lockhart. The apotheosis of self-marketing and a stranger to self-mockery, Lockhart is a self-centered, publicity-seeking celebrity author, a larger-than-life trickster figure, a latter-day P.T. Barnum, a twenty-first century Wizard of Oz. A complete humbug, in other words. Handsome, hirsute, expensively attired, and orthodontically enhanced, Lockhart is five-times winner of *Witch Weekly's* Most Charming Smile Award and, *à la* Richard Branson, "it was remarkable how he could show every one of those brilliant teeth, even when he

> wasn't talking." Like a book-writing Barry Manilow, he is adored by women of a certain age; he bestrides the best-sellers list with his arresting adventures amongst outré occultists (*Gadding With Ghouls, Holidays With Hags, Travels With Trolls,* etc.); and he is a lion of the book marketing circuit, where he draws huge crowds to his signings, readings, and fan club conventions. He even has a special quill, made from an enormous peacock feather, for such autograph-hungry occasions. Never let it be said, however, that all the attention has gone to Lockhart's head or that he has forgotten his roots. On the contrary, his secret ambition is to "rid the world of evil and market my own range of hair-care potions."
>
> Because he's worth it, presumably.

The ongoing Potter extravaganza also demonstrates that the elements of the TEASE framework do not operate in isolation. To the contrary, they overlap, meld, reinforce, and, on occasion, counteract one another. It's not like the 3Cs, 4Ps, 7Ss, or the APIC approach to the "modern" marketing concept, where everything is crystal clear and fits into nice neat categories. In theory, anyway. TEASE is an amalgam; TEASE is an admixture; TEASE is a congeries; TEASE is a grand gallimaufry. The acronym says it all. TEASE is not only about tormenting, torturing, and tantalizing consumers, through clever tricks, captivating secrets, and the contrived scarcities that create exclusivity. It's also about CAPITAL LETTERS, the big, bold, brash, bedazzling ballyhoo that inheres in amped up amplification and electrifying entertainment.

And Harry Lived Happily Ever After

Master marketeaser he may well be, but there are ominous signs on Harry Potter's star chart, especially now that the movie-based marketing has taken him in hand. Perhaps the most disconcerting indicator is that marketing fads – of which the teenage wizard is a prime example – tend to have fairly short lifelines.[34] True, Potter may turn out to be the exception that proves the rule, especially as the seven-book saga is still two volumes short of a set. But history suggests otherwise. Pet Rocks, Rubik's Cubes, Teenage Mutant Ninja Turtles, and all the rest are reminders that nothing lasts forever, pre-teen obsessions in particular.[35] What's more, the knowledge that Harry's future prospects are uncertain exacerbates marketing executives' natural short-termism. Understandably, a make-hay-while-the-sun-shines mentality tends to prevail where fads and crazes are concerned. This attitude, however, only serves to accelerate the process, since the market is quickly flooded, the cult product loses its attraction, and sated consumers soon move on to the next big thing.

Time Warner, to be sure, is well aware that the franchise must be sustained. They have repeatedly stated their determination not to kill the gaggle of golden geese that is Harry Potter. They claim to have kept a tight rein on the amount of tie-in merchandise being released in Harry's name. They contend that a trickle strategy, rather than an inundation approach, has been adhered to.[36] The evidence, however, belies the rhetoric. The market has been swamped with Potter products. Ubiquitous and overpriced, Harry Potter tie-in merchandise is unavoidable and, Great Britain excepted, not selling as well as originally anticipated. True, the wares are selling, and selling well, but not to forecast. There's nothing like display racks full of reduced-to-clear merchandise to finish off a fad in double-quick time. Movie merchandising, rather than Lord Voldemort, could be the death of Harry Potter.[37]

The big marketing issue is not that the Potter consortium – Warners, Bloomsbury, Scholastic, Mattel, Coke, etc. – is myopic or unaware of the fatal consequences of overexposure. Nor is it an inability to deploy the constituent parts of the TEASE framework. On the contrary, they are masters of trickery, exclusivity, amplification, secrecy, and entertainment. The real problem is the curse of cus-

210

tomer centricity. That is, the commonsensical yet deeply mistaken notion that disappointed, disconcerted, or disgruntled customers are bad for business. Customers must be kept happy, content, and satisfied at all times, don't you know. If Lego castles are to die for, ramp up production forthwith. Hey, the kids want more Harry Potter merchandise. Give it to them. Yesterday.

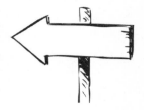

> Always remember the golden rule
> of consumer motivation:
> Wait Not, Want Not.

While such attitudes are perfectly understandable – revenue generating, furthermore – they are potentially lethal as well. When it comes to desperately-desired products like Harry Potter, less is always more.[38] Complaining customers are signs that the marketing program is working. Shrieks of consumer pain should be music to the marketers' ears. The worst thing executives can do when demand for their brand is going through the roof is to try and satisfy it right away. Not only can this cause all kinds of quality and stock control problems, but responding too readily to ravenous customers can turn them off completely and ultimately drive them away. Always remember the golden rule of consumer motivation: Wait Not, Want Not.

You've got to hold back, in other words, despite the temptation to do otherwise. The consumers won't evaporate or transfer their allegiance elsewhere. Their desire will increase rather than decrease. Their loyalty will be strengthened, not weakened. The real problem is not so much that consumers get fed up with the gotta-have-it product, but that managers get tired of tantalizing consumers and adopt a take-the-money-and-run attitude.[39] As Rowling herself seems to sense – if the inordinate delay that afflicted Volume V is any indication – it's no longer a case of Hurry Up Harry, so much as Please Pause Potter.

HOW TO GET OUT OF JAIL FREE

Majestic Marketing

The phone rings. Heavy breathing on the end of the line. A gasp. A shriek. A sigh. Who could it be? What's going on? An infatuated telemarketer perhaps? An infatuated telemarketer testing the latest can't-fail sales spiel? A satisfied consumer of *Free Gift Inside!!* – delighted, surely – who feels compelled to express their undying gratitude?

Sadly, no. The panting stops, followed by a sharp intake of breath. A frightened voice speaks up, "I want nothing more to do with whatever you people are involved in. Don't call me. Don't send me email. I am very, very serious."

Guess the consultancy report wasn't what they wanted, then. Maybe they're teasing me. Maybe they're not. Maybe the Immigration Service is trying a new tack. Maybe it's a conspiracy.

It is. A shot rings out. A bloodcurdling scream shatters the earpiece. The line goes dead.

Welcome to Majestic.[1] The latest online gaming experience from Electronic Arts, Majestic is a puzzle-solving, conspiracy-enriched mystery. Somewhat akin to the 1997 David Fincher movie *The Game*, where Conrad Van Orten (Sean Penn) gives his brother Nicholas

(Michael Douglas) a birthday present he'll never forget,[2] Majestic plunges its players into a maelstrom of mysterious phone calls, frightening faxes, cryptic emails, and bewildering websites – some genuine, some misleading – all part of a vast international conspiracy. All in real time. And all for the modest sum of $9.99 per month.[3]

Majestic's basic premise is that the player has stumbled on a government cabal related to the Majestic 12, President Truman's top-secret UFO council.[4] As the mystery deepens, however, the hapless participant is embroiled in cover ups, sudden deaths, disinformation disseminators, Deep Throat-ish revelations, and the usual conspiracy subjects – Illuminati, Rosicrucians, Freemasons, Elders of Zion, the Trilateral Commission, and many more besides. Majestic is a real time enigma, wrapped in a real time riddle, encased in a real time mystery. You don't play Majestic, Majestic plays you.[5]

Indeed, if you go to the Electronic Arts website, a curious home page awaits. Majestic, apparently, ceased and desisted after April 30, 2002.[6] Is this another twist in the Majestically mysterious plot? A fake death designed to deter all but the hardest of die-hard gamers? Unfortunately not. Majestic really did end in mid-2002. Critical acclaim for EA's gaming revolution failed to translate into bottom-line profits. Insufficient subscribers, implausible plot mechanisms, and a temporary suspension of service after 9/11, when real life conspiracy suddenly irrupted, combined to bring Majestic to an untimely end. They say its designer, Neil Young, is working on a new and improved version of the game.[7] But who really knows for sure? The Majestic mystery deepens . . .

Ogami Origami

Regardless of its afterlife in the parallel, if wacky, world of conspiracy theory, Majestic must be regarded as one strike against Secrecy. The product, innovative though it was, failed in the place that really matters. The marketplace. Secrecy isn't a sure thing, let alone the secret of success. It can be on occasion. But not on every occasion. Much depends on timing, luck, context, creativity, competitive activity, and countless other imponderables, imponderables that no amount of marketing planning can anticipate.

The same is true of Entertainment, even when it is souped up with a soupcon of secrecy. Genta Ogami may not be a household name in Peoria, IL, but he is the stuff of legend in Fukuoka, Japan.[8] Ogami is an actor. Ogami is a mediocre actor, approaching middle age. Ogami is also the self-appointed savior of the universe and the marketing genius behind Go Group.

Go Group is – or rather was – a $400 million multi-level marketing operation. The company was founded in 1995, at the very nadir of Japan's post-war economic slump, and promptly took off. In a world turned upside down, when banks paid 0% on deposits and many salarymen were saddled with enormous mortgages on apartments that had lost 80% of their value, many found it hard to resist Go's promise of easy money, returns approaching 120%, and privileged access to a range of "miracle" products that virtually sold themselves. These products included leakproof underwear, anti-cellulite creams, and Ogami's signature showstopper, "curative" tea made from specially brewed banana leaves, sourced in the deepest, darkest jungles of the Philippine Islands. The aromatic elixir, it appears, is a sure-fire cure for diabetes, obesity, and all sorts of other ailments (cellulite and anal seepage excepted, presumably).

There's more to Genta Ogami, however, than his arresting product range. The Go Group was sold with electrotaining fervor.[9] Promotional videos, starring the founder in his favorite role of marketing magus, were produced at enormous expense and supplied free of charge to investors. The scripts of these Go Group blockbusters referred to "visions," "renewal," and "salvation." The star brandished samurai swords, demonstrated his martial arts capability, and strode manfully through the jungle, wearing little more than a strategically positioned banana leaf. Ogami also made inflammatory speeches praising Japan's fighting spirit and the country's honorable achievements during the Second World War. He even persuaded the Muscles from Brussels, Jean-Claude van Damme, to appear in a big budget advertorial, alongside our kick-boxing miracle monger. How could it possibly fail?

It couldn't. Not for a while, anyway. Investors flocked to Ogami. From all over south-east Asia, they came, they saw, they contributed. At one stage, the Go Group had 20,000 members in the Philippines, 30,000 in Indonesia, and many more in Japan, mainly elderly pensioners trying to make the most for their money at a time of economic uncertainty.

In 2001, Ogami's organization acquired the Unitrust Development Bank in Manila, with assets of approximately $15 million. All seemed set fair for future expansion, investor salvation, and senior citizen security. The Go Group was going places. Unsightly cellulite would soon be history and embarrassing emissions a thing of the past.

Unfortunately, the products didn't sell. Allegations concerning the entertainer's extravagant lifestyle – fast cars, faster women, fastest pharmaceuticals – swiftly circulated and a warp speed run on the charlatan's bank transpired.[10] The foundations of his pyramid selling scheme rapidly collapsed. The tea may have been miraculous but the cash flow wasn't. A warrant was issued for the con artist's arrest. Ogami is believed to be hiding out in a secret location, where he is making a blockbuster movie that will recoup everyone's investment. Coming soon to a theater near you.

Letters Now Praise Famous Marketing Men

It is, of course, easy to be dismissive of those who fall for such patent

Ponzi schemes. However, our recent experience with crash and burn dot.coms and deified CEOs who turned out to have feet of clay – not concrete, regrettably – suggests that we shouldn't speak too soon. Tricksterism is equally ambivalent. Yes it works, as does Entertainment, as does Secrecy. But not everyone falls for it, or even realizes that they're part of the set up.

Nowhere is this better illustrated than in the reaction of service providers to Ted L. Nancy. Nancy is a professional complainer, who tests companies' customer care commitments to destruction and beyond. He writes to hotels, airlines, restaurants, and hapless celebrities with ludicrous requests, bizarre observations, and totally outlandish gripes.[11]

For example, he asked Greyhound Bus to let him travel dressed as a slab of butter. He claimed to have lost a Prussian sword when removing his pants in the men's room of Chicago's Ritz Carlton. He contacted the Brown Palace Hotel in Denver, asking after a lost tooth ("It is a small, hard, whitish object. The size of a piece of corn."). He approached a Turkish university with a request for 71 talented Turks, one with red hair, to help stage the musical *Annie in Izmir*. He tried to recruit Vaclav Havel, president of the Czech Republic, as Honorary Treasurer of the Los Angeles Vacuum Cleaner Owners' Club. He booked a room at the Beverly Hills Hotel, in the name of a two-foot-tall circus performer, Pip the Mighty Squeak, and asked for a three-foot long bed, a one-foot high dresser and a shower head mounted thirty inches off the floor ("A regular shower head blows me all over the tub.").

To cap it all, he even wrote to the irascible author of *Fear and Loathing in Las Vegas* wondering if he could purchase the great gonzo's toenail clippings for a mooted Hunter S. Thompson Mausoleum in Hollywood.

Yet as nutty as they were, virtually every one of Nancy's concerns-cum-requests was treated with due solemnity and not a little

217

deference. Such is the stranglehold of customer centricity nowadays that the obvious response – get outta here! – was unfailingly over-looked in favor of irony-free subservience. Greyhound didn't have a problem with Pat-O-Butter Man. Chicago's Ritz Hilton promised to search "high and low" for his missing saber, as did the Brown Palace for Mr Nancy's mislaid molar. The Turkish university agreed to "look very hard for" 71 student thespians, plus the requested redhead. Vaclav Havel politely declined the vacuum cleaner invitation, but sent a signed photograph instead. The Beverly Hills Hotel drew Pip's attention to its gentle, hand-held showerheads, lovingly described its low and spacious dressers, and unctuously indicated that the concierge would bend over backwards to find a smaller bed.

The Hunter S. Thompson Mausoleum, however, received short shrift from the cantankerous recluse. The words "buckshot castration" were being bandied about at one stage, apparently.

The identity of Ted L. Nancy is a closely guarded secret, not least from Hunter S. Thompson. Steve Martin, Mike Myers, and Mel Gibson, among others, have been linked to this scourge of the service economy. Jerry Seinfeld is the prime suspect, since he wrote introductions to all three *Letters From a Nut* anthologies.[12] Seinfeld, furthermore, will front an ABC television series based on the quirky correspondence, which is set to air in 2003.

For all the sophisticated CRM systems and databases beyond the CIA's wildest imaginings, many corporations misunderstand what makes twenty-first century consumers tick.

Regardless of Nancy's "true" identity, the episode demonstrates that one man's treat is another man's trick. As a burlesque on the cloying customer orientation of contemporary corporations, it is not only brilliant but a highly profitable enterprise in its own right (best selling books, prime time TV shows, etc.). As a commentary on the corporate funny bone, it is frightening, frankly. It demonstrates that, for all the talk about customer care, customer service, and getting in touch with/close to/into the minds of consumers, most companies don't know how to deal with today's marketing-savvy citizens. It shows that, for all the sophisticated CRM systems and databases beyond the CIA's wildest imaginings, many corporations misunderstand what makes twenty-first century consumers tick. It shows that just as they erroneously believe customers will reciprocate if you love them enough, so too they surmise that customer complaints, no matter how lunatic, must be handled from a prone position. The trick is on us.[13]

Voyage of the Damned

There is only one thing worse than marketers who love customers too much and that is marketers who love customers too little. Anti-customer orientation has its place, but an excess of anti is also possible. Exclusivity, as we have seen, is a powerful marketing tool in epochs of plenty, when scarcity is scarce and rarity rare. But extreme forms of exclusivity, akin to water deprivation in the desert, can give rise to drouth, delusions, and death. Voyage is a perfect case in point.[14]

The brainchild of the Mazilli family – Louise, Tiziano, Rocky, and Tatum – Voyage is an exclusive boutique. A very exclusive boutique. A very, *very* exclusive boutique. A boutique so exclusive that it makes Hermès seem vulgar, Harrods simply horrid and Tommy Hilfiger beneath contempt. The first store opened on London's trendy Fulham Road in 1991 and, by the middle of the decade, its existence was being whispered in all the right places.[15] Selling a select range

219

of top-of-the-range outfits – $5,500 T-shirts, $20,000 coats made of multi-colored ribbons, priceless bespoke items in exuberant materials like velvet, silk, fur, leather, embroidery, etc. – Voyage soon became the place to see and be seen. The clothes, indeed, had to be seen to be believed. In truth, they were pretty hard to miss.

Exclusivity, unfortunately, attracts undesirables. The act of exclusion, as previously noted, increases the appeal of what is rendered unattainable. So, in order to keep the insufficiently affluent at bay, Voyage introduced a members-only scheme in 1998. Membership was initially limited to 4,000 well-bred, well-connected, and extremely well-heeled individuals. Triple A-listed, at least. Non-cardholders were refused entry to the premises and their humiliation compounded by the infamous Voyage doorbell, which was rung by putative patrons but not necessarily answered by the preening proprietors or their snooty sales assistants. Not so much free gift inside as unbearable ignominy outside.[16]

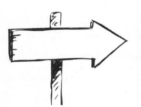

The stories of spurned celebrities precipitated a flood of applications for membership cards.

Sadly, some of those who were refused entry – and suffered the dreaded doorbell ordeal – included Madonna and Julia Roberts. Naomi Campbell, moreover, was banned after an altercation with a sales clerk who failed to open the golden portals sufficiently quickly for the piqued catwalk queen. The Mazellis, however, remained unmoved. Celebrities, it seems, are more trouble than they're worth. They expect freebies in return for their patronage. They clog up the store and make things difficult for less famous, paying customers, who spend up to $120,000 per month. Superstars, who needs them?

Needless to say, the company's closed door policy did wonders for Voyage's profile and the stories of spurned celebrities precipitated a flood of applications for membership cards. The store with "the world's least conventional approach to customer relations" had more customers and wannabe customers than it could ever hope to accommodate. A second London store was opened. Hong Kong and New York quickly followed suit. Voyage boasted of being the Most Pretentious Store in the World, with a membership limited to 60,000 cardholders. Tops.

Hubris, however, took a hand. The owners had fallen foul of the fashionistas. A self-glorifying advertising spread in the glossies further alienated the people who really matter in the dog-eat-dog catwalk world. The Mazellis were condescendingly described as an Italian Addams family, the Cosa Nostra of haut couture. Fatally, they failed to genuflect to the celebrity coven and fell out of favor as rapidly as they rose. There was widespread rejoicing among the arbiters of exclusivity when the company suddenly collapsed in February 2002, more than $5 million in debt.[17]

Voyage may be sinking but it hasn't submerged. Listing somewhat, lifeboats fully laden, the company lingers on. Production has been moved to Italy, a new outlet in Moscow is mooted and, in order to demonstrate its determination to carry on regardless, Voyage showed its first collection during the 2002 Milan Fashion Week.[18] A massive pink banner, declaiming the company's "Most Pretentious" assertion was draped over the venue's front entrance. The show commenced with models bursting through a tissue paper replica of the members-only card. A disembodied voice announced: "Rule # 1, Be Exclusive." The accompanying audio tape abandoned raucous rock music for a recording of the infamous exchange between Madonna and the conceited sales clerk who refused to admit the nabob of notoriety.[19] Notoriety has opened many doors for Madonna, but not the Mozellis'.

Brand of the Free

Although Voyage's shortcomings on the Exclusivity dimension were counterbalanced by the Amplification element of the TEASE framework, amplification too can go awry. Take America. In March 2001, Charlotte Beers was appointed Undersecretary of State for Public Diplomacy and Public Affairs.[20] Her task? Selling America the Beautiful, America the Brave, America the Brand. "She got me to buy Uncle Ben's rice," explained Secretary of State Colin Powell, the plenipotentiary behind Beers's elevation to the panjandrum of PR. "I wanted one of the world's greatest advertising experts," he went on, "because what are we doing? We're selling. We're selling a product. That product we are selling is democracy. It's the free enterprise system, the American value system. It's a product very much in demand. It's a product that is very much needed."

Although some skeptics wondered whether selling Uncle Ben's is adequate preparation for selling Uncle Sam, most commentators concurred that, if anyone is qualified to market America, that person is Charlotte Beers.[21] A charismatic Texan, who famously charmed the nation's CEOs with homely southern salutations, such as "honey," "darlin," and "y'all," she is the matriarch of Madison Avenue, the mother of all pitch battles. In a forty-year career that included two stints as chief executive of Oglivy & Mather and J. Walter Thompson respectively, the Charlotte Beers brand has been built on a mixture of flamboyance – her outfits are legendary, as are those of her pet poodle – and out-and-out audacity. She captured the Mars account by cheerfully consuming the company's dog chow in front of awe-struck executives. She casually dismantled and reassembled a power drill during her sales pitch for some serious Sears Roebuck business. She is second only to Jerry della Famina, he of the outrageous autobiography *From Those Wonderful Folks Who Gave You Pearl Harbor*, in terms of sheer marketing moxie.[22]

Beers's current task requires more than maxi-moxie, however, much less the ability to assemble an M-15 with aplomb.[23] For consumers of the American brand – that is, the rest of the world – swallowing the idea that the superpower stands for peace, freedom, tolerance, democracy, decency, opportunity, egalitarianism, and so forth is almost as difficult as swallowing Mars' driest dog treats. America, rather, comprises Those Wonderful Folks Who Gave You *Pearl Harbor*, the Movie, and crassly sought to sell it in Japan as a love story.[24] In other words, America is regarded as duplicitous at best and damnable at worst. It espouses compassion, justice, open-mindedness, generosity, honesty, and many other eminently noble aspirations. It sees itself as a shining city on a hill, the last best hope for humankind, the land of the free and home of the brave. Which of course it is. But, as Charlotte Beers's own research shows, consumers of America the Brand beg to differ. For many in the Middle East, America is a belligerent bully, a 700lb guerilla, a terrorist state that sponsors another terrorist state, and which works on the time-honored principle of do as I say not as I do.[25]

> America is a land of many talents, but its marketing talents are beyond number.

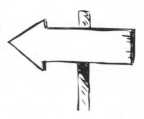

Distorted though it is, this charge of duplicitous double-dealing shouldn't really come as a surprise. It is a charge that is routinely leveled at marketing types and, if nothing else, Americans are universally regarded as consummate marketers. Marketing is the hallmark of America.[26] America is a land of many talents, but its marketing talents are beyond number. Marketing is America's biggest invisible export, by far. In functional terms, admittedly, American products aren't demonstrably superior to their international counterparts. (Anyone for French cuisine, German autos, Swiss banks, Italian fashion, Turkish coffee, Indian cinema, Japanese electronics, Chinese medicine, Mexican tequila, Spanish leather, Belgian chocolate, Irish literature, English orthodontics?) When it comes to marketing, however, America is in a league of its own. McDonald's, MTV, Disney, CNN, Microsoft, KFC, Nike, NBA, Levi's, IBM, Starbucks, P&G, Ford and, of course, the kingpins of the cola business, bear witness to the fact that, when it comes to marketing, America is top of the world, ma.

It is entirely appropriate, then, when a world-class marketer is conscripted to market the marketers du monde.[27] Yet, despite Beers's best efforts, ranging from infomercials on Saudi Arabia's Al-Jazeera satellite channel, to her "I am an American" internal marketing campaign, the so-called "biggest brand assignment in history" is proving too big for Madison Avenue's premier pitch doctor.[28] Many of her client's disgruntled customers are responding in time-honored fashion by boycotting the brand. Throughout the Arab world American products are being avoided, ignored, and unofficially embargoed. Sales of Pepsi and Coke have fallen precipitously. McDonald's restaurants are being attacked or suffering sit-in protests by unhappy eaters. Tide detergent, Heinz ketchup, Marlboro cigarettes, Pampers diapers, Estee Lauder cosmetics, Hasbro toys, Nike sneakers, Johnson & Johnson unguents, Sara Lee confections, and countless others are being cold-shouldered by supermarket shoppers throughout the Middle East, massive price cuts notwithstanding.[29]

Meanwhile, sales of locally produced alternatives, such as Zam Zam cola and Mecca cola, are growing by leaps and bounds. Based in Iran, Zam Zam operates 17 production plants, employs 7,000 people, and exports to eleven other countries, including Denmark.

Mecca cola, moreover, aims to[30] "answer the needs of world citizens by contributing to the fight against American imperialism and the fascism of the Zionist entity." A slogans go, it's not exactly the pause that refreshes. Nevertheless, Mecca cola is It for many Muslim consumers. Whether it'll be It for always remains to be seen.

The brand of the free is thus faced with a stark choice. Does it listen to its customers, as conventional marketing theory suggests? Does it alter its product formulation, in an attempt to appeal to those who can't stand the taste? Does it withdraw from the cut-throat fray and admit humiliating defeat on the hitherto triumphant marketing front? Or, does it acknowledge the simple fact that the customer isn't always right, that delighting the customer isn't necessarily the best approach, that sometimes the customer should be ignored? I know where I stand.

Time For A Take-Away

Brand America's attempted amplification, like the exclusivity of Voyage, entertainment of Ogami, trickery of Ted Nancy, and secrecy of Majestic, clearly show that the TEASE framework is far from infallible. There's no shame in that, however. Teasing, tantalizing, and tormenting the consumer is appropriate in some circumstances, but not in every circumstance. Just as it is possible to become too customer oriented – it slides imperceptibly into pestering, bothering, and stalking the consumer – so too teasing can become tiresome, irritating, and counterproductive. The appropriateness, or otherwise, of a marketeasing approach depends on the precise contextual, com-

TEASE is not a universal panacea, nor should we expect it to be.

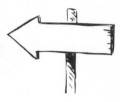

petitive, and corporate circumstances. TEASE is not a universal panacea, nor should we expect it to be. It's up to marketing executives to consider their individual situation, to decide whether TEASE is relevant, and to make the call. That's what they're paid for, after all.

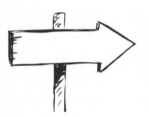

Customer orientation, too, is inappropriate on occasion.

If nothing else, TEASE indicates that there is no instant solution, or easy answer, or overarching concept, or killer app, or snappy acronym that is implementable in all circumstances.[31] Every marketing situation is different – sometimes subtly, sometimes significantly – and, therefore, what works in one setting might not work in another, be it TEASE or 4Ps. Marketease is not applicable on every occasion, nor is it applicable to every product, service, or market segment. But then again, the modern marketing concept of caring, sharing, all-hold-hands isn't always the right approach, either. Customer orientation, too, is inappropriate on occasion.

You know, we sometimes forget that the modern marketing concept was developed in a specific domain – FMCG, in the main – and, more specifically still, the concept was developed by Pillsbury.[32] It was only in the early 1970s that the idea of a universally applicable marketing concept started to emerge. There was much debate at the time, what's more, over the so-called "broadening" of the marketing concept. Subsequent empirical research has revealed that it isn't universally applicable.[33] The hi-tech sector, where customers can't really articulate their future needs, is a celebrated case in point, as are the entertainment and fashion industries. Indeed, in a world where Fast Moving Consumer Goods are no longer at the cutting edge of commercial creativity and where Fiendishly Contrived Marketing Gimmicks are the order of the day, perhaps it is time to turn to the hi-tech, hi-fashion, hi-definition holdouts for inspiration. Note, for inspiration, not a universally applicable solution.

If, however, a general rule is demanded – despite the general rule that there are no general rules – then it is often wise to do the opposite of everyone else. To buck the trend. To paddle upstream. To zig while others are zagging. When service is all, stress price (JetBlue). When retrenchment is rampant, expand rapidly (Dell). When hi-tech is the norm, try hi-touch (AOL). When utilitarianism is everywhere, emphasize esthetics (Target). When everyone is heading for the exit, occupy the entrance (Expedia.com). When customer delight is de rigueur, disregard the suckers (your company's name here).

Until such times, of course, as everyone else is doing the opposite of the opposite. Emulation, Thorstein Veblen informs us, is central to the consumer condition and the same is true of the corporate equivalent.[34] Marketing mediocrities run with the pack, follow the leader, and go with the flow. They keep up with the Joneses Inc. They buy into the latest management fad. They don't want to look old-fashioned, or reveal that they're behind the creative curve, or – heaven forbid – not au fait with the buzzword du jour. They can't allow competitors to steal a march on them, especially where new technology is concerned. They can't be seen to be selling the buggy whips of Ted Levitt, when everyone else is hawking transportation. They can't possibly abandon pandering to customers until such time as pandering is pronounced passé and persecuting consumers prevails.

It follows, then, that when the opposite of the opposite is omnipresent, true innovators do the opposite of the opposite of the opposite.

Preposterous? Perhaps. Provocative? Possibly. Perverse? Perfectly! Perversity, remember, has its place. We need perversity in order to appreciate that "normality" is a construct, a consensus, a concoction. Customer centricity is a convention – an agreement to agree – not a covenant. There's nothing inevitable, inviolate, innate, or indispensable about it.

In this regard, it is always wise to remind ourselves that consumers *aren't* paragons of virtue. It is convenient, in today's post-Enron corporate climate, a climate where big business is (rightly) at the receiving end of unceasing invective, to conclude that the customer's word is law, that consumers can do no wrong, that they're saints, angels and practically perfect in every way.

Is it any wonder that many marketing managers find it difficult to love their customers when their customers are so incorrigible, impossible, infuriating, improper?

A moment's reflection, however, reveals that they are nothing of the kind. As consumers, we illegally download music, movies, and more from the internet, while justifying our actions with self-serving, CDs-are-overpriced, the-industry-had-it-coming excuses.[35] As consumers, we understate the ages of our children at theme parks and museums, thereby saving a few bucks on entry. As consumers, we keep the change if a storekeeper makes a mistake to our advantage (hey, it was his own fault, right?). As consumers, we misappropriate bathrobes from hotels, buy fake Rolex watches in Hong Kong, and steal grapes from supermarket produce departments.

Okay, we're not talking *America's Most Wanted* here – albeit the music business has lost more to piracy than the entire cost of the

Enron scandal[36] – but the simple fact of the matter is that most consumers don't play fair with the marketing system. Is it any wonder that many marketing managers find it difficult to love their customers when their customers are so incorrigible, impossible, infuriating, improper? Is it any wonder that many customer care programs founder on the rocky shore of sales associate indifference, the poor saps who actually have to deal with double-dealing customers? Is it any wonder that paying customers and low-paid employees alike are skeptical about the customer-centric discourse disbursed by highly-paid marketing executives and consultants?

There's got to be a better way of conceptualizing the customer–marketing interface. Customer orientation doesn't cut it anymore. At least not in all circumstances.

Retromarketing Matters

The present book argues that there *is* a better way. Or, rather, a different way. It is a way that involves turning the clock back to the good old, bad old days before customerization was all, to an epoch when marketers were pranksters and proud of it.

Free Gift 14: Deja New

According to the acerbic stand-up comedian George Carlin,[37] contemporary American society suffers from a debilitating disease called "yestermania." Its principal symptom comprises an unhealthy preoccupation with times past, which is expressed through "sequels, reruns, remakes, revivals, reissues, re-releases, recreations, re-enactments, adaptations, anniversaries, memorabilia, oldies radio, and nostalgia record collections." So rampant is retrophilia, he contends,[38] that a television newscaster recently made the unforgettable announcement, "Still Ahead, A Look Back."

Although today's past times obsession hasn't quite got to Carlin's vanishing point of *vuja de*, an uncanny sense that what's happening has never happened before, *déjà vu* is definitely de rigueur.[39] The merest glance across the marketing landscape reveals that retro is all around. Old-fashioned brands, such as Airstream (caravans), Brylcreem (pomade), and Charlie (cologne) have been adroitly revived and successfully relaunched. Ostensibly extinct trade characters, like Mr Whipple, Morris the Cat, and Charlie the Tuna are cavorting on the supermarket shelves once more. Ancient commercials are being re-broadcast (Ovaltine, Alka-Seltzer); time-worn slogans are being resuscitated (Britney Spears sings "Come Alive" for Pepsi); and long-established products are being re-packaged in their original, eye-popping liveries (Necco wafers, Sun Maid raisins). Even automobiles and detergents, long the acme of marketing's new-and-improved, washes-whiter, we-have-the-technology worldview are getting in on the retrospective act, as the success of Chrysler's P.T. Cruiser and Color Protection Tide daily remind us.[40]

The service industries too have adopted a time-was ethos. Retro casinos, retro restaurants, retro ballparks, retro retail stores, retro holiday resorts, and retro rollercoasters are two a penny. The movie business is replete with remakes, prequels, sequels, and sequels of prequels (such as *Star Wars: Attack of the Clones*). Television programming is so retro – *That Seventies Show*, *Enterprise*, the all-new *Muppet Show* – that reruns of classic weather reports can't be far away. The music industry, meanwhile, is retro a-go-go. Led Zeppelin is being reinflated, or so showbiz rumors suggest. The artist formerly known as Prince is known as Prince, like before. Elton John makes his best comeback album since making his last best comeback album. Bruce Springsteen reconvenes the E-Street Band and releases its first studio set since *Born in the USA*. Elvis has reentered the building twenty-five years after his undignified departure. And U2 have reclaimed their title as the best U2 tribute band in the world. It's a beautiful payday.

Retro, moreover, is not just an American thing. In Italy management training programs based on gladiatorial contests are the fad to die for. In France old-tyme dance halls – *guingettes* – have made a dramatic comeback. In Germany a retro auto based on Hitler's limousine, the Maybach, is being manufactured by Daimler Benz and sold for $375,000 apiece. In Britain the West End is dominated by theatrical revivals, everything from *Chitty Chitty Bang Bang* to *We Will Rock You*, a musical based on Queen's greatest hits. In Ireland the *Titanic* is resurfacing once more, in a retroscape dedicated to the greatest new product failure in history. In India the diamond industry is back on top, albeit in the form of low-grade industrial stones rather than the Koh-i-noors of yore. In Afghanistan there are plans to rebuild Kabul's 500-year-old Mogul pleasure gardens as a symbol of post-Taliban regeneration. In New Zealand the tourist industry has been transformed by *Lord of the Rings*, a big budget movie of the 60s bestseller, set in a mythical landscape. In Australia the post-September 11 increase in precious metal prices, coupled with a collapsing stock market, has precipitated a retro gold rush to the outback. In Japan the tamagochi craze of ten years ago has been revived, only this time on the internet.[41]

Retro, indeed, appertains to the act of selling as well as the objects sold. Retromarketing involves both merchandise and merchandising. It represents a rejection of the hitherto ubiquitous "Benign Corporation" pose,[42] the nonsensical notion that business is here to make life better, easier, or more spiritually uplifting for consumers (Every Little Helps, Have it Your Way, Where do you Want to go Today? What Can we Do to Make it Happen?). Retromarketing, rather, spurns this pseudo empathy, pretend intimacy, and fake friendship for an open acknow- ledgement that the business of business is to sell stuff.[43] No more, no less. No airs and graces. No BS, no nonsense. No apologies. None.

231

TEASE is a manifestation of today's much-vaunted retromarketing propensity. TEASE takes us back to the time before customer coddling was marketing's philosophy of choice. TEASE takes us back to a time when stocks were scarce and sales pitches plentiful. TEASE takes us back to a time when buying a bar of soap didn't mean entering a lifetime value relationship. TEASE takes us back to a time when marketing giants, like Harry Reichenbach and Elbert Hubbard, ruled

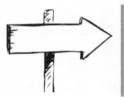

TEASE takes us back to a time when stocks were scarce and sales pitches plentiful.

the earth, a time before the drab, the desultory, the defanged, the Disneyfied version of marketing that's peddled today.

Let me give you an example. In the summer of 2002, a $5 million guerrilla marketing campaign caused much consternation in the United States. Developed by Fathom Communications, part of the Omnicom group, this exemplary example of stealthy stimulation involved sixty actors posing as tourists – particularly polite and well-dressed tourists, it has to be said. They were positioned outside leading New York landmarks, such as the Empire State Building, and inside exclusive hotels, bars, and nightclubs. When the moment was deemed ripe, Fathom's faux tourists approached innocent bystanders and asked them to take their picture. When the innocents agreed, as most of us would, they were handed the latest hi-tech gizmo from the R&D wizards at Sony Ericsson, a combination cell phone and digital camera. When the innocents expressed their admiration for this cutting-edge contribution to the telecommunications revolution, as most of us would, the benefits of the new product were enthusiastically extolled. A snip at $400. Coming soon to a Radio Shack near you. Tell all your innocent friends.[44]

Much to Fathom Communications' delight, the campaign caused an outrage. As the actors were instructed to remain silent about their connection to the manufacturers, unless directly asked, Sony Ericsson's scam attracted much anti-marketing ire and not a little media coverage.[45] Incensed consumer groups, most notably Ralph Nader's Commercial Alert, attacked the egregious organization behind the dodge. Rival marketers, affronted by the slur on the industry's good name, denounced it as "reprehensible and desperate." New Yorkers, protective of the city's tourist-friendly image, were reputed to be shocked and dismayed by Fathom Communications' heinous activities. Sony Ericsson kept its own council, however, insisting that they'd done nothing wrong. "We're not trying to deceive people or pretend we are something we're not," claimed a spokesperson. "Yes, it's a bit tongue in cheek. But it's hip and cool. Our products are best experienced in a one-to-one forum. Some of our people will, in effect, be like tourists. Basically, they will be showing that the phone can work as a digital camera."

Press #1 for "Say cheese." Press # 2 for "Closer together." Press # 3 for "Strike a pose, darling."

The When-Harry-Met-Sally Effect

Irrespective of the outcome of Sony Ericsson's pseudo event, as historian Daniel Boorstin famously termed such publicity-seeking incidents,[46] the stunt certainly succeeded in getting the contraption talked about. It'll be appearing in business books before you know it. In many respects, indeed, it is the epitome of marketease. It played a trick on consumers, but gave everyone a treat (the very thought of New Yorkers getting upset about upset tourists is priceless in itself). It imbued the product with an insouciantly exclusive air (way cool clubs, well-heeled tourists, order now to avoid disappointment). It was amplified beyond Fathom's wildest imaginings (they even sucked in professional marketers, who really should know better). It

233

exploited secrecy to telling marketing effect (the "hidden" connection to Sony is what happily antagonized the consumer activist community). Above all, it was endlessly, effortlessly, enormously entertaining (perfect fodder for midsummer media madness).

Yet for all Fathom Communications' promotional éclat, one cannot help but conclude that, as pseudo-events go, it isn't a patch on the publicity stunts that prevailed in the days prior to the "modern" marketing revolution. To cite but a single instance, eighty years before Sony Ericsson caused a sensation at the Empire State Building, the peerless press agent Harry Reichenbach was retained by the makers of Obesitea, a tea-based beverage designed for dieters and aspiring ectomorphs.[47] Harry hired a corps of couples, consisting of a slender ingénue and a decrepit old-timer, and positioned them in then fashionable New York restaurants like the Ritz, Plaza, Savoy-Plaza, and Waldorf-Astoria. During lunch, the old man ostentatiously adjusted his ear trumpet – this was in the days before hearing aids – and bellowed, "I can't hear you!" In the stunned silence that transpired, the girl shouted back, "How do I keep so slim? I drink Obesitea, of course!" To which he replied, "I still can't hear you!!" To which she countered, "Obestitea. Obestitea. I drink Obesitea!"

It was the talk of the town, by all accounts. A genuine "I'll have what she's having" moment. The When-Harry-Met-Sally Effect before Harry and Sally got acquainted.

Marketease works. Customerization works. They always have. They always will. The difficulties arise when the When-Harry-Met-Sally Effect kicks in and everyone is having what TEASE having. Or the customer-coddling alternative. Yes! Yes!! Yes!!!

How to Get Out of Jail Free?
Take a Chance.

HOW TO BAIT THE MARKETING MOUSETRAP

I'm Excited

If, by some unfortunate accident, you find yourself lost in the middle of the Australian outback, and if, perchance, you stumble across a disconcertingly jolly swagman camped by a billabong, and if, heaven forbid, he greets you with the somewhat unnerving words, "I'm excited," whatever you do, don't panic. Act normally. Fear not, my friend.

Rest assured, he's not after your koolibah. He's not about to boil your billy. He's not even asking for a waltz, Matilda. He's simply greeting you with an expression that's all the rage in Australia, and has been for the past decade. "I'm excited," is the rallying cry of ace marketing man and pitcher nonpareil, Big Kev. I'm excited just thinking about his story.

Big Kev, as his name implies, is not simply larger than life, he's larger than larger than life.[1] An energetic endomorph, Big Kev is entrepreneurship writ large. Sorry, larger. Hell's Bells, make that largest. He is the brains behind and pitchman first class for a range of eponymous cleaning products. These include Big Kev's Goo Remover, Big Kev's Mould Remover, Big Kev's Stain Free, and four more euphoniously entitled dirt busters. He started off selling his wares on a popular, family-oriented TV program, *The Bart Newton Show*, where his hyperactive, hyperspeed, hyperreal sales spiel endeared him to a mass audience. So effective was his first infomercial that the North Sydney telephone exchange couldn't cope with the strain of Stain Free-seeking shoppers and promptly collapsed. A star was born. A red giant, to be precise. Big Kev was on the roll that he'd been aeronautically designed for. And he didn't – perhaps couldn't – look back.[2]

In September 1998, the pitch perfect pitcher assembled his five bestselling products into a single multi-pack and delivered the *Citizen Kane* of infomercials – well okay, the *Star Wars* – on *Good Morning Australia*. Sales went into orbit.

A year later, Big Kev bit the bullet, broke out of the downscale, direct selling, dial 1-800 ghetto, and went to do battle with the Dark Side superpowers that dominated the household goods aisles of Australia's principal supermarkets. His product range was launched, with characteristic promotional flair, in the nation's leading chain stores, including Coles, Woolworth's, and Pick 'n' Pay.

This was followed, in August 2001, by a listing on the Australian Stock Exchange, which was heavily oversubscribed thanks to the enthusiastic support of small investors, underdog lovers, and Big Kev's big fan base. Turnover exceeded $9 million in the first trading year and, although it may be some time before profits (much less dividends) start to materialize, Big Kev Ltd is going from strength to strength.[3]

Indeed, the range has recently been extended to include laundry products and it is estimated that more than half a million Australian households swear by the big man's brand. Literally, since Consumer Reports websites suggest that Kev's latest products need a bit more R&D. As one underwhelmed purchaser stated,[4] "Face it, fatty, you're ripping off Australia by selling crap products at high prices."

Really.

Of course, it remains to be seen if Big Kev has the muscle to match Mr Muscle or any other giants of the household requisites industry. Multinationals may build their brands on banal marketing campaigns, by and large, but their pockets are deep and their horizons are long. As Tango Orange discovered in Great Britain and Jolly Cola found out to its cost in Denmark,[5] global brands are brutal competitors.

Big Kev, nevertheless, is giving it his best marketing shot. His dramatic, day-glo, spinnaker-sized shirts; his equally massive, multi-colored, Absolut-alike billboards; and his willingness to participate in anything that'll keep him in the public eye (such as a charity record with Australian rock band Mental as Anything) are wonderful examples of out-and-out, no-holds-barred, peddle-to-the-metal, marketing chutzpah. Similarly, his money-back-if-not-completely-satisfied guarantee; his outsourcing of all non-core activities except marketing; his mountainous in-store displays; his babes, babes, babes, and more babes promotional antics; and his perfectly understandable in the circumstances catchphrase, "I'm excited," are the epitome of gone-but-not-forgotten marketeasing in action. They are one part postmodern authenticity to two parts snake oil.

Big Kev, what is more, has latterly wrapped himself in the Australian flag (XXXL, naturally) in order to rally customer support against the multinational invaders who have a heinous hold on the country's bathtubs and shower curtains.[6] As a big-hearted, babe-lovin', brew-swillin', bleached blond, ostensibly unreconstructed, regular bloke, Big Kev is well placed to win the day. He is a down-to-earth Australian marketer battling in down-to-earth Australian markets. However, playing the national card is a difficult and dangerous tactic in today's branding blackjack, where products are sourced hither and yon, and global marketing is the name of the game. The big man's success is also attracting "crazy" copycats, who are being challenged in the not quite so crazy Australian courtrooms.[7]

Still, I'm excited to see if Big Kev beats the odds. Aren't you?

The Greatest

Over-the-top isn't over the hill, as our animated Antipodean amply attests. Nor is it the new kid on the marketing block, a promotional punk that can be dismissed as a flash in the PR pan. To the contrary, Big Kev is just the latest in a long line of barking barkers, as the present book demonstrates.

In an attempt, however, to extract some meaningful lessons for twenty-first century executives, it may be worthwhile returning to the fountainhead of Big Kev-style sales pitches, P.T. Barnum. It is almost impossible to do justice to Phineas Taylor Barnum, the greatest marketer on earth. Indeed, an entire industry has been built on the back of this peerless promotional polymath. Books, articles, movies, musicals, novelizations, ice-dance routines – you name it – have capitalized on the great showman's story and more interpretations are added with every passing year.[8]

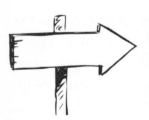

Barnum anticipated almost every marketing maneuver described in *Free Gift Inside!!*

For our present purposes, however, it is sufficient to note that Barnum anticipated almost every marketing maneuver described in *Free Gift Inside!!* To cite but a few examples: Barnum was a more adept self-publicist than Donald Trump, which is no mean achievement; Barnum not only brilliantly amplified his business through autobiography, but his marketing memoir was the best selling book of the nineteenth century, the Holy Bible excepted; Barnum anticipated Ted L. Nancy's *Letters to a Nut*, though his mooted collaboration with Mark Twain never came off; Barnum adopted the "children's friend" persona decades before Walt Disney or Harland Sanders; Barnum did a Colonel Tom Parker for a host of performance artistes, including General Tom Thumb, Jumbo the Elephant and the Swedish Nightingale, Jenny Lind; Barnum systematically offended all and sundry, *à la* Madonna, and reveled in the resultant newspaper headlines; Barnum appreciated the promotional importance of electric light long before Fred Thompson worked his Barnumesque magic at Luna Park; Barnum's Savage Girls caused the kind of marketing sensation that makes Alex Shakar's novel read like fiction; and Barnum, as previously noted, outdid Dean Kamen more than 140 years prior to the wonderful wizard of IT.[9]

As Barnum's incomparable "What is It?" indicates, the master trickster had an unerring ability to tantalize, tease, and torment the customer. Take, for instance, the Joice Heth hoax. She was the purported 161-year-old grandmother of George Washington, no less, who was exhibited around the country to huge crowds, keen to hear tales of the founding father's childhood, only to be exposed as a mere 80-year-old fake. Then there was the Feejee Mermaid stunt of 1842, which comprised the tail of a fish and the body of an orang-utan (Barnum wrote anonymous letters to the newspapers denouncing it as a fix, thereby attracting even more suckers determined to check for themselves). Then there was the "free" buffalo hunt in Hoboken, New Jersey, where the great impresario negotiated a secret cut from Hudson River ferry operators, massive crowds of New Yorkers made the daytrip, and, needless to say, the four forlorn buffaloes failed to stampede on cue. And then, of course, there was the celebrated "white" elephant episode of 1882. Disappointed with the color of his expensive acquisition – albino it wasn't – the great man gave it a couple of clandestine coats of whitewash. Mind you, this was only as a last resort. He had previously darkened the rest of the herd. Beat that, Komar and Melamid![10]

While there were many more deceptions where the white elephant came from, it has become popular in recent years to deny that Barnum was a trickster through and through.[11] Increasingly, the Prince of Humbugs is portrayed as a kind of customer coddler, as someone who never believed "there's a sucker born every minute," as the very antithesis of the cozening, conniving charlatan he actually was. Although national heroes are regularly reinvented to suit the sensibilities of each rising generation, this latter-day attempt to

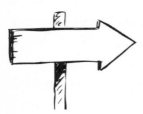

People like to be deceived, provided the deception is artful, creative, and, ideally, astonishing.

whitewash Barnum simply won't wash. He may be the biggest bull elephant in marketing's majestic herd, but a white elephant he definitely wasn't. Barnum believed in bilking his customers. He reveled in it. He boasted about it. He considered himself the very best in the customer bilking business, which he was. He diddled them repeatedly, what's more. He did it without respite. He ripped them off and they came back for more. And more. And more. And they loved him for it.[12]

240

Perhaps better than anyone else, before or since, Barnum understood that people like to be deceived. Provided, that is, the deception is artful, creative, and, ideally, astonishing.[13] As the continuing popularity of puzzles, crosswords, stage magicians, and suchlike daily reminds us, artful deception has an appeal all of its own. There is an important difference, Barnum explained in his 1866 book *Humbugs of the World*, between outright fraud, which is not only dishonest but bound to fail sooner or later, and his signature style of humbuggery, which swindled – yes, swindled – people in a playful, preposterous, pranksterish, and (extremely) profitable way.[14] It involved attracting audiences through ostentation, display, and downright deviousness, while ensuring that the imposture was worth the money. For Barnum, the ultimate swindler is the person who fails to appreciate the importance of friendly swindling, light-hearted chicanery, and playful deception. The contemporary marketing community, characterized by its obsession with absolute integrity, po-faced probity, and the-customer-is-always-right self-righteousness, is a perfect example of what he abhorred.

Yes, Barnum conned his customers. But he conned them in such a cunning way that they couldn't get enough of it. They connived in his conning. His tricks not only contained a treat, but the treat often turned out to be yet another trick.[15]

Yes, Barnum was thrifty with the truth, not to say an outright liar. However, lies are part of what makes people human. As psychological research consistently shows, falsehoods help sustain social cohesion and dissimulation is central to worldly success, some say to the advance of civilization.[16]

Yes, when push comes to shove, I suppose Barnum can be considered customer oriented. He was oriented toward tricking 'em, toying with 'em, two-timing 'em, taking 'em for a ride. A ride of a lifetime. Obsequious he wasn't. Servility didn't come into it. Pander to their needs? I don't think so.

You don't need to either. Unctuousness, obsequiousness, and the customer's will be done, aren't always necessary and aren't necessarily the best way to achieve marketing excellence. Customerization schmusterization, I say.

Gentlemanly Jim

Although even the most customer-committed marketing executive might be prepared to concede that Barnum was brilliant – beyond brilliant – some might be inclined to temper this concession with the observation that his achievements were service sector specific. Bamboozling and ballyhoo are standard practice in show business, but cut much less ice elsewhere. Granted, Big Kev is holding up his hyperbolic end in the noisome netherworld of grime-encrusted shower curtains and behind-the-fridge fungal jungles. However, razzamatazz is much less effective in the hard-hearted, horny-handed, huckster-buster battleground that is B2B. Isn't it?

'Fraid not. If anything, it's the complete opposite. Just as consumers are convinced that advertising works on everyone except themselves – a delusion that advertisers exploit with impunity[17] – so too B2B types tell themselves that they are immune to hoopla, they can see through hype, they never fall for Barnumesque hullabaloo. This belief makes them all the more susceptible, as the career of "Diamond" Jim Brady brilliantly demonstrates.[18]

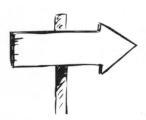

They remind us that marketing *is* vulgar and that vulgarity has its place.

Famously described in a mid-50s issue of *Fortune* as "the greatest capital goods salesman who ever lived," James Buchanan Brady is a half-forgotten footnote in the history of marketing.[19] He's almost forgotten, I suspect, because of the sheer vulgarity of his promotional activities, which comprised an indelicate combination of glitz, graft, gifts, grifts, and gross-out. They were, nonetheless, strikingly effective. They remind us that marketing *is* vulgar and that vulgarity has its place.

The eldest son of an alcoholic tavern owner, Jim Brady not only fought his way out of the Bowery but, perhaps more than almost anyone, came to symbolize the gaudiness of the Gilded Age. He began as a bellhop in the St James' Hotel, Lower Broadway; moved on to a porter's position at Grand Central Station; and, after studying business administration in night school, became a straight-commission salesman for Manning, Maxwell, and Moore, manufacturers of railroad equipment. If ever a market and marketer were made for each other, it was the Iron Horse and Diamond Jim. He was selling rail cutters, flatbed trucks, signaling equipage, and so forth at a time when railroads were spreading like laughter lines across the face of the American continent.

Although demand exceeded supply and selling railroad requisites wasn't exactly a hard station – the words "candy," "baby," and "taking" spring to mind – the industry was characterized by intense rivalry between competing capital goods manufacturers. Jim Brady, moreover, was only one among hordes of sales representatives riding and retailing the rails.[20] What raised him substantially above the rest was his exuberance, his excess, his blarney, his boisterousness, his very himself-ness. That is to say, he created a persona – a living legend – that he perpetuated by *being* Diamond Jim. He was larger than life at a time when larger than life was the norm. He was huge. Literally. His appetite was gargantuan. He ate for his country. He ate the entire contents of his country. He would have eaten the country itself, had it been served on a silver platter. He was, in fact, one of the country's natural wonders, a tourist attraction of monumental proportions, who was particularly partial to monumental portions. For the celebrity restaurateur George Rector,[21] Diamond Jim represented "the best 25 customers I ever had."

Nowadays, we are appalled by the very thought of ostentatious obesity. One hundred years ago, however, bigness bespoke success and few were bigger or more successful than Diamond Jim Brady. He was a billboard-sized billboard for himself. An illuminated billboard, to boot. Early on in his selling career, Brady discovered that dia-

He was a billboard-sized billboard for himself.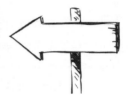

monds opened doors. The flash of a diamond ring, or tiepin, or coat button, guaranteed the best hotel room, restaurant table, or seat at the theater. Hot rocks also eased his passage past outer office receptionists, secretaries, and low-level functionaries of big chief buyers. People remembered the scintillating salesperson, moreover. They wanted to do business with someone who looked like a million dollars, who smelled of money, who dangled de Beers from every fold of his mammoth hide.

And Diamond Jim didn't disappoint. At all times, he was peppered with precious stones. From the tip of his jewel-encrusted cane to the trimming on his suspenders, he sparkled like an iridescent hippopotamus. He also sported a massive money belt, filled to overflowing with diamonds of every size, shape, and color, which he happily displayed to astonished customers and fellow salespersons. He was a walking jewelry store. He owned thirty themed "sets" of rings, cufflinks, waistcoat buttons, belt-buckles, collar studs, and suchlike. These included the Racing Set, the Transport Set, and the so-called Number One Set, which when fully in place made him look like Luna Park at twilight.[22]

The Gilded Age, to be sure, was coming down with over the top marketing persons. What lifted Jim above the hyperbolic herd – and ensured that the sale was made before he broached it – was his sheer ebullience. Diamond Jim collected favors the way he downed Chesapeake Bay oysters. In enormous quantities. He rarely visited customers after the first few years; they came to him. Blessed with a bottomless expense account, he showed them the fleshpots of New York. He plied them with food, drink, and their every heart's desire: diamonds, dancers, and the demi-monde included. He knew everyone, everyone knew him, and he never forgot a thing. He kept careful track of his beneficiaries and Gotham City alumni. Every month, he sent them enormously expensive hampers, huge boxes of candy, and other top-drawer luxuries, just to remind them of their indebtedness.

Now don't mistake any of this for customer orientation. To the contrary, it was closer to extortion, intimidation, blackmail. Brilliantly disguised, diamond-studded blackmail, admittedly, but it was blackmail all the same. He didn't so much cuddle his customers as put the squeeze on them.

In return for his ceaseless free gifts, Brady was repaid with orders, with favors, with the low down from Wall Street, which he never failed to act upon. True, by today's standards he stands accused of free gift insider dealing, as it were, but he demonstrates that over-the-top and more-more-more work just as well in capital goods as they do in the service sector. Ask Larry Ellison.[23]

The B-Team

Diamond Jim Brady may be moldering in his grave, alongside P.T. Barnum, but his marketing soul goes marching on. Indeed, the history of twentieth century marketing reveals a long line of men and women who kept the Barnum and Brady show going. These include Sol Bloom, the inventor of World's Fair midways;[24] John M. Burke, the promotions Svengali behind Buffalo Bill;[25] Walford Bodie, a popular Progressive Era electrotherapist;[26] Bruce Barton, the marketing man everybody knew in the 1920s;[27] Edward Bernays, the self-styled "Father of Public Relations," whose principal inter-war client was himself;[28] Russell Birdwell, the early post-war spin doctor who vies with Harry Reichenbach as the all-time master of ballyhoo;[29] Al Braverman, an early-70s boxing promoter who briefly got the better of Don King;[30] Jim and Tammy Bakker, the PTL network pioneers who discovered that, although a camel can't pass through the eye of a needle, the Lord can be sold in a Brady-like manner;[31] Harold Bloom, a larger than life literary critic who commands the front pages and gets the John Grisham treatment in bookstores, despite being a scholarly pariah;[32] Richard Branson, the P.T. Barnum of the airline industry, especially now that Doug Kelleher is ensconced in the Pitch and Yaw Hall of Fame;[33] Trevor Beattie, the fiendish adman behind FCUK and many other equally noisome commercials;[34] David Blaine, the marketing-minded street magician, whose extravagant events – being buried alive, being encased in a block of ice, standing on a 100 ft pole for two days etc. – attract world-wide audiences for what are, in fact, very old magic tricks;[35] and, of course, our own our very own Big Kev, Australia's excited entrepreneur and the Barnum of bathtubs.

In our world of identical products, indistinguishable brands, and same-old-same-old marketing campaigns, it is necessary to stand proud, to stand tall, to shill, shill, and shill again.

246

Although it is difficult to ignore such marketing exemplars, it is easy to dismiss what they do as B-team marketing, as outmoded marketing, as all style and no substance marketing. But such critiques fail to appreciate that there is a massive, monumental, magniloquent side to marketing, a side that aspires to stand out from the crowd, a side that is needed now more than ever. In our world of identical products, indistinguishable brands, and same-old-same-old marketing campaigns – the axis of equal – it is necessary to stand proud, to stand tall, to shill, shill, and shill again.

Marketing, we sometimes forget, is about extravagance, about exuberance, about more-more-more. Marketing is shop-til-you-drop, the-ultimate-driving-machine, the-best-a-man-can-get, the-world's-favorite-airline. It is the Whopper, the Monster Burger, the Big Kahuna burger, the New Double Rodeo Cheeseburger, the Big Bertha golf club, the Bigger Bertha golf club, the Biggest Bertha golf club. It is the mega mall, the hypermarket, the category killer, the acme, the apogee, the ultimate, the de luxe, the double-ply, the triple-strength, the blockbuster, the colossus, the extravaganza, the cheapest, the largest, the mostest, the greatest show on earth. Marketing is Big Gulp. Marketing is Extra Large. Marketing is Super-Duper. Super-Duper Extra Large Big Gulp Marketing is the answer to our prayers. It is the marketeaser's catechism. Go forth and multiply.

Who Moved My Market?

Before you hit the ballyhoo trail, however, let me make a couple of concluding points. First, Super-Duper Extra Large Big Gulp Marketing is not simply about personalities, be it Barnum, or Brady, or Bernays. Granted, the line between marketing figurehead and corporate body is often difficult to draw. Richard Branson *is* Virgin. Michael Dell *is* Dell Computers, near enough. Martha Stewart *is* Martha Stewart Inc, a not so good thing, sometimes.

But Big Gulp Marketing (for short) is also applicable in an organizational sense. Boeing, for instance, is a BGM that has consistently

247

made extremely big, extremely bold, extremely brash moves.[36] It has bet-the-corporation on several occasions, such as during the development of the 707, the 737, and, most dramatically, the 747. The last of these was widely disparaged as an enormous white elephant that would never take off, let alone fly like Dumbo. According to *Built to Last*, Boeing is characterized by its commitment to BFHG (Big Fat Hairy Goals), enormously ambitious objectives that enthuse the organization and help it achieve the impossible.[37] Boeing even bombs spectacularly, as its recent failure to outfox Airbus clearly shows (see Free Gift 15). Phil Condit, however, is a master trickster (low key version) and he has done much to put Boeing back on Big Gulp track.

Free Gift 15: Boeing, Boeing, Bon

In his eponymous biography, the celebrity CEO Jack Welch tells a revealing tale about Phil Condit, his equal and opposite number at Boeing.[38] According to Welch, GE was pitching to supply engines for the Seattle planemaker's extra-long-range version of the 777. They cut a deal over dinner, but Condit demanded that Welch remain silent on the subject while their respective negotiating teams thrashed things out between them. The great man agreed. With Neutron Jack effectively sidelined, Boeing's negotiators extracted concession after concession from GE and eventually signed an extremely favorable contract. There is no suggestion that Condit acted improperly, because he never consented to reciprocal silence. Nevertheless, his ability to spike GE's greatest weapon speaks volumes about his marketing abilities. The fact that Jack happily recounts the story, without apparently realizing he'd been had, says even more about Condit's sublime salesmanship. Yet, for all his prodigious marketing gifts, not even the Welch squelcher could prevent the disaster that befell Boeing in the late 1990s.

With sales of $53 billion and a workforce of 168,000, Boeing is America's second largest corporation and its biggest exporter.[39] In many ways, it is the General Motors of the airline business. It sells everything from family saloons (737), through impressive people movers (747), to top of the range roadsters (the mooted, much-vaunted Supercruiser). Like GM, moreover, Boeing's ageing marques are beginning to lose their luster – the elephantine 747, in particular – and facing ever-stiffer competition. Airbus, the European consortium, now offers a suite of models that are higher spec and cheaper to operate than Boeing's barnstorming brands. While Condit's squadron still controls the civil, if far from friendly skies, the Airbus formation is becoming more and more of a threat. Depending on how the figures are calculated – orders, ex-factory, in service, etc. – the Toulouse-based upstart's market share is somewhere between 40-50%. And increasing.[40]

In an attempt to combat the trans-Atlantic threat, Boeing made a mistaken move downmarket during 1997. It slashed prices dramatically and, in the ensuing buying frenzy, found that it couldn't cope with the increased demand. Suppliers found it impossible to keep up, orders didn't get delivered on time, expensive penalty clauses were invoked by irate airlines, half-completed aircraft glutted the assembly plants, the 25% increase in efficiency that was supposed to compensate for the price cuts never materialized, the factories were closed for a month in a desperate attempt to restore order, and, when the dust had finally settled, a write-off totaling $4 billion was announced, which plunged the company into the red.[41]

Boeing's blue light special, so to speak, had backfired disastrously. The stock price promptly collapsed by one third. Wall Street was baying for blood – which it got in the form of top marketing gun, Ron Woodard – and by 1999 rumors of a GE-led takeover or break-up abounded. To cap it all, the price-cutting paroxysm failed to dent Airbus's advance. The European interloper actually managed to increase its market share, despite Boeing's "buy one get one free" fusillade. To add insult to injury, Airbus announced plans for a double-

249

decker, 550- passenger super-jumbo, the A380, which will compete head-to-head with Phil Condit's flagging flagship.

Boeing's once-stellar reputation, clearly, was rapidly plummeting to earth. The company's turn-of-the-century difficulties were deepened by a sudden slowdown in new aircraft orders, precipitated by the Asian financial crises, and the dreadful aftermath of 9/11, when four of its planes were used in the attacks; 30,000 workers were laid off and the civil aviation industry was thrown into turmoil and restructuring. The post-Enron accounting scandals also briefly washed over Boeing, albeit its "progressive accounting" procedures are commonplace within the aerospace sector. However, the extent of the crisis is illustrated by Boeing's rapidly diminishing output. It delivered 620 planes in 1999, 527 in 2001 and is slated for 275 in 2003.[42]

Condit, nevertheless, has lost none of his marketing touch. A brilliant piece of brinkmanship embroiled the cities of Chicago, Denver, and Dallas in a no-holds barred scrap to secure Boeing's corporate headquarters. Since acquiring McDonnell Douglas in 1997, the company has built up its presence in the hitherto-avoided defense sector, though it lost a $400 billion battle for the Joint Strike Fighter to Lockheed Martin. All sorts of aviation services, such as air traffic management systems, administering air force bases, in-flight broadband communications capability, and integrated warfare solutions, are also being targeted.

The behemoth, in short, is becoming less and less dependent on the notoriously cyclical civil aviation business (down from 85% to 50% of sales). Even here, however, Condit has regained the high conceptual ground with his vision of the Sonic Cruiser, an exclusive, 200-passenger, business class-biased, Mach 1 with plenty to spare Beamer. Equally compelling is the sheer creative panache behind Boeing's Blended Wing Body, a radically different aviation solution, based on stealth fighter technology. Boeing, Boeing, Bon? Not if Condit has anything to do with it.

Another important point to take away with you is that BGM is only one side of the marketeasing equation. Alongside over-the-top, marketease embraces hard-to-get. The marketeasing concept, to repeat the lessons outlined in the first half of *Free Gift Inside!!*, involves refusing to pander to customers' every need, it involves

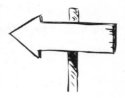

You want it? Can't have it!
Try again later, pal . . .

making life deliciously difficult for them, it involves tantalizing, teasing, and tormenting, it involves tapping into the primal principle, familiar to seducers and seductresses since time immemorial, that absence makes the heart grow fonder and that unattainability increases desire. Marketing, to put it bluntly, involves a three-stage sequence of caring for customers: You want it? Can't have it! Try again later, pal . . .

Now, this does not mean that marketers should spit in their customers' faces or gaily greet them with "Have a nasty one, you SOB." Nor does it mean that customer-centric marketing doesn't work any more. Nothing could be further from the truth. Customer orientation works and works very well, as the marketing record shows. Customers are a good thing by and large, provided they're kept well downwind. The problem is that nowadays every organization is customer led, driven, focused or whatever. Contemporary customers are aware of this. They make use of it. They are familiar with the marketing concept. They know us just as well as we know them.

Indeed, it is arguable that all the genuflecting, kow-towing, and hug-a-customer crapola has turned their heads, inflated their egos, increased their demands, and made life increasingly difficult for the marketing fraternity. That's not necessarily a bad thing, of course.

251

From a societal perspective it's excellent news. However, it means that marketers are caught in a vicious circle, whereby the more they provide, the less consumers appreciate; the more they pander, the greater consumers' expectations; the more they pamper, the harder consumers are to please; the more they prostrate themselves, the lower they descend in consumers' esteem. The "Battle in Seattle" has a message for us all. But it's not the message of *more* customer orientation.

A Better-baited Mousetrap

What marketing really needs, in conclusion, is a better-baited mousetrap. It is a commonplace of modern marketing ideology that building better mousetraps doesn't work. They don't work because all mousetraps are pretty much of a muchness and, therefore, snares need to be placed in the path of pesky consumers (or consumice, if you prefer). The rodent trapper's task, according to conventional wisdom, is to find out where the critters are and, better yet, identify where they're headed. Discover, though ongoing market research, what kind of cheese they like and pile it high, certainly higher than the competition. Sit back. Wait. Dispose of the corpses. Or, for relationship marketing mousetraps, release the cuddly little creatures from the foam rubber cross-bar, pat them gently on the head, and ask them nicely to call again.

Most infestation authorities agree that this modern marketing mousetrap works very well and has done for a long time. Unfortunately, the mice have become wise to the mechanism. More and more cheese is required to attract them, and they are becoming increasingly fussy eaters. A better bait is necessary, a bait that is so delicious, so alluring, so difficult to get hold of that the mice are fighting among themselves to put their heads on the block. So many mice, so little time, so hard to kill them all at once.

Now, some of the old mousehands among you may be tempted to dismiss this attractive trapping option. It only works for showbiz mice, or fashion conscious mice, or baby mice that don't know any better. Not so, my friend. Quite apart from the truism that every mouse is a showbiz mouse these days, and notwithstanding the fact that the modern marketing mousetrap made its name in the FMCG sector (Fat Mouse Capturing Gadget), before spreading to every conceivable nook and cranny, there is enough evidence from sufficient spheres to show that better baited mousetraps work in most places. They may work best on showbiz mice, or baby mice, or way cool mice wearing designer Rodent Raybans. But, as the present book has demonstrated, they can catch big, burly B2B rats as well.

I Can't Believe I Read the Whole Thing

Better-baited mousetraps are what marketease is all about. Marketing, as we have seen, is an amalgam of over-the-top and hard-to-get. Over-the-top works perfectly well on its own, as P.T. Barnum and Big Kev prove. Hard-to-get works equally well in isolation, as de Beers and the Hermès Birkin bear witness. However, when hard-to-get and over-the-top are used in hard-to-top combination, as in the case of Madonna's Drowned World tour or *The Producers*, which was the hot Broadway ticket until recently,[43] the resultant mix is a Big Gulp marketing mousetrap masterpiece.

If you need a closing aphorism that captures the marketeasing process – and a business book's not a business book without a snappy aphorism – then it would have to be: Limit. Limn it. Large it. Restrict the amount of product that's available. Wrap it in an aura of mystery and exclusivity. And get it shouted about by all and sundry. Limit. Limn it. Large it. Limit. Limn it. Large it. One more time, Limit, limn it, large it.

Okay, okay, it's not in the same league as Elbert Hubbard (who coined the original "Build a better mousetrap" aphorism and shamelessly attributed it to Emerson). But it'll keep us going until I return with *Money Back Guarantee!!* Ciao.

How to Bait the Marketing Mousetrap?
Go to http://www.sfxbrown.com for further free gifts inside!!

NOTES AND REFERENCES

Preface: Got Them Old, B1–B2, US Visitors' Visa Blues

1. My perennial point-of-entry difficulties, rest assured, are not due to a history of prior misdemeanors, held on the Immigration Service's bulging database. I got away with most of those! The hassles, rather, simply reflect the fact that the postmodern physiognomists on duty just don't like the look of me. Incidentally, for an intriguing discussion of "they" – as in "they say" – see Douglas Rushkoff, *Coercion* (Boston: Riverhead Books, 1999).

2. In saying this, I appreciate that I'm taking a risk. Offending the Immigration Service is unwise at the best of times. Offending them in print is a serious error of judgement. My future point-of-entry experiences could prove interesting.

3. I should immediately acknowledge that there is a groundswell of anti-customer sentiment among marketing gurus and commentators. Check out Robert Jones, *The Big Idea* (London: HarperCollins, 2000), as well as Jonas Ridderstrale and Kjell Nordstrom, *Funky Business* (London: FTCom, 2000). I'll be considering these critiques in Lesson Three. It is

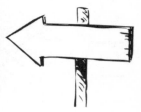

The vast majority of marketing textbooks . . . prescribe how things ought to be done. "Must" is their favorite word.

also important to distinguish between descriptive and prescriptive, positive and normative, "is" and "ought." The vast majority of marketing textbooks are normative, inasmuch as they prescribe how things ought to be done. "Must" is their favorite word (as in companies "must" adopt CRM, micromarketing, STP, or whatever). The present book, in the main, describes rather than prescribes. It deals with things as they are, not as they "ought" to be. There is no ought in marketing. Ought ought to be outlawed, as it were.

4. This hard-to-get, over-the-top combination can also be expressed in terms of *Will & Grace*. Hard-to-top is embodied in the form of Jack "justJack" McFarland. The remaining three-word combo, get-over-the, is embodied in, who else, Karen.

5. As strict grammarians will readily inform you, "free gift" is a pleonasm, an example of egregious linguistic redundancy, akin to "true fact." Gifts are inherently free, after all. Except in marketing!

FREE GIFT INSIDE!!

Lesson One: How to Win Business and Infuriate People

1. Most mainstream marketing textbooks adopt a "converting the heathens" approach. They work on the basic assumption that ignorance of marketing principles is widespread and that enlightenment is therefore necessary. This may have been an appropriate approach forty years ago, when ignorance really was widespread, but it is totally inappropriate to the present circumstances, where everyone is fully au fait with marketing. The contemporary challenge involves "preaching to the converted," convincing those who believe in customer orientation that there are alternative pathways to marketing salvation.

2. Even those books that criticize the consumer (cf Jones, 2000, and Ridderstrale and Nordstrom, 2000 noted above), continue to insist that customer orientation is marketing's be and end all.

3. As P.J. O'Rourke, the right-wing humorist, aptly observes in *The CEO of the Sofa*, "The modernists believed that artistic creativity – like the manufacture of kitchen appliances or flint spear points – should progress. This is like believing that sex appeal should progress. Sandra Bullock has a marvelous behind. Now if only she could grow a third buttock" (New York: Atlantic Monthly Press, 2001, p. 81).

4. Kevin Drawbaugh, *Brands in the Balance* (New York, Reuters, 2001).

5. Lucy Kellaway, *Sense and Nonsense in the Office* (London: FTCom, 2000, pp. 121–2).

6. Mark Earls, *Welcome to the Creative Age: Bananas, Business and the Death of Marketing* (New York: John Wiley, 2002, p. 60).

7. Andy Raskin, "What's an MBA Really Worth?" *Business 2.0*, July 2002, www.business2.com; Ridderstrale and Nordstrom, *Funky Business*, op. cit., p. 22.

"Less is more," says Mies van der Rohe. "Less is a bore," says Robert Venturi. In marketing, however, more's the bore.

8. "Less is more," according to modernist architect Mies van der Rohe. "Less is a bore," says postmodernist architect Robert Venturi. In marketing, however, more's the bore.

9. OK, I am that "learned marketing philosopher." A similar more-is-less stance is described by Joe Owen in *Management Stripped Bare: What They Don't Teach You at Business School* (Milford, CT: Kogan Page, 2002, p. 126). He calls it the Mars Bar Lesson.

10. Bill Bryson, "For Your Convenience," in *Notes From a Big Country* (London: Transworld, 1998, pp. 299–302).

11. Michael Moore, *Stupid White Men . . . and Other Sorry Excuses for the State of the Nation* (New York: HarperCollins, 2001).

12. Justin Martin, "Ignore Your Customer," *Fortune*, May 1, 1995, pp. 83–6; Paul Blumberg, *The Predatory Society: Deception in the American Marketplace* (New York: Oxford University Press, 1989); A. Larry Elliot and Richard J. Schroth, *How Companies Lie: Why Enron is Just the Tip of the Iceberg* (London: Nicholas Brealey, 2002); Manuel P. Asensio, *Sold Short: Uncovering Deception in the Markets* (New York: John Wiley, 2001).

13. Richard Johnson, "FoodFella," *Sunday Times Magazine*, July 14, 2002, pp. 52–9.

14. The best summary of the Beanie Babies phenomenon is contained in Pauline Maclaran and Alan Sangster, "Beanie Babies and The End – A Postmodern Perspective," *Proceedings of the Academy of Marketing Conference*, 2000. See also Gary Samuels, "Mystique Marketing," *Forbes*, October 21, 1996, pp.226–7; Benjamin Fulford, "Don't Flood the Market," *Forbes*, December 28, 1998, p.56; Holly Stowe and Carol Turkington, *The Complete Idiot's Guide to Beanie Babies* (New York: Alpha Books, 1998); Stephen Geraint, "The Meaning of Beanies," *The Times Weekend*, July 17, 1999, pp. 1–2; Nicholas Whittaker, *Toys Were Us: A Twentieth-Century History of Toys* (London: Orion, 2001).

15. For the obsessives among you, The Original Nine are Cubbie the Bear, Legs the Frog, Patti the Platypus, Spot the Dog, Squealer the Pig, Flash the Dolphin, Splash the Whale, Chocolate the Moose and Punchers the Lobster.

16. Gary Cross, *Kids' Stuff: Toys and the Changing World of American Childhood* (Cambridge, MA: Harvard University Press, 1997).

17. Stowe and Turkington, *The Complete Idiot's Guide to Beanie Babies*, op. cit., p. 12.

18. Maclaran and Sangster, op. cit.

19. Quoted in Samuels, "Mystique marketing," op. cit., p. 277.

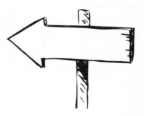

Do android marketers dream of fleecing the customer?

20. Some of the more imaginative Beanie lovers have noted Ty Inc's phonic resemblance to the Tyrrell Corporation in *Blade Runner*. Perhaps Ty's a rogue marketing replicant, unpredictable and a law unto himself. Do android marketers dream of fleecing the customer, I wonder?

21. William Shaw, "Bag Ladies," *Life, The Observer Magazine*, October 28, 2001, pp. 42; Karen Wheeler, "The Next Bag Thing," *Financial Times' How to Spend It*, March 2002, p. 55; Claudia Croft, "It's in the Bag," *Sunday Times Style*, March 24, 2002, p. 7; Michael Harvey, "Handbags at Dawn," *The Times Magazine*, September 7, 2002, pp. 54–7.

22. Angela Buttolph et al., *The Fashion Book* (New York: Phaidon, 1998); Georgina O'Hara Callan, *Fashion and Fashion Designers* (London: Thames & Hudson, 1998); Colin McDowell, *Fashion Today* (New York: Phaidon, 2000); Claire Wilcox, *Bags* (London: V&A Publications, 1999).

23. Shaw, "Bag Ladies," op. cit., p. 41.

24. "Coulda, Woulda, Shoulda," episode eleven of the fourth series (written by Jenny Bicks, directed by David Frankel).

25. Hermès contemporary cachet also owes much to the acumen of deconstructor-in-chief Martin Margiela. An edgy fashion designer, famous for combining unusual materials in an idiosyncratic, inside-out manner and for mounting shows in the most insalubrious venues, such as wastegrounds, disused metro stations, "secret" venues, and suchlike,

Margiela was brought in to oversee the repositioning of the brand in the mid-1990s. He succeeded triumphantly.

26. "Ford Thunderbird Sports Roadster Concept," www.ford.com.

27. James R. Healey, "Nostalgic T-bird is Fun, but Could Get Better," *USA Today*, June 8, 2001, p. 12D; Jim Mateja, "T-bird Cruises Back into Ford's Lineup," *Chicago Tribune*, May 27, 2001, Section 12, pp. 1, 10.

Lesson Two: How to Cope With Canny Customers

1. Ratnesar, Romesh, "Chaos Incorporated," *Time*, July 23, 2001, pp. 33–6; Emma Bircham and John Charlton, eds, *Anti-Capitalism: A Guide to the Movement* (London: Bookmarks, 2001); Jane Pavitt, ed., *Brand.New* (London: V&A Publications, 2000); Peter York, "Branded," *Times Magazine*, October 14, 2000, pp. 30–34.

2. Alexander Cockburn, Jeffrey St. Clair and Allan Sekula, *Five Days That Shook the World: Seattle and Beyond* (New York: Verso, 2000).

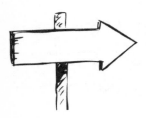

Generation ® is proving so popular that it has been formally registered and should be referred to as Generation ®®.

3. Kalle Lasn, *Culture Jam: How to Reverse America's Suicidal Consumer Binge – And Why We Must* (New York: Quill, 2000). Generation ® is pretty resonant, I'm sure you agree. Perhaps I should register the concept before greedy advertising agencies get their grubby mitts on it. From henceforth, therefore, Generation ® should be referred to as Generation ®®. Actually, Generation ®® is pretty good too. Maybe I should register that as well, just to be on the safe side. From this day forward, Generation ®® must be referred to as Generation ®®® (and so on ad infinitum). Ignore this injunction at your peril.

4. Michael Elliott, "Death in Genoa," *Time*, July 30, 2001, pp. 22–3; Aaron Bernstein et al., "Time to Regroup," *Business Week*, August 6, 2001, pp. 26–8; Rod Nordland and Christopher Dickey, "First Blood," *Newsweek*, July 30, 2001, pp. 20–3; James Harding, "I'm Ready to Fight...This is a War," *Financial Times*, July 21, 2001, p. 1.

5. José Bové and François Dufour, *The World is Not For Sale: Farmers Against Junk Food* (New York: Verso, 2001).

6. Noreena Hertz, *The Silent Takeover: Global Capitalism and the Death of Democracy* (London: Heinemann, 2001).

7. *The Economist*, "Brands: Who's Wearing the Trousers?" *The Economist*, September 8, 2001, pp. 26–8.

8. Naomi Klein, *No Logo: Taking Aim at the Brand Bullies* (London: HarperCollins, 2000). On Klein, see for example: Gaby Wood, "Look, No Brands . . ." *Observer Review*, November 12, 2000, p. 3; Marcel Knobil, "No Logo – No Comeback," *Observer Business*, December 3, 2000, p. 4; Katharine Viner, "Hand-to-Brand Combat," *Guardian Weekend*, September 23, 2000, pp. 12–21.

NOTES AND REFERENCES

9. *The Economist*, "Brands: Who's Wearing the Trousers?" op. cit., p. 26.

10. James Dugdale, "Diary," *Sunday Times Culture*, January 28, 2001, p. 37.

11. Quoted in *The Economist*, "Leaders: The Case for Brands," *The Economist*, September 8, 2001, p. 11.

12. Surely, it won't be long before No Logo T-shirt wearing protesters storm the offices of *No Logo*'s publisher and a bestselling book is written about the event. *No No Logo*, no doubt. Anyone for *No No No Logo . . . No No No No Logo . . .*?

13. *Financial Times*, "Corporate Social Responsibility," March 11, 2002, p.14; Mike Bygrave, "Where Did All the Protesters Go?" *Observer*, July 14, 2002, pp. 24–5; Marcia Vickers et al., "How Corrupt is Wall Street?" *Business Week*, May 13, 2002, pp. 34–40; Terry Slavin, "New Rules of Engagement," *Observer*, September 1, 2002, p.11; The Brookings Institute, *Corporate Social Responsibility* (Washington, DC: Brookings Institute, 2002).

14. Douglas B. Holt, "Poststructuralist Lifestyle Analysis: Conceptualizing the Social Patterning of Consumption in Postmodernity," *Journal of Consumer Research*, 23 (March), 1997, pp. 326–50; Douglas B. Holt, "Why Do Brands Cause Trouble? A Dialectical Theory of Consumer Culture and Branding," *Journal of Consumer Research*, 29 (1), 2002, pp. 70–90.

15. David Lewis, *The Soul of the New Consumer. Authenticity: What We Buy and Why in the New Economy* (London: Nicholas Brealey, 2000).

16. Christopher Parkes, "Real People Lift Ratings for US Broadcasters," *Financial Times*, September 7, 2002, p. 17.

17. Morris B. Holbrook, "The Millennial Consumer Enters the Age of Exhibitionism – A Book Review Essay, Part 2," *Consumption, Markets and Culture*, 5 (2), 2002, pp. 113–51.

18. Dalya Alberge, "Stuckists Give Their Rivals the Brush-off," *The Times*, July 20, 2002, p. 7.

19. Vanessa Juarez and Ana Figueroa, "Paging Dr Phil," *Newsweek*, September 16, 2002, p. 98.

20. Stephen Brown, *Postmodern Marketing* (London: Routledge, 1995)

21. Michael Bracewell, *The Nineties: When Surface Was Depth* (London: Flamingo, 2002, p. 50).

22. Stephen Brown and Anthony Patterson, "Knick-knack Paddy-whack, Give a Pub a Theme," *Journal of Marketing Management*, 16 (6), 2000, pp. 647–62.

23. Umberto Eco, *Reflections on The Name of The Rose* (London: Minerva, 1985).

24. This is analogous, in certain respects, to the point made by Alex Shaker in his novelistic analysis of the "post-ironic" consumer. See Free Gift 3.

25. Earls, *Welcome to the Creative Age*, op. cit., p. 62.

26. Stephen Brown, "The Retromarketing Revolution," *International Journal of Management Reviews*, 3 (4), 2001, pp. 303–20.

27. The literature on Starbucks is, well, voluminous. See for example, Nancy F. Koehn, *Brand New: How Entrepreneurs Earned Consumers' Trust from Wedgwood to Dell* (Boston, MA: Harvard Business School Press, 2001); Marc Gobé, *Emotional Branding: The New Paradigm for Connecting Brands to People* (New York: Allworth Press, 2001); Thomas Gad, *4-D Branding: Cracking the Corporate Code of the Network Economy* (Harlow: Financial Times Prentice Hall, 2001); Barry J. Gibbons, *Dream Merchants and HowBoys: Mavericks, Nutters and the Road to Business Success* (Oxford: Capstone, 2002); Mark Pendergrast, *Uncommon Grounds: The History of Coffee and How It Transformed Our World* (New York: Basic Books, 1999).

28. Howard Schultz, *Pour Your Heart Into It: How Starbucks Built a Company One Cup at a Time* (New York: Hyperion, 1997).

29. Mick Jackson, dir., *L.A. Story* (Hollywood, CA: Universal Studios, 1990).
30. Schultz adapted the "third place" concept from Ray Olderburg's classic book, *The Great Good Place: Cafes, Coffee Shops, Community Centers, Beauty Parlors, General Stores, Bars, Hangouts, and How They Get You Through the Day* (New York, Paragon, 1989).

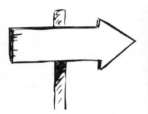

Howard Schultz adapted the "third place" concept from Ray Olderburg's classic book, *The Great Good Place*.

31. Alison Maitland, "Bitter Taste of Success," *Financial Times*, March 11, 2002, p. 14.
32. Oliver Burkeman and Emma Brockes, "Trouble Brewing," *Guardian G2*, December 3, 1999, pp. 1–3.
33. Maitland, "Bitter Taste of Success," op. cit., p. 14.
34. Quoted in Maitland, ibid.
35. Rushkoff, *Coercion*, op. cit; Jeffrey Robinson, *The Manipulators: A Conspiracy to Make Us Buy* (London: Simon and Schuster, 2000); D. Butler et al., "Attention All Shoppers," *Time*, August 2, 1999, pp. 38–43; Paco Underhill, *Why We Buy: The Science of Shopping* (New York: Orion, 1999); Gary Cross, *An All-Consuming Century: Why Commercialism Won in Modern America* (New York: Columbia University Press, 2000); James Twitchell, *AdCult USA: The Triumph of Advertising in American Culture* (New York; Columbia University Press, 1996).
36. Vance Packard, *The Hidden Persuaders* (New York: David McKay, 1957). On the impact of Packard's polemic, see Daniel Horowitz, *Vance Packard and American Social Criticism* (Chapel Hill: University of North Carolina Press, 1994), and Thomas Hine, *Populuxe: From Tailfins and TV Dinners to Barbie Dolls and Fallout Shelters* (New York: MJF Books, 1999).
37. Jonathan Bond and Richard Kirshenbaum, *Under the Radar: Talking to Today's Cynical Consumer* (New York: John Wiley, 1998, p. 92).
38. See, for example, the series of articles by Stephanie O'Donohoe: "Raiding the Postmodern Pantry: Advertising Intertextuality and the Young Adult Audience," *European Journal of Marketing* 31 (3/4), 1997, pp. 234–54; "Living With Ambivalence: Attitudes to Advertising in Postmodern Times," *Marketing Theory* 1 (1), 2001, pp. 91–108; "Beyond Sophistication: Dimensions of Advertising Literacy," *International Journal of Advertising* 17 (4), pp. 467–82 (with Caroline Tynan).
39. Stephen Brown, "Tradition on Tap: The Mysterious Case of Caffrey's Irish Ale," *The Marketing Review*, 1 (2), 2000, pp. 137–63.
40. Quoted by Jane Pavitt, "Diesel: For Successful Branding?" in Jane Pavitt, ed., *Brand.new* (London; V&A Publications, 2000, p. 64). On Diesel generally: Angela Buttolph et al., *The Fashion Book*, op. cit.; Georgina O'Hara Callan, *Fashion and Fashion Designers*, op. cit.; Colin McDowell, *Fashion Today*, op. cit.; Ted Polhemus, *Diesel: World Wide Wear* (London: Thames & Hudson, 1998). Diesel, incidentally, has recently addressed the hypocrisy of anti-capitalist riots – the ad depicts protesters holding up pro-Diesel placards – thereby adding another intriguing twist to marketer-consumer counterpoint.

41. Martin, "Ignore Your Customer," op. cit.
42. Clayton M. Christensen, *The Innovator's Dilemma: When New Technologies Cause Great Firms to Fail* (Boston, MA: Harvard Business School Press, 1997). See also Geoffrey A. Moore, *Crossing the Chasm: Marketing and Selling Technology Products to Mainstream Customers* (New York: Capstone, 1998); Fiona Harvey, "Dare to be Different," *Financial Times*, October 1, 2002, pp. 10–11.
43. Martin, "Ignore Your Customer," op. cit.
44. Lois Rogers, "Heart Pumps to Help Patients in Transplant Queue," *Sunday Times*, March 3, 2003, p. 15.

Lesson Three: How to Handle How-to Marketing Books

1. Marianne Wilson, "Levi's Fashions a New Attitude," *Chain Store Age*, 75 (10), October 1999, pp. 134–6; Owen Thomas, "The Perfect Fit," *Time Digital Magazine*, 4 (6), 1999, p. 1.
2. Ed Cray, *Levi's* (Boston: Houghton Mifflin, 1978); Graham Marsh and Paul Trynka, *Denim: From Cowboys to Catwalks – A Visual History of the World's Most Legendary Fabric* (London: Aurum Press, 2002).
3. www.levistrauss.com; Wilson, "Levi's Fashions a New Attitude," op. cit.
4. www.levi.com/original_spin
5. Don Peppers and Martha Rogers, *The One to One Future: Building Relationships One Customer at a Time* (New York: Bantam, 1993).
6. Jean Baudrillard, *The Illusion of the End*, trans. Chris Turner (London: Polity, 1992). See also Oliver Bennett, *Cultural Pessimism: Narratives of Decline in the Postmodern World* (Edinburgh: Edinburgh University Press, 2001); Nicholas Campion, *The Great Year: Astrology, Millenarianism and History in the Western Tradition* (New York: Penguin, 1994); Morris Berman, *The Twilight of American Culture* (New York: W.W. Norton, 2000).
7. Jack Trout, *Big Brands, Big Trouble: Lessons Learned the Hard Way* (New York: John Wiley, 2001).

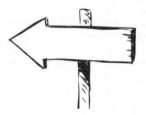

A delivery schedule that was closer to Pony Express than Federal Express.

8. It must be stressed that far from all of Levi's problems were customerization related. True, the Original Spin venture was an extremely expensive experiment. It antagonized traditional channel partners, most notably Sears and Penney's, and created all sorts of logistical headaches. What's more, the bells-and-whistles body scanning technology, which was supposed to capture detailed consumer data for customized products and analogous micro-marketing purposes, turned out to be rather less efficient than the good old-fashioned tape measure. The company's so-called "Customer Service Supply Chain," an ambitious $850million re-engineering operation that involved the construction of five new distribution centers and the reorganization of just about everything else, was an

equally expensive folly. It not only increased Levi's distribution costs drastically but slowed retailer restocking to 27 days, a delivery schedule that was closer to Pony Express than Federal Express. Levi's lack of consistency in its communications strategy – the late 90s were characterized by constant chopping and changing – coupled with associated PR disasters and competitors' understandable determination to capitalize on the corporation's evident confusion, also added to the iconic organization's woes. These are excellently dissected in Trout, *Big Brands, Big Trouble*, op. cit., pp. 67–75.

9. Laura Craik, "The Rebirth of Cool," *Guardian G2*, October 22, 1999, pp. 10–11; Alice Z. Cuneo, "Levi's Makes Move to Drop All Hype and Push Products," *Advertising Age*, April 17, 2000, pp. 4, 69; Jane Simms, "When Brands Bounce Back," *Marketing*, February 15, 2001, pp. 26–7; Louise Lee, "Can Levi's Be Cool Again?" *Business Week*, March 13, 2000, pp. 144–8.

10. Chris Sanderson, "New Old Levi's," *Esquire*, September 2002, pp. 46–50.

11. Sergio Zyman, *The End of Marketing as We Know It* (New York: HarperCollins, 1999).

12. Regis McKenna, *Total Access: Giving Customers What They Want in an Anytime, Anywhere World* (Boston, MA: Harvard Business School Press, 2002).

13. Elliott Ettenberg, *The Next Economy: Will You Know Where Your Customers Are?* (New York: McGraw-Hill, 2002).

14. Bernd H. Schmitt, *Experential Marketing* (New York: Free Press, 1999); B Joseph Pine II and James H. Gilmore, *The Experience Economy: Work is Theatre and Every Business a Stage* (Boston, MA: Harvard Business School Press, 1999).

15. John F. Sherry, Jr., ed., *Servicescapes: The Concept of Place in Contemporary Markets* (Chicago: NTC Books, 1998); Stephen Brown and John F. Sherry, Jr., eds, *Time, Space, and the Market* (New York: M.E. Sharpe, 2002).

16. Paul Dickinson and Neil Svensen, *Beautiful Corporations: Corporate Style in Action* (London: Pearson, 2000); Bernd Schmitt and Alex Simonson, *Marketing Aesthetics: The Strategic Management of Brands, Identity, and Image* (New York: Free Press, 1997).

17. Emanuel Rosen, *The Anatomy of Buzz: Creating Word-of-Mouth Marketing* (New York: Doubleday, 2000); Seth Godin, *Unleashing the Ideavirus*, Dobbs Ferry: Do You Zoom, 2000).

18. Why stop at greed? See Marc Lewis, *Sin to Win: Seven Deadly Steps to Success* (Oxford: Capstone, 2002); Jesper Kunde, *Corporate Religion: Building a Strong Company Through Personality and Corporate Soul* (London: Pearson, 2000); Andrew Finan, *Corporate Christ* (Chilford: Management Books, 1998).

19. Anita Roddick, *Business as Unusual: The Triumph of Anita Roddick* (London: Thorsons, 2001); Ben Cohen and Jerry Greenfield, *Ben and Jerry's Double-Dip: How to Run a Values-led Business and Make Money, Too* (New York: Fireside, 1998).

20. Luke Sullivan, *"Hey, Whipple, Squeeze This." A Guide to Creating Great Ads* (New York: John Wiley, 1998); Adam Morgan, *Eating the Big Fish: How Challenger Brands Can Compete Against Brand Leaders* (New York, John Wiley, 1999).

21. Peter Doyle, *Value-Based Marketing: Marketing Strategies for Corporate Growth and Shareholder Value* (Chichester: John Wiley, 2000); Tim Ambler, *Marketing and the Bottom Line: The New Metrics of Corporate Wealth* (London: Financial Times Prentice Hall, 2000).

22. John Grant, *The New Marketing Manifesto: The 12 Rules for Building Successful Brands in the 21st Century* (London: Orion, 1999).

23. Philip Kotler, Dipak C. Jain, and Suvit Maesincee, *Marketing Moves: A New Approach to Profits, Growth, and Renewal* (Boston, MA: Harvard Business School Press, 2002, p. 27).

24. A particularly fine example of this perspective is Patricia B. Seybold, *The Customer Revolution: How to Thrive When Customers Are in Control* (New York, Business Books, 2002). The *reductio ad absurdum*, however, is surely the "prosumer" movement. Prosumers are members of the general public, recruited by marketers as putative new product developers. They come up with innovative ideas and pass judgement on the ideas of others. P&G sets great store by the prosumer, apparently, and several specialist providers, such as Infonic and Added Value, also exist. While prosumption undoubtedly has its place, not least as a

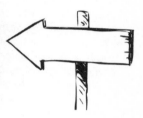

> It's a bit like asking heart transplant patients to come up with a better way of doing a triple bypass.

brand loyalty building exercise, the NPD prowess of consumers is debatable at best and negligible at worst. Consumers, in general, are ill-equipped to make meaningful marketing contributions. Richard Munn, co-founder of much-admired, multi-award-winning design consultancy, WHM, puts it this way: "We don't allow ourselves to get swayed by democracy. Consumers do not have a vision. Designers have the esthetic sense, not shoppers. People tend to want what they already have, until you show them something different." As De Capote notes, "It's a bit like asking heart transplant patients to come up with a better way of doing a triple bypass." (See Conor Dignam, "Prosumer Power," *Marketing*, March 14, 2002, pp. 24–5; Fiona Harvey, "Dare to be Different," *Financial Times Creative Business*, October 1, 2002, pp. 10–11; Roger De Capote, "Kreative Konsumers," *Marketing Week*, September 12, 2002, p. 31.)

25. Shira P. White, *New Ideas About New Ideas: Insights on Creativity from the World's Leading Innovators* (New York: Financial Times Prentice Hall, 2002); Robert I. Sutton, *Weird Ideas That Work: 11$^1/_2$ Ways to Promote, Manage, and Sustain Innovation* (New York: Penguin, 2001).

26. The conventional approach to arts marketing is exemplified by Philip Kotler and Julia Scheff, *Standing Room Only: Strategies for Marketing the Performing Arts* (Boston, MA: Harvard Business School Press, 1997). An alternative standpoint is argued by many of the contributors to Stephen Brown and Anthony Patterson, eds, *Imagining Marketing: Art, Aesthetics, and the Avant-Garde* (London: Routledge, 2000).

27. Quoted in Chris Roberts, "On the Other Hand There's a Fist," *Uncut* 53, October 2001, pp. 88–90.

28. Alex Shakar, *The Savage Girl* (New York: HarperCollins, 2001).

29. Shakar, ibid., p. 51.

30. Stephen Brown, *Marketing: The Retro Revolution* (London: Sage, 2001).

31. Patent medicine purveyors, for example, were the *experiential* marketers of the late nineteenth century; Marshall Field was a past master of in-store *environment* creation; Maxfield Parrish espoused marketing *esthetics* long before Bernd Schmitt was born; the history of marketing *ephemerality* reveals that it is anything but (think door-to-door selling, periodic markets, itinerant peddlers, etc.); the founder of BBDP, Bruce Barton, was

evangelizing in the mid-1920s; the "truth in advertising" movement, an *ethical* eschewal of hard sell tactics, predates the First World War; forty-odd years ago, Jerry della Famina had *eccentricity* off pat, as evinced by his arrestingly titled autobiography, *From Those Wonderful Folks Who Gave You Pearl Harbor*; and marketers' $E = MC^2$ mentality, the belief that marketing is a science, or on the cusp of becoming one, is seventy-five years old if it's a day.

32. Philip Kotler's contributions to marketing thought are considered in Stephen Brown, "The Specter of Kotlerism," *European Management Journal*, 20 (2), 2002, pp. 129–46.

33. Quoted in Earls, *Welcome to the Creative Age*, op. cit., p. 62.

34. On the increasingly identikit nature of contemporary brands, see for example: Kevin Keller "The Brand Report Card," in *Harvard Business Review on Marketing* (Boston, MA: Harvard Business School Press, 2002, pp. 1–24). The Clone Radio quote is from Queens of the Stone Age, *Songs For the Deaf* (Los Angeles: Interscope Records, 2002).

35. Al Ries and Jack Trout, *Positioning: The Battle for Your Mind* (New York: McGraw-Hill, 1981).

36. Derek Ralston, "False Assumptions," *Financial Times Creative Business*, September 10, 2002, p. 15.

37. The literature on Elbert is somewhat limited. An excellent overview is contained in Alf H. Walle and Marcella Brimo "From Soap to Society: Elbert Hubbard and his Saga of Selling" in Stanley C. Hollander and Terence Nevett, eds, *Marketing in the Long Run* (East Lansing: Michigan State University, 1985, pp. 239–256). See also Freeman Champney, *Art and Glory: The Story of Elbert Hubbard* (Kent, OH: Kent State University Press, 1983), and Marie Via and Marjorie Searl, eds, *Head, Heart and Hand: Elbert Hubbard and the Roycrofters* (Rochester, NY: University of Rochester Press, 1994).

38. The great and good replied with disdainful condescension, which The Mother of All Hubbards readily reprinted and gleefully glossed, while watching *The Philistine*'s circulation figures mount rapidly. Parodies proliferated – such as *The Bilioustine* by minor poet B.L. Taylor – as did scholarly mockeries of his over-the-top stylistic excesses.

39. After selling his share of Larkin Soap in 1895, Elbert traveled the capitals of Europe, where he encountered the work of William Morris and the Arts and Crafts movement. Inspired by Morris's Kelmscott experiment, Hubbard established Roycroft on his return and everything he did thereafter – pamphlets, periodicals, publicity – was designed to keep Roycroft in the limelight.

40. A colophon, by the way, is a printer's mark, one of which served as Roycroft's distinctive logo. A colophon is also an inscription at the end of many medieval books, somewhat akin to contemporary Acknowledgements, containing details of the title, author, date of publication, and so forth. Hubbard's books often contained rococo colophons – Here endeth our Little Journey, written at the desk of Fra Elbert, in the sleepy hamlet of East Aurora, etc. – and parodists had a field day with this aspect of his output.

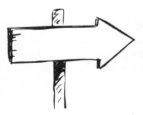

There is room in business for all your religion, all your poetry, all your love.

41. Certainly, Hubbard's spiritual approach to doing business is very much in keeping with twenty-first century sentiment. Consider for example: "When I want to hear really good sermons nowadays, we attend a weekly lunch of the ad club, and listen to a man who deals in ways and means and is intent in bringing about paradise, here and now," "There is room in business for all your religion, all your poetry, all your love;" "Business is beautiful and it is fast becoming so." His extensive writings are still in print. A useful assemblage can be found in *The Philosophy of Elbert Hubbard* (Kila, MT: Kessinger Publishing, reprint of Roycrofter original, 1930).

42. From a marketing perspective, it made eminent sense to publish such material under the Hubbard brand name – any number of celebrity authors operate similar policies these days – but, from the literary–scholarly standpoint of the time, it represented a scandalous affront.

43. Quoted in Walle and Brimo, "From Soap to Society," op. cit., p. 253.

Now That's What I Call Marketing #1

1. Marwood Darlington, *Irish Orpheus: The Life of Patrick S. Gilmore, Bandmaster Extraordinary* (Philadelphia: Olivier Maney Klien, 1950). The wider musical context is comprehensively covered in Ronald L. Davis's three-volume study, *A History of Music in American Life* (Huntington, NY: Krieger, 1980).

2. Neil Harris, "John Philip Sousa and the Culture of Reassurance," in Neil Harris, *Cultural Excursions: Marketing Appetites and Cultural Tastes in Modern America* (Chicago: University of Chicago Press, 1990, pp. 198–232).

3. Adam Carse, *The Life of Jullien: Adventurer, Showman-Conductor and Establisher of the Promenade Concerts in England, Together With a History of Those Concerts up to 1895* (Cambridge: W. Heffer and Sons, 1951).

4. Darlington, *Irish Orpheus*, op. cit., pp. 54–5.

5. Davis, *A History of Music in American Life, Volume II – The Gilded Years, 1865–1920*, op. cit., p. 4.

6. Darlington's somewhat hagiographic biography underplays the professional disaster that was the World Peace Jubilee. The true situation is described by Davis, ibid., pp. 3–5.

7. There are several excellent, if rather dated, biographies of Lillian Russell. For example: Parker Morell, *Lillian Russell: The Era of Plush* (Garden City, NY: Garden City Publishing, 1943); James Brough, *Miss Lillian Russell: A Novel Memoir* (New York: McGraw-Hill, 1978); John Burke, *Duet in Diamonds* (New York: G.P. Putnam's, 1972).

8. Quoted in Burke, *Duet in Diamonds*, op. cit., pp. 23, 24.

9. Quoted in Morell, *Lillian Russell*, op. cit., p. 165.

Lesson Four: How to Trump the Trick-or-Treat

1. Donald J. Trump with Tony Schwartz, *The Art of the Deal* (New York: Random House, 1987, p. 123).

2. Trump, ibid., p. 36.

3. For general biographical background on The Donald, see: Gwenda Blair, *The Trumps: Three Generations That Built an Empire* (New York: Simon and Schuster, 2000); John R. O'Donnell, *Trumped! The Inside Story of the Real Donald Trump – His Cunning Rise and Spectacular Fall* (New York: Simon and Schuster, 1991); Harry Hurt III, *Lost Tycoon: The*

Many Lives of Donald Trump (New York: Norton, 1993); Mark Singer, "Trump Solo," in David Remnick, ed., *The New Gilded Age:* The New Yorker *Looks at the Culture of Affluence* (New York: Random House, 2000, pp. 43–64).

4. When I originally wrote this sentence in mid-2002, it read: "He has his name on more buildings than McDonald's." Then, characteristically, The Donald got his name on McDonald's as well, thanks to his contribution to the company's "Big'N'Tasty" campaign, which commenced in October 2002. The McDonald, as ever, is ahead of the curve.

5. In addition to *The Art of the Deal*, Trump has written several book-length updates, which disburse his trademark combination of autobiography and how-to business advice: Donald J. Trump with Charles Leerhsen, *Trump: Surviving at the Top* (New York, Random House, 1990); Donald J. Trump with Kate Bohner, *Trump: The Art of the Comeback* (New York: Times Books, 1997); Donald J. Trump with Dave Shiflett, *Trump: The America We Deserve* (Los Angeles, Renaissance Books, 2000).

6. As, for example, in Chicago during 2001. See Abigail Rayner, "The Sky's Still the Limit for Trump" *Times*, August 9, 2002, p. 29; Blair, *The Trumps*, op. cit.

7. Trump, *The Art of the Deal*, op. cit., p. 37.

8. There is a prodigious academic literature on tricksterism. See, for example, Lewis Hyde, *Trickster Makes This World: Mischief, Myth, and Art* (New York: Farrar, Straus and Giroux, 1998); William J. Hynes and William G. Doty, eds, *Mythical Trickster Figures* (Tuscaloosa: University of Alabama Press, 1993); Zeese Papanikolas, *Trickster in the Land of Dreams* (Lincoln: University of Nebraska Press, 1995); Lori Landay, *Madcaps, Screwballs and Con Women: The Female Trickster in American Culture* (Philadelphia: University of Pennsylvania Press, 1998); Beatrice K. Otto, *Fools Are Everywhere: The Court Jester Around the World* (Chicago: University of Chicago Press, 2001).

9. For an excellent discussion of marketing and tricksterism, check out Kent Grayson, "The Dangers and Opportunities of Playful Consumption," in Morris B. Holbrook, ed., *Customer Value: A Framework for Analysis and Research* (New York: Routledge, 1999, pp. 105–25). Incidentally, "sizzle" and "servility" refer to two main schools of marketing thought. The "modern" marketing concept of Phil Kotler, Ted Levitt, and Peter Drucker is predicated on servility. The "premodern" marketing concept of P.T. Barnum and Harry Reichenbach (see Tango below) is premised on sizzling. Today's "postmodern" marketing concept represents a tongue-in-cheek return to the sizzling marketease of yesteryear.

10. Earl Shorris, *A Nation of Salesmen: The Tyranny of the Market and the Subversion of Culture* (New York: Avon, 1994). Also, Cynthia Crossen, *Tainted Truth: The Manipulation of Fact in America* (New York: Touchstone, 1996); Blumberg, *The Predatory Society*, op. cit.; Rushkoff, *Coercion*, op. cit.

11. John Heilemann, "Machine of Dreams," *Vanity Fair*, May 2002, pp. 120–4, 158–66. Also www.segway.com

12. Alfred Lubrano, "An Inventor's Project Starts a National Buzz," *Philadelphia Inquirer*, January 21, 2001, p. 1; Joseph P. Shapiro and Nancy Shute, "The Ginger Riddle: What is the Greatest Thing Since Sliced Bread?" January 22, 2001, www.usnews.com; CBS News, "The Wizard of IT," February 6, 2001, www.cbsnews.com

13. Troy Wolverton, "Amazon Takes Orders for 'Ginger'," January 27, 2001, www.seattletimes.com

14. Al Ries and Laura Ries, *The Fall of Advertising and the Rise of PR* (New York: HarperBusiness, 2002).

15. Heilemann, "Machine of Dreams," op. cit., p. 122.

16. *The Economist*, "Is that IT?" December 6, 2001, www.economist.com

17. Heilemann, "Machine of Dreams," op. cit., p. 165.

18. At the time of writing (Feburary 2003), the Segway is still unavailable to the general public, though extensive trials are allegedly underway in the B2B market (US Mail, police forces, municipal services, etc.). The omens thus far are not good. Several cities have cited it as a potential traffic hazard, a number of senior executives have quit the ailing company, and the reported price point-cum-distribution strategy seems, well, somewhat quirky ($4,950, only available through Amazon.com). See Faith Keenan, "Is Segway Going Anywhere?" *Business Week*, January 27, 2003, p. 43; John Harlow, "Hollywood Called Up to Kickstart Super-Scooter," *Sunday Times*, January 26, 2003, p.24.

19. Barnum's version of "What is It?" is covered in most biographies of the great impresario. For more detailed discussion, see James W. Cook, *The Arts of Deception: Playing With Fraud in the Age of Barnum* (Cambridge, MA: Harvard University Press, 2001, esp. Chapter 3, "Describing the Nondescript").

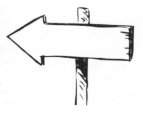

He came not from the wilds of New Guinea but from the wilds of New Jersey.

20. In reality, "What is It?" was a "microcephalic black dwarf" called William Henry Johnson (Philip B. Kunhardt et al., *P.T. Barnum: America's Greatest Showman*, New York: Knopf, 1995, p. 149). By all accounts, Johnson was an affable, urbane, and well-spoken gentleman, who disdained the credulous audiences that unfailingly fell for Barnum's tomfoolery. He came not from the wilds of New Guinea but from the wilds of New Jersey. His performance was carefully scripted; his appearance was altered to emphasise its "bestiality"; he was taught a "jungle language" newly invented by the imperishable impresario; and, although he remained a staple of the Barnum and Bailey sideshow for decades thereafter, Johnson never revealed the master marketer's trickery.

21. Papanikolas, *Trickster in the Land of Dreams*, op. cit.

22. William Castle, *Step Right Up! I'm Gonna Scare the Pants Off America* (New York: Putnam's, 1976).

23. Candice Jacobson Fuhrman, *Publicity Stunt: Great Staged Events That Made the News* (San Francisco, CA: Chronicle Books, 1989), pp. 58–9.

24. Ralph Rugoff, "Keep on Taking the Tableaux," *Financial Times Weekend*, October 30, 1999, p. vii.

25. Ed Vuilliamy, "If This is Art, I'm an Elephant," *Observer*, March 26, 2000, p. 9.

26. JoAnn Wypijewski, *Painting By Numbers: Komar and Melamid's Scientific Guide to Art* (Berkeley: University of California Press, 1997).

27. Wypijewski, ibid., p. 75.

28. HHCL, *Tango 1991–2001: Ten Years of Disruption* (London, HHCL Report, 2002). Also, Grant, *The New Marketing Manifesto*, op. cit., pp. 212–16; Earls, *Welcome to the Creative Age*, op. cit., pp. 102–3.

29. Warren Berger, *Advertising Today* (New York: Phaidon, 2001).

30. Brown, *Postmodern Marketing*, op. cit.

31. Grant, *The New Marketing Manifesto*, op. cit., p. 123.

32. Brilliantly effective though this prank proved, it is by no means original. The peerless press agent Harry Reichenbach got there first. In the early days of the movies, individual motion pictures had to be sold to distributors and exhibitors. Given the glut of

This box holds the thing most dear to both of us.

all-but-identical products, this was an extremely hard sell. Reichenbach, nevertheless, rose to the challenge by means of an innovative direct mailing. As he explains in is auto-biography, "Each exhibitor received a personal letter on hotel stationery written in a femi-nine hand addressed him by his first name. It said in part, 'I know you never expected to hear from me again, dear, but I couldn't help it. I am sending you this key and in the next few days you will receive a box which it will unlock. This box holds the thing most dear to both of us. I know when you receive it you will act like a man. Until then, as ever, Your Natalie'" (Harry Reichenbach, *Phantom Fame*, New York: Simon and Schuster, 1931, p. 147). Harry let the exhibitors stew for a while – one apparently confessed to an extra-marital fling, others wracked their brains about the mysterious Natalie – then took out massive ads in a movie trade paper. These contained the secret box; the key opened the box; and inside lay another ad for National Pictures Inc (or "Natalie," as it was popu-larly known).

33. Sales figures quoted in Branwell Johnson, "Buried Treasure," *Marketing Week*, April 25, 2002, pp. 22–5.

34. Richard Lacayo, "Search for a Perfect Pitch," *Time*, July 23, 2001, p. 45; Teresa Howard, "Freebies Take on Brash New Form," *USA Today*, May 15, 2001, pp. B1–2.

35. The psychology of claquing is considered by Robert B. Cialdini, *Influence: Science and Practice* (Boston: Allyn and Bacon, 2001, pp. 134–6).

36. As Cook puts it in his detailed study of artful deception, "none of the tricksters . . . simply peddled deception as an end in itself . . . the deception always involved at least a modi-cum of narrative – an entertaining story that delivered the trick." (*The Arts of Deception*, op. cit., p. 17).

37. Leslie Miller, "Locked In and Can't Go Back," *USA Today*, May 29, 2001, p. 3D. On the gen-eral problem of striking the right balance, see for example Michael McCarthy, "Recent Crop of Sneaky Ads Backfires," *USA Today*, July 17, 2001, p. 3B; Edward Iwata, "Officials Say Deceptive Tech Advertising On Rise," *USA Today*, May 29, 2001, p. B1.

38. The 419 Fraud takes its name from the eponymous article of the Nigerian penal code. It is an online scam which promises "investors" a percentage of millions of dollars allegedly stuck in Nigerian bank accounts, accounts that can only be released by bribing govern-

ment officials. The victim is asked to pay an upfront fee, or "transfer tax," in order to help grease the necessary palms. But payouts never arrive. The only return an investor sees is additional requests for further financial advances. This continues until the patsy catches on. The 419 Fraud is Nigeria's fourth biggest industry, apparently. The South African Reserve Bank bilk is a variation on the same theme. See Peter Warren, "Online Fraud: The Nigerian Sting," *The Business*, August 19, 2002, p.24; Conal Walsh, "Fraud That Will not Die," *Observer*, September 29, 2002, p. 3; *The Economist*, "Scam of Scams," *The Economist*, August 24, 2002, p. 62.

39. Trump, *The Art of the Deal*, op. cit., p. 41.

40. Benjamin Franklin's fondness for tomfoolery is summarized in Gordon Stein and Marie J. MacNee, *Hoaxes! Dupes, Dodges, & Other Dastardly Deceptions* (Detroit, MI: Visible Ink, 1995, pp. 127–30).

41. Harold Bloom, *Genius: A Mosaic of One Hundred Exemplary Creative Minds* (London: Fourth Estate, 2002).

42. Terence Brown, *The Life of W.B. Yeats* (Dublin: Gill & Macmillan, 1999).

43. Aedh Aherne, "Chronicles of the Celtic Marketing Circle, Part I: The Paradise Parchment," *Marketing Intelligence and Planning*, 18 (6/7), 2000, pp. 400–413.

44. Stephen Brown and Anthony Patterson, "A Taste of Paradise," special double issue of *Marketing Intelligence & Planning*, 18 (6/7), 2000.

45. Fuhrman, *Publicity Stunt*, op. cit.

Lesson Five: How to Employ Exclusivity Effectively

1. Susan Dobscha and Ellen Foxman, "Women and Wedding Gowns: Exploring a Discount Shopping Experience," in Eileen Fischer and Daniel L. Wardlow, eds, *Gender, Marketing and Consumer Behavior*, Fourth Conference Proceedings (San Francisco: Assocation for Consumer Research, 1998, pp. 131–41).

2. George E. Berkley, *The Filenes* (New York: Branden, 1998).

3. Cialdini, *Influence*, op. cit., p. 205.

4. Cialdini, ibid., pp. 203–32.

5. Fulford, "Don't Flood the Market," op. cit.

6. Fulford, ibid., p. 56.

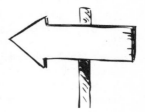

A fine description of the boiler room experience is contained in *Trading With the Enemy.*

7. A fine description of the boiler room experience is contained in Nicholas W. Maier, *Trading With the Enemy: Seduction and Betrayal on Jim Cramer's Wall Street* (New York: HarperBusiness, 2002). See also, Robert J. Stevenson, *The Boiler Room and Other Telephone Sales Scams* (Urbana: University of Illinois Press, 1998).

8. Cialdini, *Influence*, op. cit., p. 205.

9. Stephen Brown, *Songs of the Humpback Shopper (and Other Bazaar Ballads)*, www.sfxbrown.com. On eBay see, Randall E. Stross, *eBoys* (New York, Crown, 2000).

10. *Newsweek, The World in 2012, Newsweek*, special double issue, September 16–23, 2002.

11. Scott B. Pruden, "Krispy Kremes: The Sweetest Sacrament," May 27, 2001, www.waysouth.com; Theresa Howard, "Who Needs Ads When You've Got Hot Doughnuts Now?" *USA Today*, May 31, 2001, p. 3B; company history and financial figures available from www.kkd.com

12. Ries and Ries, *The Fall of Advertising*, op. cit., p. 135.

13. On cult brands generally, see: Melanie Wells, "Cult Brands," *Forbes*, April 16, 2001, pp. 198–205; Robert V. Kozinets, "Utopian Enterprise: Articulating the Meanings of *Star Trek*'s Culture of Consumption," *Journal of Consumer Research*, 28 (June), 2001, pp. 67–88; John W. Schouten and James H. McAlexander, "Subcultures of Consumption: An Ethnography of the New Bikers," *Journal of Consumer Research*, 22 (June), 1995, pp. 43–61.

14. *The Economist*, "One-downmanship," *The Economist*, September 14, 2002, p. 74.

15. Matthew Hart, *Diamond: The History of a Cold-Blooded Love Affair* (London: Fourth Estate, 2002).

16. Hart, ibid., p. 138.

17. James B. Twitchell, *Living It Up: Our Love Affair With Luxury* (New York: Columbia University Press, 2002).

18. James B. Twitchell, "De Beers: A Good Campaign is Forever," in James B. Twitchell, *Twenty Ads That Shook the World* (New York: Three Rivers, 2000, pp. 88–101).

19. Hart, *Diamond*, op. cit.

20. Greg Campbell, *Blood Diamonds: Tracing the Deadly Path of the World's Most Precious Stones* (Boulder, CO: Westview, 2002).

21. Wells, "Cult Brands," op. cit. See also Emily Davies, "Preppy Tommy Comes Back From the Ghetto," *The Times T2*, March 24, 2003, p. 11. The Lexus dilemma is discussed in Chester Dawson, "Lexus' Big Test. Can it Keep its Cachet and Appeal to the Young?" *BusinessWeek*, March 24, 2003, pp. 48–51.

22. Wells, ibid., p. 203.

23. Cialdini, *Influence*, op. cit., p. 79

24. Ridderstrale and Nordstrom, *Funky Business*, op. cit., pp. 76–84.

25. Robert H. Frank, *Luxury Fever: Why Money Fails to Satisfy in an Era of Excess* (New York: Free Press, 1999).

26. Sara Gay Forden, *The House of Gucci: A Sensational Story of Murder, Madness, Glamour and Greed* (New York: HarperCollins, 2000); de Agostini UK Ltd, *Fragrance and Fashion* (Enderby: Silverdale, 2000); Angela Buttolph et al., *The Fashion Book*, op. cit.; Georgina O'Hara Callan, *Fashion and Fashion Designers*, op. cit.

27. Kevin Drawbaugh, "Back From the Brink: Gucci and Brand Rescue," in *Brands in the Balance*, op. cit., pp. 182–98.

28. By the middle of 2002, however, rumors were circulating that Gucci had over-extended the brand once again. See for example, Ben Bold, "Is Gucci for the Masses Damaging the Brand?" *Marketing*, October 10, 2002, p. 15.

29. Drawbaugh, op. cit., p.184.

30. Alden Hatch, *American Express 1850–1950: A Century of Service* (Garden City, NJ: Country Life, 1950); Peter Z. Grossman, *American Express: The Unofficial History of the People Who Built the Great Financial Empire* (New York: Crown, 1987); Jon Friedman and John Meehan, *House of Cards; Inside the Troubled Empire of American Express* (New York: Putnam, 1992).

31. The inside story of the marketing campaign behind the inaugural Amex card launch is told in Lester Wunderman, *Being Direct: Making Advertising Pay* (New York: Random House, 1996).

32. George Ritzer, *Expressing America: A Critique of the Global Credit Card Society* (Thousand Oaks, CA: Pine Forge, 1995).

33. Friedman and Meehan, *House of Cards*, op. cit.

34. Ritzer, *Expressing America*, op. cit., p. 41.

35. Jean-Marie Dru, *Beyond Disruption: Changing the Rules in the Marketplace* (New York: John Wiley, 2002).

36. *The Economist*, "American Express Catch Up," *The Economist*, April 24, 1997, www.economist.com

37. Only joking! To paraphrase rock music journalist Joe Queenan, if you're asking *me* for advice, your brand must *really* be in trouble.

38. Nicholas Wapshott, "Why Canaries Are Flying Off Their Perch," *The Times*, November 2, 2001, p. 3.

Lesson Six: How to AMPLIFY

1. Jeevan Vasagar, "Amusement at Cleaner's Judgement on Hirst's Art," *Guardian*, October 20, 2001, pp. 1, 20.

2. *Guardian*, "The Art of Rubbish: You Couldn't Make It Up – Or Could You?" *Guardian*, October 20, 2001, p. 23.

3. Although *Untitled* may be the most cost-effective of Damien Hirst's publicity stunts, it is by no means the most dramatic. That honor goes to *Hymn*, an exact replica of a child's anatomical toy. The bright plastic plaything, a cut-away of the human torso complete with internal organs, eye sockets, and cranial cavity, is manufactured by Hasbro and retails at $24. Hirst, however, cast a 20-foot-high version of it in bronze, sold the piece for $2.2 million to Charles Saatchi, and generated more free publicity than Richard Branson in his pomp.

4. For biographical background on Damien Hirst, see for example: Julian Stallabrass, *High Art Lite: British Art in the 1990s* (London: Verso, 1999); Matthew Collings, *Blimey! From Bohemia to Britpop: The London Artworld From Francis Bacon to Damien Hirst* (London: 21 Publishing, 1997); Matthew Collings, *Art Crazy Nation: The Post-Blimey! Art World* (London: 21 Publishing, 2001). Also useful is the series of interviews, Damien Hirst and Gordon Burn, *On the Way to Work* (London: Faber and Faber, 2001).

5. Not least Hirst's debauched publicity stunts. He has variously opened a theme restaurant which displayed his abbatoiral acumen to startling effect; released several disgustatory singles with rock band Fat Les; published a deeply pretentious autobiography, *I Want to Spend the Rest of My Life Everywhere With Everyone, One to One, Always, Forever, Now*; and, at all times, worked on his pants-dropping, cigarette-puffing, cheeky-chappie, gutter-press-pleasing artistic persona.

6. John A. Walker, *Art and Outrage: Provocation, Controversy and the Visual Arts* (Sterling, VA: Pluto, 1999); Anthony Julius, *Transgressions: The Offence of Art* (London: Thames and Hudson, 2002).

7. John Seabrook, *Nobrow: The Culture of Marketing – The Marketing of Culture* (New York: Knopf, 2000).

271

8. Stephen Brown and Anthony Patterson, "Figments for Sale: Marketing, Imagination and the Artistic Imperative," in Stephen Brown and Anthony Patterson, *Imagining Marketing*, op. cit., pp. 4–32.

9. Hirst and Burn, *On the Way to Work*, op. cit., p. 105.

10. In mid-2002, one of Hirst's signature spot paintings was sent into deep space, much to the amusement of newspaper columnists.

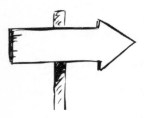

We live in a post-PR world.

11. A similar argument is made by Ries and Ries in *The Fall of Advertising and the Rise of PR*, though they fail to note that, in our marketing- and PR-savvy society, we are not dealing with public relations in a traditional sense. We live in a post-PR world. See also, Thomas H. Davenport and John C. Beck, *The Attention Economy: Understanding the New Currency of Business* (Boston, MA: Harvard Business School Press, 2001).

12. Boorstin, *The Image*, op. cit.

13. Gerry Khermouch and Jeff Green, "Buzz Marketing," *Business Week*, July 30, 2001, pp. 50–6; Renee Dye, "The Buzz on Buzz," *Harvard Business Review*, 78 (November), 2000; Godin, *Unleashing the Ideavirus*, op. cit.

14. Cosmo Landesman, "Whassup? We're Just Chillin', Man," *Sunday Times*, October 8, 2000, p. 5; Jim Kirk, "Talk Value Creates name for Scarpelli," *Chicago Tribune*, June 3, 2001, Section 5, pp.1, 7.

15. See for example: Jim Davies, *The Book of Guinness Advertising* (London: Gullane, 1998); Jeff Manning, *Got Milk: The Book* (Rocklin, CA: Prima, 1999); Jay Schulberg, *The Milk Mustache Book: A Behind-the-Scenes Look at America's Favorite Advertising Campaign* (New York: Ballantine, 1998); Alfredo Marcantonio and David Abbott, *Remember Those Great Volkswagen Ads?* (London: Enterprise Millenium, 2000); Bob Stoddard, *Pepsi 100 Years* (New York: General, 1998); *Sears Roebuck and Company Catalogue – 100th Anniversary Edition* (Berlin: Verlag, 1998); Marie Melillo, *The Ultimate Barbie Doll Book* (New York: Krause, 1996).

16. Fay Weldon, *The Bulgari Connection* (London: Flamingo, 2001); Anne Hanley, "All That Glitters," *Voyager*, May 2002, pp. 44–8.

17. Richard W. Lewis, *Absolut Book. The Absolut Vodka Advertising Story* (Boston, MA: Journey Editions, 1996); Carl Hamilton, *Absolut: Biography of a Bottle* (New York: Texere, 2000).

18. Eric Culp, "Olympic Champ Quietly Going for Gold at Absolut," *The Business*, September 9, 2002, p. 8.

19. Lewis, *Absolut Book.*, op. cit., pp. 4–5.

20. Malolm Gladwell, *The Tipping Point: How Little Things Can Make a Big Difference* (London: Little Brown, 2000); Stephen Bayley, "Only Connect," *Observer Review*, May 21, 2000, p.

13. See also, Malcolm Gladwell, "Clicks and Mortar," in Remnick, *The New Gilded Age*, op. cit., pp. 125–38.

21. Daragh O'Reilly, "Nice Video, Shame About the Scam: Pedagogical Rhetoric Meets Commercial Reality at Stew Leonard's," Academy of Marketing Conference, July 2000.

22. Naturally, I'm reluctant to name, and thereby amplify, the amplifier concerned. You'll have to track the quack yourself.

> There is a dangerous downside to the executive autobiography. Almost inevitably, the CEO will begin to believe his or her own publicity.

23. There is, I should perhaps add, a dangerous downside to the executive autobiography. Almost inevitably, the CEO will begin to believe his or her own publicity, albeit not entirely for narcissistic reasons. Decades of psychological research demonstrate that when people write something down about themselves, they adapt their personality accordingly. They *become* the persona they describe, and act in a manner that is consistent with this characterization. CEOs, in short, take their cue from the semi-fictional character described in the autobiography and, while this may seem innocent enough, the formulaic nature of such texts contain the seeds of corporate destruction. Thus, they unfailingly refer to the great man's customer orientation, even though this statement is pure ideology. In a market-oriented world, where no CEO can openly admit that customers are a pain in the butt or that they can be safely ignored (just think of Wall Street's reaction), it goes without saying that their triumphs are predicated on customer centricity. The products sell, therefore the customers must be satisfied, therefore the executive is customer oriented, at an intuitive level possibly. In reality, the executive may have teased, tormented, and tantalized customers en route to the top, but the ideology of customer orientation doesn't allow this to appear in the official autobiography. Unfortunately, the corporate chickens come home to roost when the once-successful executive becomes the customer-hugging character described in the book and things start falling apart. It is often said that Tom Peters is the kiss of corporate death, in that the companies he mentions in his blockbusters often go belly up before the paperback edition hits the bookstands. This is true and empirically proven. But the reason it is true has nothing to do with Peters's reputation as the Death Watch Beetle of the business community. It is because the companies concerned adapt themselves to the fictional, unfailingly customer-oriented, organization described in Tom Peters's bestseller. The fault does not lie with Tom, Tom the piper's son, but with the companies who dance to the Pied Peters Piper's tune. Just a hypothesis of mine, you understand...

24. Brown, *Marketing: The Retro Revolution*, op. cit., pp. 170–1. Incidentally, have you ever noticed that the figure for free, shock-horror publicity is *always* $100 million? Just as the consumer is reportedly exposed to 3000 advertising messages per day, so too the monetary value of amplification unfailingly comes out at a round $100 million. Something tells me we're in guesstimate territory.

25. Jonathan Schroeder, "Edouard Manet, Calvin Klein, and the Strategic Use of Scandal," in Stephen Brown and Anthony Patterson, *Imagining Marketing*, op. cit., pp. 36–51.

26. Harriet Lane, "Beattie Mania," *The Observer Magazine*, January 28, 2001, pp. 10–14; Grant, *The New Marketing Manifesto*, op. cit., pp. 220–2; Brown, *Marketing: The Retro Revolution*, op. cit., p. 167.

27. Ralph Rugoff, "Empty Window Dressing," *Financial Times Weekend*, October 28, 2000, p. 7. In this regard, it will be interesting to monitor the impact of current mayor Mike Bloomberg's ban on smoking. Will it encourage rather than discourage smokers? Time will tell. See for example, Nicholas Wapshott, "Smokers of New York Fight Ban to Clear the Air," *Times*, August 24, 2002, p. 15.

28. Cialdini, *Influence*, op. cit., pp. 214, 223. I can confirm this finding from personal experience. As child, I well remember the kerfuffle that surrounded Monty Python's "sacrilegious" movie, *The Life of Brian*. It was banned in my hometown of Belfast, but screened in a nearby suburb. That suburban cinema did its best business ever. The lines stretched several times round the block. The word of mouth was incredible. Even people who didn't like Monty Python were raving about it. The movie played to packed houses in the suburbs until such time as Belfast City Council rescinded the ban; it faded fairly rapidly thereafter.

29. Fuhrman, *Publicity Stunt*, op. cit., pp. 144–5.

30. The same principle applies in almost every sphere of human endeavor – politics (Gore/Bush), science (Newton/Leibniz), technology (Gates/Ellison), music (Beatles/Stones), art (Picasso/Matisse), literature (Mailer/Capote), television (Leno/Letterman), comics (Superman/Batman) and, not least, professional sport, where two much-hyped combatants square off against each other (Ali/Foreman, McGwire/Sosa, Borg/McEnroe).

31. Ries and Ries, *The Fall of Advertising*, op. cit., p. 99

32. Ries and Ries, ibid., p. 102.

33. Adam Sage, "Art World Fumes as the Car in Front is a Picasso," *Times*, January 15, 2000, p. 6.

34. Joanna Smith Rakoff, "Great Expectations," *Guardian G2*, November 9, 2001, pp. 2–3.

35. *The Economist*, "Sticky Issue," *The Economist*, August 24, 2002, p. 57.

36. Stephen Baker and Christina White, "Why 'Porno Chic' is Riling the French," *Business Week*, July 30, 2001, p. 47.

37. Jon Henley, "Campaign to Turn Tide of Sexist Ads," *Guardian*, November 11, 2000, p. 21; Charles Bremner, "Bitches Bare Teeth Over Nude Dahl," *Times*, November 11, 2000, p. 6.

38. Matt Haig, *Mobile Marketing: The Message Revolution* (London: Kogan Page, 2002); Jane Simms, "Is This the Way to Project Your Figures?" *The Business*, September 9, 2002, p. 9.

39. *The Economist*, "Revenge of the Nerds," *The Economist*, July 27, 2002, p.73.

40. *Sunday Times*, "Reinventing a Career Can be a Bit of a Steal," *Sunday Times*, November 10, 2002, p. 17.

41. Hannah Jones, "Jacko: Relive That Incredible Documentary," *heat*, February 15–21, 2003, pp 28–30.

42. OK, I made this one up. But it sounds plausible, no? The gory details of Treacy and Wiersema's attempted payola are recounted in John Micklethwait and Adrian Wooldridge, *The Witch Doctors: Making Sense of the Management Gurus* (New York: Times Business, 1996).

Lesson Seven: How to Sell Sham Secrets

1. Douglas Rogers, "News of the World," *Times Magazine*, June 29, 2002, p. 12.
2. Quoted in Rogers, "News of the World," ibid., p.12.
3. Daniel Pipes, *Conspiracy: How the Paranoid Style Flourishes and Where It Comes From* (New York: Free Press, 1997).
4. Pipes, *Conspiracy*, op. cit.; Peter Knight, *Conspiracy Culture: From Kennedy to the X Files* (New York: Routledge, 2000); Al Hidell and Joan D'Arc, *The Conspiracy Reader* (New York: Citadel, 1998); Mark Fenster, *Conspiracy Theories: Secrecy and Power in American Culture* (Minneapolis, MN: University of Minnesota Press, 1999); Jim Marrs, *Rule By Secrecy* (New York: Perennial, 2000); Timothy Melley, *Empire of Conspiracy: The Culture of Paranoia in Postwar America* (Ithaca, NY: Cornell University Press, 2000).
5. The less said about cabbalistic symbols on dollar bills, the better.
6. Khermouch and Green, "Buzz Marketing," op. cit., pp. 55–6.
7. Even I, in my innocence, got caught up in the cinematic conspiracy. A few weeks after *AI's* premiere, at the height of the promotional frenzy, I presented a paper at an academic marketing conference. Ordinarily, my presentations are greeted with silence, somnambulance,

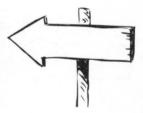

He thought I was channeling *AI* central, that I was a stooge for Spielberg and his heinous Dreamworks henchpersons!

and the occasional satisfied snore. But, on this occasion, I was accosted by an agitated delegate, who waxed lyrical about my remarkable marketing insights. Naturally, I enquired about the specifics of his enthusiasm, and it transpired that I'd used several crucial code words in the course of my presentation. He thought I was channeling *AI* central, that I was a stooge for Spielberg and his heinous Dreamworks henchpersons! I immediately denied any involvement, but that simply increased his conviction. In the wacky world of conspiracy theories, a denial's as good as a confession.

8. www.luckystar.com; Shaun Phillips, "Shine Your Heavenly Body Tonight," *Esquire*, September 2002, pp. 94–8.
9. Wunderman, *Being Direct*, op. cit., pp. 119–29.
10. I'm speculating, of course, but I suspect that Bezos got the "gold box" idea from Malcolm Gladwell's *Tipping Point*, which includes a version of Wunderman's Colorado story.
11. Richard Hofstader, *The Paranoid Style in American Politics and Other Essays* (New York: Knopf, 1965).
12. Kennedy statistic quoted in Pipes, *Conspiracy*, op. cit., p. 15. On related matters, see Michael Shermer, *Why People Believe Weird Things* (New York: Freeman, 1997); Stuart A. Vyse, *Believing in Magic: The Psychology of Superstition* (New York: Oxford University Press, 1997).
13. The literature on Elvis is almost beyond measure. The classic study is Peter Guralnick's two-volume epic: *Last Train to Memphis: The Rise of Elvis Presley* (Boston, MA: Little

Brown, 1994) and *Careless Love: The Unmaking of Elvis Presley* (Boston, MA: Little Brown, 1999). Presley's wider musical context is expertly dissected by Peter Doggett in *Are You Ready for the Country: Elvis, Dylan, Parsons and the Roots of Country Rock* (New York: Viking, 2000). The numerologists' notion of a 2001 comeback was based on the following calculations: when you add the year of his death (1977), to the day he died (16), and the number of the month he died (8), you get 2001 (Elvis's theme tune, remember!). By the way, there is no significance – repeat, *no* significance – attached to the fact that this is the thirteenth footnote in the seventh chapter of *Free Gift Inside!!* None whatsoever…

14. The twenty-fifth anniversary commemoration of Presley's demise threw up dozens of examples of anti-Parker diatribe. See for example Rose Clayton and Dick Heard, *Elvis By Those Who Knew Him Best* (London: Virgin, 2002) and Paul Simpson, *The Rough Guide to Elvis* (London: Rough Guides, 2002).

15. True, Elvis was successful before the Colonel took him in hand, albeit on a relatively small scale, in a regional market, and in a musical genre that lacked cross-over appeal. Elvis, what's more, would doubtless have made it under the tutelage of any other reasonably competent manager. Nevertheless, he owed an *awful* lot to Parker.

16. Sean O'Neal, *My Boy Elvis: The Colonel Tom Parker Story* (New York: Barricade Books, 1998).

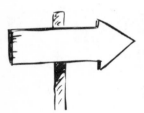

Parker set up a "pet cemetery" on waste ground behind the Tampa animal shelter and made a fortune from fake funeral services.

17. He set up a "pet cemetery" on waste ground behind the Tampa animal shelter, engraved a tombstone for an non-existent canine called "Spot," ostentatiously placed it over an unoccupied grave, and, incorrigible charlatan that he was, made a fortune from fake funeral services.

18. Not everyone appreciated the Colonel's promotional stunts, it has to be said. Eddie Arnold terminated his association with him after the Colonel falsely announced in *Variety* that the singer was booked solid for a year. The ruse worked brilliantly, as promoters desperately tried to squeeze into the crooner's "crowded" schedule and paid over the odds to do so. Arnold was affronted, the Colonel was dismissed and Elvis reaped the benefit.

19. Parker, indeed, adapted the same approach to every aspect of Presley's career, from the scheduling of new releases (which were delayed until 1 million advance sales – an eminently marketable statistic – were racked up) and the composition of album liner notes (all information concerning studio and recording personnel was removed in order to increase the King's mystique), through the lucrative "tour" by Elvis's gold Cadillac (which attracted huge crowds, desperately hoping that the automobile's owner would show up too), to the day-to-day man management of "My Boy Elvis" himself (Parker kept Presley in comparative penury in order to increase his control over him).

20. Unless, of course, there are submininal embeds in mainstream marketing textbooks. Stranger things have happened . . . you feel drowsy reading them, right? There's definitely something going on . . .

21. William Poundstone, *Big Secrets: The Uncensored Truth About All Sorts of Stuff You Are Never Supposed to Know* (New York: Quill, 1983).

22. A fascinating inventory of health and beauty ballyhoo is contained in David Armstrong and Elizabeth Metzger Armstrong, *The Great American Medicine Show: Being An Illustrated History of Hucksters, Healers, Health Evangelists, and Heroes from Plymouth Rock to the Present* (New York: Prentice Hall, 1991).

23. The academic literature on gift giving and consumption festivals is vast. It is expertly summarized by Russell W. Belk, "Studies in the New Consumer Behavior," in Daniel Miller, *Acknowledging Consumption: A Review of New Studies* (London: Routledge, 1995, pp. 58–95).

24. James O'Shea and Charles Madigan, *Dangerous Company: The Consulting Powerhouses and the Businesses They Save and Ruin* (London: Nicholas Brealey, 1999). For an example of such outlandish claims, see Sergio Zyman, *The End of Advertising As We Know It* (New York: John Wiley, 2002, p. 234).

25. Blumberg, *Predatory Society*, op. cit.

26. Profitable though mysteries are, the commodification of conspiracy cuts both ways. When Tropical Fantasy, a soft drink, was launched in the early 1990s, it was rumored that the beverage was manufactured by the Ku Klux Klan and contained "stimulants to sterilize the black man" (Pipes, *Conspiracy*, op. cit., p. 3). Although subsequent investigations revealed that the accusations were groundless – the product was made in Brooklyn by a predominantly African-American workforce – sales plummeted by approximately 70%. All sorts of other products, such as Kool and Uptown cigarettes, Troop sport clothing, Church's Fried Chicken and Snapple soft drinks, have suffered similar slanders and similar fates at the checkout.

27. John Ed Pearce, *The Colonel: The Captivating Biography of the Dynamic Founder of a Fast Food Empire* (Garden City, NY: Doubleday, 1982); Col. Harland Sanders, *Life As I Have Known It Has Been Finger Lickin' Good* (Carol Stream, IL: Creation House, 1974). See also John A. Jakle and Keith A. Sculle, *Fast Food: Roadside Restaurants in the Automobile Age* (Baltimore: Johns Hopkins University Press, 1999); Eric Schlosser, *Fast Food Nation: What the All-American Meal is Doing to the World* (New York: Houghton Mifflin, 2001).

28. R. David Thomas, *Dave's Way: A New Approach to Old-fashioned Success* (New York: Putnam, 1991).

29. Jakle and Sculle, *Fast Food*, op. cit.

30. The tradition continues with "Buckethead," the mysterious lead guitarist with Guns N' Roses. No one knows who he is and Axl's not saying. All we know for certain is that he bestrides the stage wearing a facemask whilst sporting a natty KFC bucket. The Colonel may be long gone, but KFC product placement is not dead.

31. Poundstone, *Big Secrets*, op. cit., pp.13–21.

32. James E. Collins and Jerry I. Porras, *Built to Last: Successful Habits of Visionary Companies* (New York: Random House, 1994).

33. Suffice it to say that the "secrecy" ruse is still widely used in fast food, most recently in the upscale chain Chipotle (the secret of which is that it's a – shock, horror! – McDonald's subsidiary).

34. Cialdini, *Influence*, op. cit., terms this the Rejection-then-Retreat principle. It involves making a large request (buy the more expensive item), followed by a smaller request (less expensive item) after the large request has been rejected. People are prone to make the smaller purchase because of the salesperson's apparent concession (lower price). The rules of reciprocity demand that an equal and opposite "concession" is made by the customer. Ring up that sale!

35. Cialdini, *Influence*, op. cit., pp. 100–4.

36. Reichenbach, *Phantom Fame*, op. cit.

37. Warren Berger, "Just Do It Again," *Business 2.0*, September 2002, pp. 76–84.

38. Mike Daisy, *Twenty-one Dog Years: Doing Time @ Amazon.com* (London: Fourth Estate, 2002).

39. Stephen Brown, "The Three Rs of Relationship Marketing: Retroactive, Retrospective, Retrogressive," in Thorsten Hennig-Thurau and Ursula Hansen, eds, *Relationship Marketing: Gaining Competitive Advantage Through Customer Satisfaction and Customer Retention* (Berlin: Springer-Verlag, 2000, pp. 393–413).

40. A recent Gallup poll on attitudes to a variety of professions, showed that advertisers ranked second lowest in the public's overall estimation, one place below insurance salesmen and one place above car dealers (quoted in Ries and Ries, *The Fall of Advertising*, op. cit., pp. 2–3).

41. Robert Greene, *The Art of Seduction* (New York: Viking, 2001).

42. Greene, *The Art of Seduction*, ibid.

Lesson Eight: How to Entertain When Entertainment is Everywhere

1. Brown, *Postmodern Marketing*, op. cit.

2. Roy Porter, *Quacks: Fakers and Charlatans in English Medicine* (Charleston, SC: Tempus, 2000); Edwin A. Dawes, *The Great Illusionists* (London: David & Charles, 1979).

3. Blaine McCormick, "Benjamin Franklin: Founding Father of American Management," *Business Horizons*, 44 (1), 2001, pp. 2–10.

4. Armstrong and Armstrong, *The Great American Medicine Show*, op. cit., p. 186.

5. Pine and Gilmore, *The Experience Economy*, op. cit.

6. Porter, *Quacks*, op. cit., pp. 144–6.

7. For example, when Graham took the Temple of Health and Hymen on tour at the end of its West End run, many provincial magistrates were less than enamored by the prospect of his libidinous lectures. They were banned, takings were sequestered, and he was gaoled on more than one occasion. Down but not out, the megaquack abandoned his electro-magnetic approach, sold the celebrated celestial bed, and eventually saw the light. As a

Assisted by a bevy of amply upholstered, if lightly draped, beauties he championed the curative properties of mud-baths.

born-again evangelist, Graham changed his name to Servant of the Lord O.W.L. [O Wonderful Love] and toured the county espousing a quasi-pantheistic creed, which coupled the divinity of Christ as Redeemer with the healing powers of Nature. Assisted by a bevy of amply upholstered, if lightly draped, beauties he championed the curative properties of mud-baths, Mother Earth, and the heavenly Father. To prove his point, the Servant of the Lord O.W.L. had himself repeatedly buried, buck-naked, in a freshly-dug pit, whilst lecturing to groups of bemused onlookers. Not everyone, of course, had the time or indeed the inclination to indulge in such painstaking treatments, so he developed a short-order version of his remedial regime for particularly time-poor patients. Namely, a sod of turf attached to the chest.

8. Patricia Fara, *An Entertainment for Angels: Electricity in the Enlightenment* (Duxford: Icon, 2002).
9. There are several excellent biographies of Edison. The classic statement is Matthew Josephson, *Edison: A Biography* (New York: McGraw-Hill, 1959).
·10. Peter Drucker, for example, repeatedly takes Edison to task for his marketing and managerial shortcomings. However, as Andre Millard argues in *Edison and the Business of Innovation* (Baltimore: Johns Hopkins University Press, 1990), "Drucker has accepted the part of the Edison myth that depicts him as the eccentric inventor too concerned with experiments to bother with business affairs... This image was useful in the constant litigation that threatened to take up all his time. Called to the stand, Edison could claim ignorance and therefore innocence of the unsavoury wheeling and dealing of the business world. This stance helped foster the myth of the great inventor and poor businessman. Edison took great pains not to alter this perception, and for good reason... His business associates knew a different Edison, a shrewd calculating man who exercised fine judgement of the marketplace." (p.50).
11. Josephson, *Edison*, op. cit., p. 137.
12. See Paul Israel, *Edison: A Life of Invention* (New York: John Wiley, 1998).
13. Israel, *Edison*, ibid., pp 167–90.
14. Interestingly, Edison tried the same knocking copy approach at the end of the decade, when Westinghouse's AC generators challenged his proprietary DC system. The Wizard's unsavory PR man – one Harold Brown – dramatically demonstrated the dangers inherent in AC by publicly electrocuting a veritable menagerie of dogs, cats, cows, horses, pigs, and sheep, claiming that the creatures would have survived had DC been used instead. This not only stirred up the anti-AC wrath of the SPCA (Society for the Prevention of Cruelty to Animals), but it also eventually led (in August 1890) to the development of the electric chair as a means of disbursing capital punishment. Yet despite the best efforts of this "macabre Barnum," who actually challenged George Westinghouse to a death-by-electrocution duel, the much superior AC system eventually carried the day. See Michael White, "The Battle of the Currents," in *Rivals: Conflict as the Fuel of Science* (London: Secker and Warburg, 2001, pp. 133–75). Also useful is H.W. Brands, *The Reckless Decade: America in the 1890s* (Chicago: University of Chicago Press, 2002).
15. Israel, *Edison*, op. cit., pp. 377–8.
16. David Nasaw, *Going Out: The Rise and Fall of Public Amusements* (Cambridge, MA: Harvard University Press, 1993).
17. Nasaw, *Going Out*, ibid. The broader context of electricity's reception and development in the US is cogently explained by David E. Nye, *Electrifying America: Social Meanings of a New Technology 1880–1940* (Cambridge, MA: MIT Press, 1990). The period after 1940 is

covered in Richard Rudolph and Scott Ridley, *Power Struggle: The Hundred-Year War Over Electricity* (New York: Harper and Row, 1986).

18. Robert W. Rydell, *All the World's A Fair: Visions of Empire at American International Expositions, 1876–1916* (Chicago; University of Chicago Press, 1984).

19. Judith A. Adams, *The American Amusement Park Industry: A History of Technology and Thrills* (Boston, MA: Twayne, 1991).

20. Woody Register, *The Kid of Coney Island: Fred Thompson and the Rise of American Amusements* (New York: Oxford University Press, 2001).

21. Nasaw, *Going Out*, op. cit., p. 83.

22. Quoted in Adams, *The American Amusement Park Industry*, op. cit., p. 50.

23. John F. Kasson, *Amusing the Million: Coney Island at the Turn of the Century* (New York: Hill and Wang, 1978).

24. Rem Koolhaas, "Coney Island: The Technology of the Fastastic," in *Delirious New York: A Retroactive Manifesto for Manhattan* (New York: Monacelli, 1994, pp. 28–79).

25. Mark Dery, *The Pyrotechnic Insanitarium: American Culture on the Brink* (New York, Grove, 1999).

26. Nicholas Wapshott, "Revival Hopes for Faded Glory of Coney Island," *The Times*, July 27, 2002, p. 21.

27. Kasson, *Amusing the Million*, op. cit., p. 106.

28. See for example, Sherry, *Servicescapes*, op. cit.; Brown and Sherry, *Time, Space, and the Market*, op. cit.; Mark Gottdiener, *The Theming of America: Dreams, Visions, and Commercial Spaces* (Boulder, CO: Westview, 1997); Ralph Rugoff, *Circus Americanus* (New York: Verso, 1995); Ada Louise Huxtable, *Architecture and Illusion* (New York: Free Press, 1997).

29. Mike Clarke-Madison, "Museums For the Masses," *Hemispheres*, September 2002, pp. 50–8.

30. Clarke-Madison, ibid., p. 50.

31. Stephen Brown et al., "Presenting the Past: On Marketing's Reproduction Orientation," in Stephen Brown and Anthony Patterson, eds, *Imagining Marketing: Art, Aesthetics and the Avant-Garde* (London: Routledge, 2000, pp. 145–91).

32. Brown, *Postmodern Marketing*, op. cit.

33. White, *New Ideas About New Ideas*, op. cit., p. 115.

34. The literature on Las Vegas is vast. I found the following particularly helpful: Sally Denton and Roger Morris, *The Money and the Power: The Making of Las Vegas and Its Hold on America 1947–2000* (New York: Knopf, 2001); Pete Early, *Super Casino: Inside the "New" Las Vegas* (New York, Bantam, 2000); Mark Gottdiener et al., *Las Vegas: The Social Production of an All-American City* (Malden, MA: Blackwell, 1999); Jay Tolson, "The Face of the Future," *US News and World Report*, June 11, 2001, pp. 48–56.

35. See, for example, the contributions to Mike Tronnes, ed., *Literary Las Vegas: The Best Writing About America's Most Fabulous City* (New York: Henry Holt, 1995).

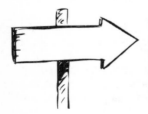

Recent reports from some *very* disgruntled customers suggest that Oracle is reverting to type.

36. Mike Wilson, *The Difference Between God and Larry Ellison: God Doesn't Think He's Larry Ellison* (New York: Quill, 1997).

37. Florence M. Stone, *The Oracle of Oracle* (New York: AMACOM, 2002); Stuart Read, *The Oracle Edge* (Holbrook, MA: Adams Media, 2000). See also, David A. Kaplan, "Oz," in, *The Silicon Boys and Their Valley of Dreams* (New York: Perennial, 2000, pp.119–54.)

38. Not just in the early days; recent reports from some *very* disgruntled customers suggest that Oracle is reverting to type. See for example, Ian Mount "Out of Control," *Business 2.0*, August 2002, www.business2.com; Eric Hellweg, "Oracle's Larry Ellison, a Solitary Man," *Business 2.0*, July 15, 2002, www.business2.com

39. Wilson, *The Difference*, op. cit., p. 239.

40. White, *Rivals*, op. cit., p. 352.

41. Wilson, *The Difference*, op. cit., p. 171.

42. Wilson, ibid., p.126.

43. Another example of Ellison's ability to charm all comers occurred during Team Oracle's 2002 bid for the America's Cup. When asked how his team would celebrate if they carried the venerated trophy back to the United States, Larry replied, "Oh, I think the usual quiet style that our sailing team has established over its many years. We'll probably drive out to a book store, have a cappuccino, pick up a couple of hard-back books, give each other a hug, and go to sleep by 9 o'clock." (See Edward Gorman, "Curiosity Draws Ellison Towards his Limits," *The Times*, October 4, 2002, p. 40.)

44. Wilson, ibid., p. 232.

45. Brown, *Marketing: The Retro Revolution*, op. cit.

46. Michael J. Wolf, *The Entertainment Economy: The Mega-Media Forces That are Reshaping Our Lives* (New York: Random House, 1999); Neal Gabler, *Life The Movie: How Entertainment Conquered Reality* (New York, Vintage, 1998); Dery, *The Pyrotechnic Insanitarium*, op. cit.

Now That's What I Call Marketing #2

1. Darden Asbury Pyron, *Liberace: An American Boy* (Chicago: University of Chicago Press, 2000); Bob Thomas, *Liberace: The True Story* (New York: St. Martin's, 1987); Liberace, *Liberace: An Autobiography* (New York: Putnam's, 1973); Liberace, *The Wonderful, Private World of Liberace* (New York: Harper and Row, 1986).

2. Pyron, *Liberace*, op. cit., pp. 286, 372, 379, respectively.

3. Pyron, *Liberace*, ibid., p. 156.

4. Pyron, *Liberace*, ibid., p. 165.

5. In an attempt to cool the entertainment industry's mid-fifties ardor, Liberace demanded the unprecedented sum of $50,000 per engagement. This was a fee he thought couldn't possibly be met, but the Riviera Hotel in Las Vegas leapt at the opportunity. He opened on April 20, 1955, with a spectacular show featuring the copious costume changes that subsequently became his trademark. The Last Frontier, Liberace's previous residency, responded with a rising young rock and roller from Tupelo, Mississippi, who made his Las Vegas debut during the 1956 season. It was a disaster, though the magnanimous victor went out of his way to pitch for the punk and gave him some advice on the necessary glitz, glamour, and grandiloquence of Vegas-style showmanship. Elvis never forgot his generosity, apparently. Every time Liberace opened a casino season thereafter, the King sent him a guitar-shaped bouquet of flowers.

6. Lewis MacAdams, *The Birth of the Cool: Beat, Bebop, and the American Avant-Garde* (New York: Free Press, 2001); David Halberstam, *The Fifties* (New York: Fawcett Columbine, 1993); David Sterritt, *Mad to be Saved: The Beats, the 50s, and Film* (Carbondale, IL: Southern Illinois University Press, 1998).

7. Michael Segell, "It's All Wunnerful for Liberace: An Extraordinary Visit with the Gilded Cherub of American Camp," *Rolling Stone*, October 1, 1981 (quoted in Pyron, *Liberace*, op. cit., p. 283).

8. Marc Cooper wryly describes the museum thus: "Far be it for me to rob the reader of the joy of discovering the contents of this temple on his or her own, but let me advise that when you make the pilgrimage, don't forget your sunglasses. The glare is vicious: here's the rhinestone-covered Baldwin grand piano, the coordinated rhinestone-covered Rolls-Royce (if you have trouble finding it just look for the Rolls painted like an American flag next to it), the rhinestone-and-coral pink convertible VW with a Rolls grille, the collection of rhinestone-studded velvet capes, yet one more rhinestone-covered grand piano, and the rhinestone-covered frame around the picture of Liberace and Tony Orlando." (p.342 in "Searching for Sin City and Finding Disney in the Desert," Mike Tronnes, ed., *Literary Las Vegas*, op. cit., pp. 325–50).

9. Pyron, *Liberace*, op. cit., p. 451.

10. J. Randy Taraborrelli, *Madonna: An Intimate Biography* (London: Pan, 2002); Andrew Morton, *Madonna* (London: Michael O'Mara, 2001); Christopher Anderson, *Madonna Unauthorized* (New York: Simon and Schuster, 1991); Robert Matthew Walker, *Madonna: The Biography* (New York: Sidgwick and Jackson, 1991).

11. Matthew Rettenmund, *Encyclopedia Madonnica* (New York: St. Martin's, 1995).

12. Carol Benson and Allan Metz, eds, *The Madonna Companion: Two Decades of Commentary* (New York: Schirmer, 1999).

13. Luc Sante, "Unlike a Virgin" (p.236 in Benson and Metz, *The Madonna Companion*, ibid., pp. 232–40).

14. Quoted in Taraborrelli, *Madonna*, op. cit., p. 217.

15. In many ways, Madonna's marketing strategy is reminiscent of Colonel Tom Parker's Presleymarketing policy, discussed in Lesson Seven. Madonna, indeed, believes that there is an affinity between herself and the King, largely because he died on her nineteenth birthday. However, when compared directly with Elvis, as she was after her infamous "Like a Virgin" performance on MTV (a postmodern reprise of Presley's bump and grind on the Milton Berle show of June 5, 1956), she tartly replied, "I never had someone like Colonel Parker propping me up or telling me what to wear or think or do...I did it all on my own" (p. xiii in Steve Dougherty, "Introduction: The Madonna Legend," Benson and Metz, eds, *The Madonna Companion*, op. cit., pp. xiii-iv).

16. Steven Daly, "Madonna Marlene," *Vanity Fair*, October 2002, p. 226.

17. Robert LaFranco, "The Rolling Stone Money Report," *Rolling Stone*, July 2002, p. 65.

18. Quoted in Taraborrelli, *Madonna*, op. cit., p. 244.

19. John Skow, "Madonna Rocks the Land" (p. 114 in Benson and Metz, eds, *The Madonna Companion*, op. cit., pp. 109–16.)

20. Q Magazine, "Madonna," *Q*, September 2002, p. 86.

Lesson Nine: How to Do a Harry Potter

1. Joanne K. Rowling, *Harry Potter and the Philosopher's Stone* (London: Bloomsbury, 1997); *Harry Potter and the Chamber of Secrets* (London: Bloomsbury, 1998); *Harry Potter and the Prisoner of Azkaban* (London: Bloomsbury, 1999); *Harry Potter and the Goblet of Fire* (London: Bloomsbury, 2000).

2. Sean Smith, *J.K. Rowling: A Biography* (London: Michael O'Mara, 2001); Philip Nel, *J.K. Rowling's Harry Potter Novels: A Reader's Guide* (New York: Continuum, 2002); Marc Shapiro, *J.K. Rowling: The Wizard Behind Harry Potter* (New York: St Martin's Griffin, 2000); Lindsey Fraser, *An Interview With J.K. Rowling* (London: Mammoth, 2000); Lindsey Fraser, *Conversations With J.K. Rowling* (New York: Scholastic, 2001).

3. Gaynor Pengelly, "Just Married and now J.K. Rowling Tops Britain's Highest Earning Women," *Mail on Sunday*, December 30, 2001, pp. 16–17; *Mail on Sunday, Rich Report 2002*, pp. 44–45.

4. Brian MacArthur, "Rowling Books a Place in Publishing History," *The Times* December 21, 2001, p. 8; Andrew Blake, *The Irresistible Rise of Harry Potter* (London: Verso, 2002).

5. Anthony Holden, "So Farewell, Harry Potter," *The Observer Review*, July 9, 2000, p.11.

6. Stephen Brown, "Marketing for Muggles: The Harry Potter Way to Higher Profits," *Business Horizons*, 45 (1), 2002, pp. 6–14.

7. *The Times*, "Potter's Wizardmanship: The Strongest Spell is the Book That You Cannot Put Down," *The Times*, July 8, 2000, p. 21.

8. Brown, "Marketing for Muggles," op. cit.

9. See for example: Julia Eccleshare, *A Guide to the Harry Potter Novels* (London: Continuum 2002); Sharon Moore, *We Love Harry Potter: We'll Tell You Why* (New York: St Martin's Griffin, 1999); Elizabeth D. Schafer, *Exploring Harry Potter* (London: Ebury, 2000); David Colbert, *The Magical Worlds of Harry Potter* (Wrightsville Beach, NC: Lumina, 2001); Allan Zola Kronzek and Elizabeth Kronzek, *The Sorcerer's Companion: A Guide to the Magical World of Harry Potter* (New York: Broadway, 2001); Bill Adler, *Kids' Letters to Harry Potter From Around the World* (New York: Carroll and Graf, 2001); Michael Gerber, *Barry Trotter and the Unauthorized Parody* (New York: Simon and Schuster, 2001); www.harrypotterguide.co.uk

10. Vanessa Thorpe, "Harry Potter Beats Austin in Sale Rooms," *Observer*, January 20, 2002, p. 11.

11. Oliver August, "Harry Potter and the Chinese Pirates," *The Times*, September 27, 2000, p. 21; Oliver August, "China is First With the New Harry Potter," *The Times*, July 24, 2002, p. 1.

12. Emma Cochrane, "Harry Potter and the Big Screen Adventure," *Empire*, December 2001, pp. 56–75; Jeff Jensen and Daniel Fierman, "Inside Harry Potter," *Entertainment Weekly*, September 2001, 28–38; Leslie Bennetts, "Something About Harry," *Vanity Fair*, October 2001, pp. 300–21.

13. Sam Tanenhaus, "Return to Hogwarts," *Vanity Fair*, October 2002, pp. 172–5; Chris Hewitt, "Problem Child," *Empire*, October 2002, pp. 36–43.

14. Instalment Three, *The Prisoner of Azkaban*, will be directed by Alfonso Cuaron (of *A Little Princess* fame) and released in November 2004.

15. Pravina Patel, "Harry Potter Fans Start Boycott of Film Merchandise," *Mail on Sunday*, February 25, 2001, p. 35.

16. Penelope Dening, "Selling Harry Potter," *Irish Times Weekend*, November 10, 2001, p. 1; Alice Fowler, "Who's Counting on Harry?" *You Magazine*, October 7, 2001, pp. 40–4.

17. John Harlow and Maurice Chittenden, "Movie Pirates Cash in on Harry Potter Mania," *Sunday Times*, November 4, 2001, p. 24.

18. Fowler, "Who's Counting on Harry?" op. cit.

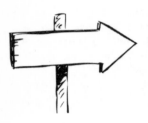

Harry, believe it or not, has even been credited with saving Christmas.

19. Actually, the sky doesn't do justice to it, since the network television rights for the first movie have recently been sold for $49 million. If that isn't stratospheric, I don't know what is. Additionally, Harry has even been credited with saving Christmas. In the aftermath of 9/11, when consumers were circumspect and retail store owners seriously worried, Hogwarts' anti-Grinch attracted recalcitrant shoppers into the stores and succeeded in prising open nervous parents' pocket books.

20. Brown, "Marketing for Muggles," op. cit.

21. *Marketing Business*, "Marketing Magic," *Marketing Business*, November 2001, pp. 10–13; *Marketing Week*, "Harry Potter," *Marketing Week*, Effectiveness Awards 2001, pp. 6–7.

22. Stephen Brown, "Torment your Customers (They'll Love It)," *Harvard Business Review*, 79 (9), 2001, pp. 82–8.

23. Stephen Brown, "Who Moved my Muggle?: Harry Potter and the Marketing Imaginarium," *Marketing Intelligence and Planning*, 20 (3), 2002, pp. 134–48.

24. Anthony Holden, "Why Harry Potter Doesn't Cast a Spell Over Me," *Observer Review*, June 25, 2000, pp. 1–2.

25. *Harvard Business Review*, "A Conversation With Literary Critic Harold Bloom," *Harvard Business Review*, 79 (5), 2001, pp. 63–8.

26. Harold Bloom, *Stories and Poems for Extremely Intelligent Children of All Ages* (New York: Scribner, 2001).

27. Jack Zipes, "The Phenomenon of Harry Potter, or Why All the Talk," in *Sticks and Stones: The Troublesome Success of Children's Literature from Slovenly Peter to Harry Potter* (New York: Routledge, 2001, pp. 170–89).

28. June Cummins, "Read Between the Lines for a Lesson in Consumer Coercion," *The Times Higher*, December 21, 2001, pp. 26–7.

29. David Ignatius, "The Anti-marketing Wizard," *The Washington Post*, June 25, 2000, p. B7.

30. Quoted in Fowler, "Who's Counting on Harry?" op. cit., p. 44.

31. Blake, *The Irresistible Rise of Harry Potter*, op. cit.; Brown, "Marketing for Muggles," op. cit.

32. For example, when Harry Potter was snubbed by the jury of a prominent literary prize, sponsored by Whitbread, the ensuing eruption of pro-Potter public approval must have been music to the ears of Bloomsbury's marketing department, albeit the official response

was one of "anger and disappointment" (just as it was when *The Sunday Times* "controversially" excluded the Potter books from its prestigious best-sellers list).

33. Rowling, *Harry Potter and the Prisoner of Azkaban,* op. cit., p. 137.

34. Stephen Brown, "Harry Potter and the Marketing Mystery," *Journal of Marketing,* 66 (1), 2001, pp. 126–30.

35. Paul Kirchner, *Forgotten Fads and Fabulous Flops* (Los Angeles: General Publishing, 1995); Dan Epstein, *Twentieth-Century Pop Culture* (London: Carlton, 1999).

36. Fowler, "Who's Counting on Harry?" op. cit.

37. As Fowler, ibid., p. 44, rightly puts it, "When children are playing on their Harry Potter computer games, building their model Hogwarts and eating Harry Potter chocolate, will they hunger for books five, six and seven with the same ferocity as they have done in the past? Faced with immense commercial pressure, will Rowling retain her freshness and deftness of touch? Could Harry Potter, so loved for the past four years, be so ubiquitous that he simply becomes boring?"

38. Ries and Ries, *The Fall of Advertising,* op. cit., p.108.

39. David A. Aaker, *Building Strong Brands* (New York: Free Press, 1996).

Lesson Ten: How to Get Out of Jail Free

1. *Newsweek,* "A Game That Calls *You* Up," *Newsweek,* August 20, 2001, p. 10; Janelle Brown, "Paranoia For Fun and Profit," August 10, 2001, www.salon.com

2. David Fincher, dir., *The Game* (Los Angeles: Universal Pictures, 1997).

3. Marc Saltzman, "Majestic Turns the Tables on PC Gamers," *USA Today,* August 21, 2001, www.usatoday.com; Dan Caines, "EA Looking Majestic," February 27, 2001, www.suite101.com

4. Vincent Lopez, "Majestic: Is EA's Online Gamble Really the Next Step Forward in Gaming?" *PC Games,* August 17, 2001, www.pc.ign.com

5. Brett Sporich, "Gamer has 'Majestic' Hopes," *The Hollywood Reporter,* August 24, 2001, www.hollywoodreporter.com; Alex Caris, "Majestic by Electronic Arts," August 13, 2001, www.gamezilla.com

6. www.ea.com/worlds/games/pw_majstc

7. Adam Wisniewski, "Fear Factor," *Time Out New York,* August 16–23, 2001, www.timeoutny.com

8. Michael Sheridan, "Samurai Tea Miracle Rips Off Investors," *The Sunday Times,* June 16, 2002, p. 24.

9. Sheridan, "Samurai Tea," ibid.

10. Sheridan, "Samurai Tea," ibid. A depressingly similar story is recounted in Ellen Joan Pollock, *The Pretender: How Martin Frankel Fooled the Financial World and Led the Feds on One of the Most Publicized Manhunts in History* (New York: Wall Street Journal Books, 2002)

11. Ted L. Nancy, *Letters From a Nut* (New York: Avon, 1997); Ted L. Nancy, *More Letters From a Nut* (New York: Bantam, 1998); Ted L. Nancy, *Even More Letters From a Nut* (New York: St Martin's, 2000).

12. John Harlow, "Seinfeld Fingered as the Merry Prankster, *Sunday Times,* June 30, 2002, p. 24; Oliver Burkeman, "Is Jerry the Joker?" *Guardian Unlimited,* July 3, 2002, www.guardian.co.uk; Kimberly Potts, "TV Scoop," *E! Online,* August 7, 2002, www.eonline.com

13. Some of us are wondering how ABC will respond when it is flooded with quirky complaints from hoteliers, whose facilities are filled with Nancy fans searching for allegedly missing incisors and purported Prussian cutlasses . . .

14. Julie Burchill, "Voyage of the Damned," *Guardian*, February 1, 2002, pp. 4–5.

15. Suzy Menkes, "Voyage to Indian Summer of Exotic and Erotic Clothes," *International Herald Tribune*, September 1, 1998, www.iht.com

16. Burchill, "Voyage of the Damned," op. cit.

17. Laura Peek, "Snoot Boutique Hits the Rocks," *The Times*, February 1, 2002, p. 9.

18. Lisa Armstrong, "Elitist Voyage Leads the Dash for Trash," *The Times*, March 6, 2002, p. 11.

19. Jane Barrett, "Fashion's Rebels Without a Cause go on New Voyage," March 6, 2002, www.news.yahoo.com

20. Douglas Harbrecht, "Building Brand America," *Business Week*, December 10, 2001, www.businessweek.com; Alexandra Starr, "Charlotte Beers' Toughest Sell," *Business Week*, December 17, 2001, www.businessweek.com; *The Economist*, "From Uncle Ben's to Uncle Sam," *The Economist*, February 21, 2002, www.economist.com

21. David Benady, "Fighting Talk," *Marketing Week*, November 8, 2001, pp. 24–7.

22. Jerry della Famina, *From Those Wonderful Folks Who Gave You Pearl Harbor: Front-line Dispatches From the Advertising War* (New York: Simon and Schuster, 1970).

23. Ashley Alsup, "Selling the Stars and Stripes," *Observer*, December 2, 2001, p. 7.

24. Josh Chetwynd, "Pearl Harbor Built on 'Titanic' Formula," *USA Today*, May 25, 2001, pp. 1B–2B; Mike Clark, "Pearl Harbor Sputters – Until the Japanese Show Up," *USA Today*, May 25, 2001, p. E1.

25. Thus it expects compliance with nuclear and chemical weapons proliferation protocols, yet exempts itself from the same controls. It demands fair trade and free elections in return for US aid, despite its own electoral shortcomings (the November 2000 debacle) and blatant protectionism (farm subsidies, steel tariffs, drug testing rigmaroles, preferential defense procurement procedures). It insists, though its de facto control of the WTO, IMF, and World Bank, that it's the American economic way or the highway, as newly impoverished citizens of Argentina, Brazil, and Eastern Europe know only too well. It pollutes the global environment with impunity – while gorging on our planet's non-renewable natural resources – yet refuses to sign up to the Kyoto protocol on global warming (for fear that it might damage the American economy).

26. Mark Hertsgaard, *The Eagle's Shadow: Why America Fascinates and Infuriates the World* (London: Bloomsbury, 2002); Ziauddin Sardar and Merryl Wyn Davies, *Why Do People Hate America?* (Cambridge: Icon, 2002); Bryan Appleyard, "Why Do They Hate America?" *The Sunday Times*, September 23, 2001, section 4, pp. 1–2.

27. In fairness, Charlotte Beers is trying to sell the fact that there is more to America than marketing and militarism, a far from easy task. The 9/11 catastrophe and its aftermath

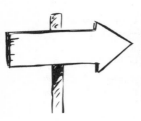

From Those Wonderful Folks Who Gave You *The Simpsons*. Homer's where the heart is.

have made a difficult task next to impossible. So wide is the perceived discrepancy between the brand's promise (life, liberty, and the pursuit of happiness) and performance (naked commercialism meets tawdry materialism) that Beers might be better off marketing marketing – From Those Wonderful Folks Who Gave You *The Simpsons* – since it is America's brilliantly marketed popular culture that enthralls and enraptures the rest of the world. Homer's where the heart is.

28. Richard Tomkins, "Brand of the Free," *Financial Times*, October 20, 2001, p. 12. Beers, perhaps unsurprisingly, resigned as ambassador-at-large in mid-March 2003.

29. Michael Theodoulou et al., "Cola Wars as Islam Shuns the Real Thing," *The Times*, October 11, 2002, p. 3.

30. Theodoulou et al., "Cola Wars," ibid.

31. The principal problem with the traditional customer-oriented marketing concept – or, for that matter, any sure-fire management remedy, from re-engineering to CRM – is that it is supposed to be universally applicable. In practice, admittedly, nostrums like CRM are adapted to specific organizational circumstances; and rightly so. In principle, nevertheless, they are presented as corporate cure-alls, instant alleviants for every imagined organizational ailment. It is ironic that, in our era of mass customization, management consultants continue to intimate that one size fits all in the market for management consultancy. The inevitable upshot of this have-model-will-travel mentality is that modern marketing has a cookie-cutter, sausage-machine, seen-one-seen-them-all quality, with only minor variations on the established APIC paradigm.

32. See Brown, *Postmodern Marketing*, op. cit.

33. Brown, *Postmodern Marketing*, ibid.

34. Veblen's continuing relevance to contemporary marketing is discussed in Brown, *Marketing – The Retro Revolution*, op. cit.

35. An excellent review of this topic is contained in Vincent-Wayne Mitchell and Ka Lun Chan, "Investigating UK Consumers' Unethical Attitudes and Behaviours," *Journal of Marketing Management*, 18 (1–2), 2002, pp. 5–26.

36. Nick Paton-Walsh, "The Great Rock and Roll Swindle," *Q Magazine*, August 2002, pp. 96–100.

37. George Carlin, *Brain Droppings* (New York: Hyperion, 1997).

38. Carlin, ibid., p. 111.

39. George Carlin, *Napalm and Silly Putty* (New York: Hyperion, 2001).

40. Stephen Brown, Robert V. Kozinets and John F. Sherry, Jr., "Still Ahead, A Look Back: Reconnoitering Retromarketing," (Northwestern University, Kellogg School of Management, Working Paper, 2002).

41. Stephen Brown, Robert V. Kozinets and John F. Sherry, Jr., "Revival of the Fittest," (Northwestern University, Kellogg School of Management, Working Paper, 2002).

42. Bracewell, *The Nineties*, ibid., p. 22.

43. A good example of this no-nonsense stance is Burch's campaign for a commonsense approach to business. In essence, this involves turning back to the sales manuals of the 1950s and relearning the lost art of selling, even down to resurrecting FBI (Features, Benefits, Incentives). Retromarketing redux. See Geoff Burch, *Writing on the Wall: The Campaign for Commonsense Business* (Oxford: Capstone, 2002).

44. Suzanne Vranica, "Sony Ericsson Campaign Uses Actors to Push Camera-Phone in Real Life," *Wall Street Journal*, July 31, 2002, www.wsj.com. On guerrilla marketing generally see Jay Conrad Levinson, *Guerrilla Marketing* (New York: Aspatore, 2001).

45. Chris Ayres, "Sony Ericsson Develops Guerrilla Marketing," *The Times*, August 1, p. 23; Vranica, "Sony Ericsson Campaign," op. cit.

46. Daniel J. Boorstin, *The Image: A Guide to Pseudo Events in America* (New York: Harper & Row, 1961).

47. The Obesitea story, strangely enough, doesn't feature in Reichenbach's autobiography, *Phantom Fame*, op. cit. It is recounted by Edward L. Bernays in his voluminous memoirs, *Biography of an Idea* (New York: Simon and Schuster, 1965).

Lesson Eleven: How to Bait the Marketing Mousetrap

1. www.bigkev.com.au

2. *Sydney Morning Herald*, "Thumbs Up from Big Kev," www.smh.com.au, March 25, 2002.

3. *Australian Financial Review*, "Big Kev's Ltd," www.afr.com, July 29, 2002; www.bigkev.com.au, op. cit.; Shaw Stockbroking, "Big Kev Meets Forecasts," www.egoli.com.au, September 12, 2001.

4. Posted by kirkbright on Australian Consumer Forum, October 31, 2001, www.auschange.org.

5. Soren Askegaard and Fabian F. Csaba, "The Good, the Bad, and the Jolly: Taste, Image and the Symbolic Resistance to the Coca-colonisation of Denmark," in Brown and Patterson, eds, *Imagining Marketing*, op. cit., pp. 124–40.

6. Anna-Rose Stancombe, "Australian Brands," *Th!nk: Marketing and Brand Knowledge*, www.think.d4cmillerhare.com, October 2001.

7. Big Kev's Ltd, Corporate Announcements, June 7, 2002 (Interlocutory Injunctions), May 23, 2002 (Application of Injunction), May 20, 2002 (Proceedings Against Chemical House Pty Ltd), February 25, 2002 (Vigorous Defence of Legal Action), February 6, 2002 (Vigorous Defence of Legal Action), etc., etc. Source: www.bigkev.com.au

8. Brown, *Marketing: The Retro Revolution*, op. cit., p. 234.

9. Kunhardt et al., *P.T. Barnum*, op. cit.

10. Stephen Brown, "The Unbearable Lightness of Marketing," in Stephen Brown et al., eds, *Romancing the Market* (London: Routledge, 1998, pp. 255–77).

11. Joe Vitale, *There's A Customer Born Every Minute: P.T. Barnum's Secrets to Business Success* (New York: Anacom, 1998); Morris B. Holbrook, "Let the Retro Marketing Revolution Roll," *Journal of the Academy of Marketing Science*, in press.

12. Brown, *Marketing: The Retro Revolution*, op. cit., pp. 55–72.

13. Terence Whalen, "Introduction: P.T. Barnum and the Birth of Capitalist Irony," in *The Life of P.T. Barnum, Written by Himself* (Urbana: University of Illinois Press, 2000, original 1855, pp. vii–xxxvii).

14. P.T. Barnum, *The Humbugs of the World: An Account of Humbugs, Delusions, Impositions, Quackeries, Deceits, and Deceivers Generally, in All Ages* (Amsterdam: Fredonia Books, 2001, original 1866).

15. Cook, *The Arts of Deception*, op. cit.

16. See for example, Evelin Sullivan, *The Concise Book of Lying* (New York: Farrar, Straus and Giroux, 2001); Jeremy Campbell, *The Liar's Tale: A History of Falsehood* (New York: Norton, 2001).

17. Twitchell, *AdCult USA*, op. cit.; Cialdini, *Influence*, op. cit.

18. H. Paul Jeffers, *Diamond Jim Brady: Prince of the Gilded Age* (New York: John Wiley, 2001); Burke, *Duet in Diamonds*, op. cit.

19. *Fortune*, "The Greatest Capital Goods Salesman of Them All," *Fortune*, October 1954.

20. A good description is found in Richard S. Tedlow, "Andrew Carnegie: From Rags to Richest," *Giants of Enterprise: Seven Business Innovators and the Empires They Built* (New York: HarperBusiness, 2001, pp. 19–71).

21. Quoted in Jeffers, *Diamond Jim Brady*, op. cit., p. 4.

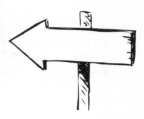

Brady started a dairy farm in New Jersey, where the milk was collected in golden buckets.

22. The Brady illuminations were priceless talking points. However, they were just the settings for Diamond Jim's publicity stunts, which ensured that he was never far from the front pages. He owned the first horseless carriage in New York City and had footmen uniformed to match the automobile's plush upholstery. He embraced the bicycle craze and had a custom-built, gold-plated, diamond-dappled, mother-of-pearl inlaid, specially-strengthened tricycle and hired a mighty-thewed flunky to do the pedaling. He owned a stable of thoroughbred racehorses; started a dairy farm in New Jersey, where the milk was collected in golden buckets; and, when his constitution started to give out under the gastronomic strain, encouraged the rumors that he'd had a stomach transplant – an elephant's stomach transplant!

23. Naturally, your honor, I hesitate to make a direct comparison between Diamond Jim Brady and Happy as Larry Ellison. However, there are definite parallels. Both are larger than life characters. Both made their name in cutting edge industries. Both use(d) their personal possessions, and overpowering personalities, to peerless promotional effect. Both have voracious appetitites, though for Jim's Chesapeake Bay oysters, read Larry's unlimited arm candy.

24. Sol Bloom, *The Autobiography of Sol Bloom* (New York: Putnam's, 1948).

25. Robert A. Carter, *Buffalo Bill Cody: The Man Behind the Legend* (New York: John Wiley, 2000).

26. Dawes, *The Great Illusionists*, op. cit.

27. Brown, *Marketing: The Retro Revolution*, op. cit., pp. 39–54.

28. Larry Tye, *The Father of Spin: Edward L. Bernays and the Birth of Public Relations* (New York: Crown, 1998).

29. Fuhrman, *Publicity Stunt*, op. cit.

30. Jack Newfield, *Only in America: The Life and Crimes of Don King* (New York: William Morrow, 1995).

31. R. Laurence Moore, *Selling God: American Religion in the Marketplace of Culture* (New York: Oxford, 1994).

32. Stephen Brown, "Marketing and Literature: The Anxiety of Academic Influence," *Journal of Marketing*, 63 (January), 1999, pp. 1–15.

33. Richard Branson, *Losing My Virginity* (London: Virgin Books, 1999).

34. Harriett Lane, "Beattie Mania," op. cit.

35. David Blaine, *Mysterious Stranger* (London: Channel 4 Books, 2002).

289

36. Robert J. Sterling, *Legend and Legacy: The Story of Boeing and Its People* (New York: St. Martin's, 1992).
37. Collins and Porras, *Built to Last*, op. cit.
38. Jack Welch, *Jack: What I've Learned Leading a Great Company and Great People* (New York: Warner Books, 2001, pp. 177–9).
39. *The Economist*, "It's a Desert Out There," www.economist.com, January 24, 2002; David Gow, "The Vintage Visionary," *Guardian*, July 13, 2002, p. 30.
40. Airbus has now overtaken Boeing. It won the contract to supply European low-cost carrier Easyjet in October 2002, despite Boeing's best negotiating efforts. This contract has considerable symbolic significance, moreover, since Boeing has completely dominated the low-cost carrier segment hitherto. (See Carol Matlack and Stanley Holmes, "Look Out, Boeing," *Business Week*, October 28, 2002, pp. 20–1; *The Economist*, "Bashing Boeing," *The Economist*, October 19, 2002, pp. 87–8; Oliver Morgan, "Embattled Seattle Flies on One Wing," *Observer Business*, September 8, 2002, p. 4; *The Economist*, "Towards the Wide Blue Yonder: Special Report Boeing v Airbus," *The Economist*, April 27, 2002, pp. 75–7; Tony Dawe, "Sonic Cruiser v Super-Jumbo," *The Times*, July 18, 2002, p. 34; Russell Hotten, "Boeing Takes a Chance on a New Flight Path," *The Times*, July 27, 2002, p. 48.)
41. *The Economist*, "Hard Man Harry," www.economist.com, June 7, 2001; *The Economist*, "Building a New Boeing," www.economist.com, August 10, 2000; *The Economist*, "Fearful Boeing," www.economist.com, February 25, 1999.
42. Gow, "The Vintage Visionary," op. cit.
43. Actually, it still is. Or it was when I tried (and failed) to get tickets in September 2002.

ACKNOWLEDGEMENTS

Although I have written several books in the past – still available from all good thrift shops, used bookstores, and remainder bins everywhere! – this is the first time I've written for a managerial readership. I would, therefore, like to thank Richard Burton of Capstone for taking a chance on this idiosyncratic venture. Grace Byrne and John Moseley, also of Capstone-Wiley, helped bring the book to fruition, as did ace copyeditor Kate Santon. Thank you all. Julia Kirby, senior editor at *Harvard Business Review*, kept the faith when my spirits were particularly low, for which I am very grateful. My sister-in-law, Shirley, and her husband, Alun, kindly persuaded me not to mention their companies, since I am the kiss of corporate death. Above all, however, I'd like to thank my wife, Linda, and three daughters, Madison, Holly, and Sophie, for putting up with the attention deficit, yet again.

INDEX